A Guide to Econometrics

A Guide to Econometrics

SECOND EDITION

Peter Kennedy

The MIT Press
Cambridge, Massachusetts

MIT Press editions, 1979 and 1985

First published in 1979 by Martin Robertson and Company Ltd.
Second Edition published by
Basil Blackwell Ltd
108 Cowley Road, Oxford OX4 1JF, UK

Library of Congress Cataloging-in-Publication Data

Kennedy, Peter, 1943–
  A guide to econometrics.

  Bibliography: p.
  Includes index.
  1. Econometrics. I. Title.
HB139.K45   1985   330′.028   85–16677
ISBN 0–262–11110–1 (hard)
       0–262–61043–4 (paper)

Printed and bound in Great Britain

Contents

Preface

In the preface to the first edition of this book, I made the bold claim that the majority of instructors do not feel that this book is needed whereas students are unanimously of the opposite opinion. I am sorry to report that I must continue to make that claim: too many students have told me that they learned of the book from fellow students rather than from their instructors. The great success of the first edition is due to this word-of-mouth phenomenon.

What is it about this book that students have found to be of such value? This book supplements econometrics texts, at all levels, by providing an overview of the subject and an intuitive feel for its concepts and techniques, without the usual clutter of notation and technical detail that necessarily characterize an econometrics textbook. It is often said of econometrics textbooks that their readers miss the forest for the trees. This is inevitable – the terminology and techniques that must be taught do not allow the text to convey a proper intuitive sense of 'What's it all about?' and 'How does it all fit together?' All econometrics textbooks fail to provide this overview. This is not from lack of trying – most textbooks have excellent passages containing the relevant insights and interpretations. They make good sense to instructors, but they do *not* make the expected impact on the students. Why? Because these insights and interpretations are broken up, appearing throughout the book, mixed with the technical details. In their struggle to keep up with notation and to learn these technical details, students miss the overview so essential to a real understanding of those details. This book provides students with a perspective from which it is possible to assimilate more easily the details of these textbooks.

The basic structure of this book remains unchanged from the first edition. Following an introductory chapter, the second chapter discusses at some length the criteria for choosing estimators, and in doing so develops many of the basic concepts used throughout the book. The third chapter provides an overview of the subject matter, presenting the five assumptions of the classical linear regression model and explaining how most problems encountered in econometrics can be interpreted as a violation of one of these assumptions. The fourth chapter discusses some concepts of inference to provide a foundation for later chapters. The next six chapters each deal with a violation of one of these assumptions of the classical linear regression model, describe their implications, and suggest means of resolving the resulting estimation problems. The final five chapters address selected topics.

Changes from the first edition are both numerous and major. The chapters on specification and multicollinearity have been completely rewritten. The five selected topics treated in the final chapter of the first edition have been upgraded to separate chapters, incorporating within them expanded discussion of a variety of topics (e.g., distributed lags, pretest estimators, Stein estimators). In earlier chapters new sections on Monte Carlo studies and on LR, W and LM statistics have been added, and discussion of several topics (e.g., maximum likelihood, non-nested hypothesis tests, principle components) has been expanded. The Ballentine is exploited in several places as an expository device. And throughout, minor changes have been made to update material in light of new results in the literature.

To minimize readers' distractions, there are no footnotes. All references, peripheral points and details worthy of comment are relegated to a section at the end of each chapter entitled 'General Notes'. The few technical discussions that appear in the book are placed in end-of-chapter sections entitled 'Technical Notes'. Students are advised to wait until a second or third reading of a chapter before attempting to integrate the material in the General or Technical Notes with the body of the chapter. A glossary explains common econometric terms not found in the body of this book.

Shortcomings of this book are my responsibility, but for improvements I owe many debts. In addition to those cited in the first edition, I must add Terry Seaks, Shyam Kamath, Josef Bonnici, several anonymous reviewers and scores of students, both graduate and undergraduate, whose comments and reactions have all played a role in shaping this second edition. Barb Clark provided expert typing. I would especially like to thank those students who have written to me and my publishers to thank us for having produced this book. Authors seldom receive such plaudits; I found them inspiring, rendering the preparation of this second edition almost a pleasure.

Dedication

To ANNA and RED
who, until they discovered what an econometrician was, were very impressed that their son might become one. With apologies to K. A. C. Manderville, I draw their attention to the following, adapted from *The Undoing of Lamia Gurdleneck*.

'You haven't told me yet,' said Lady Nuttal, 'what it is your fiancé does for a living.'

'He's an econometrician,' replied Lamia, with an annoying sense of being on the defensive.

Lady Nuttal was obviously taken aback. It had not occurred to her that econometricians entered into normal social relationships. The species, she would have surmised, was perpetuated in some collateral manner, like mules.

'But Aunt Sara, it's a very interesting profession,' said Lamia warmly.

'I don't doubt it,' said her aunt, who obviously doubted it very much. 'To express anything important in mere figures is so plainly impossible that there must be endless scope for well-paid advice on how to do it. But don't you think that life with an econometrician would be rather, shall we say, humdrum?'

Lamia was silent. She felt reluctant to discuss the surprising depth of emotional possibility which she had discovered below Edward's numerical veneer.

'It's not the figures themselves,' she said finally, 'it's what you do with them that matters.'

1. Introduction

1.1 What is Econometrics?

Strange as it may seem, there does not exist a generally accepted answer to this question. Responses vary from the silly 'Econometrics is what econometricians do' to the staid 'Econometrics is the study of the application of statistical methods to the analysis of economic phenomena', with sufficient disagreements to warrant an entire journal article devoted to this question (Tintner, 1953).

This confusion stems from the fact that econometricians wear many different hats. First, and foremost, they are *economists*, capable of utilizing economic theory to improve their empirical analyses of the problems they address. At times they are *mathematicians*, formulating economic theory in ways that make it appropriate for statistical testing. At times they are *accountants*, concerned with the problem of finding and collecting economic data and relating theoretical economic variables to observable ones. At times they are *applied statisticians*, spending hours with the computer trying to estimate economic relationships or predict economic events. And at times they are *theoretical statisticians*, applying their skills to the development of statistical techniques appropriate to the empirical problems characterizing the science of economics. It is to the last of these roles that the term 'econometric theory' applies, and it is on this aspect of econometrics that most textbooks on the subject focus. This guide is accordingly devoted to this 'econometric theory' dimension of econometrics, discussing the empirical problems typical of economics and the statistical techniques used to overcome these problems.

What distinguishes an econometrician from a statistician is the former's preoccupation with problems caused by violations of statisticians' standard assumptions; owing to the nature of economic relationships and the lack of controlled experimentation, these assumptions are seldom met. Patching up statistical methods to deal with situations frequently encountered in empirical work in economics has created a large battery of extremely sophisticated statistical techniques. In fact, econometricians are often accused of using sledgehammers to crack open peanuts while turning a blind eye to data deficiencies and the many questionable assumptions required for the successful application of these techniques. Valavanis has expressed this feeling forcefully:

1

Econometric theory is like an exquisitely balanced French recipe, spelling out precisely with how many turns to mix the sauce, how many carats of spice to add, and for how many milliseconds to bake the mixture at exactly 474 degrees of temperature. But when the statistical cook turns to raw materials, he finds that hearts of cactus fruit are unavailable, so he substitutes chunks of cantaloupe; where the recipe calls for vermicelli he uses shredded wheat; and he substitutes green garment dye for curry, ping-pong balls for turtle's eggs, and, for Chalifougnac vintage 1883, a can of turpentine. [1959, p. 83]

Criticisms of econometrics along these lines are not uncommon. Rebuttals cite improvements in data collection, extol the fruits of the computer revolution and provide examples of improvements in estimation due to advanced techniques. It remains a fact, though, that in practice good results depend as much on the input of sound and imaginative economic theory as on the application of correct statistical methods. The skill of the econometrician lies in judiciously mixing these two essential ingredients; in the words of Malinvaud:

The art of the econometrician consists in finding the set of assumptions which are both sufficiently specific and sufficiently realistic to allow him to take the best possible advantage of the data available to him. [1966, p. 514]

Modern econometrics texts try to infuse this art into students by providing a large number of detailed examples of empirical application. This important dimension of econometrics texts lies beyond the scope of this book. Readers should keep this in mind as they use this guide to improve their understanding of the purely statistical methods of econometrics.

1.2   The Disturbance Term

A major distinction between economists and econometricians is the latter's concern with disturbance terms. An economist will specify, for example, that consumption is a function of income, and write $C = f(Y)$ where C is consumption and Y is income. An econometrician will claim that this relationship must also include a *disturbance* (or *error*) term, and may alter the equation to read $C = f(Y) + \varepsilon$ where ε (epsilon) is a disturbance term. Without the disturbance term the relationship is said to be *exact* or *deterministic*; with the disturbance term it is said to be *stochastic*.

The word 'stochastic' comes from the Greek 'stokhos' meaning a target or bull's eye. A stochastic relationship is not always right on target in the sense that it predicts the precise value of the variable being explained, just as a dart thrown at a target seldom hits the bull's eye. The disturbance term is used to capture explicitly the size of these 'misses' or 'errors'. The existence of the disturbance term is justified in three main ways. (Note: these are not mutually exclusive.)

(1) *Omission of the influence of innumerable chance events* Although income might be the major determinant of the level of consumption, it is not the only determinant. Other variables, such as the interest rate of liquid asset holdings, may have a systematic influence on consumption. Their omission constitutes one type of *specification error*: the nature of the economic relationship is not correctly specified. In addition to these systematic influences, however, are innumerable less systematic influences such as weather variations, taste changes, earthquakes, epidemics and postal strikes. Although some of these variables may have a significant impact on consumption, and thus should definitely be included in the specified relationship, many have only a very slight, irregular influence; the disturbance is often viewed as representing the net influence of a large number of such small and independent causes.

(2) *Measurement error* It may be the case that the variable being explained cannot be measured accurately, either because of data collection difficulties or because it is inherently unmeasurable and a proxy variable must be used in its stead. The disturbance term can in these circumstances be thought of as representing this measurement error. Errors in measuring the explaining variable(s) (as opposed to the variable being explained) create a serious econometric problem, discussed in chapter 8. The terminology *errors in variables* is also used to refer to measurement errors.

(3) *Human indeterminancy* Some people believe that human behaviour is such that actions taken under identical circumstances will differ in a random way. The disturbance term can be thought of as representing this inherent randomness in human behaviour.

Associated with any explanatory relationship are unknown constants, called *parameters*, which tie the relevant variables into an equation. For example, the relationship between consumption and income could be specified as

$$C = \beta_1 + \beta_2 Y + \varepsilon$$

where β_1 and β_2 are the parameters characterizing this consumption function. Economists are often keenly interested in learning the values of these unknown parameters.

The existence of the disturbance term, coupled with the fact that its magnitude is unknown, makes calculation of these parameter values impossible. Instead, they must be *estimated*. It is on this task, the estimation of parameter values, that the bulk of econometric theory focuses. The success of econometricians' methods of estimating parameter values depends in large part on the nature of the disturbance term; statistical assumptions concerning the characteristics of the disturbance term, and means of testing these assumptions, therefore play a prominent role in econometric theory.

1.3   Estimates and Estimators

In their mathematical notation, econometricians usually employ Greek letters to represent the true, unknown values of parameters. The Greek letter most often used in this context is beta (β). Thus, throughout this book, β is used as the parameter value that the econometrician is seeking to learn. Of course, no one ever actually learns the value of β, but it can be estimated: via statistical techniques, empirical data can be used to take an educated guess at β. In any particular application, an estimate of β is simply a number. For example, β might be estimated as 16.2. But in general, econometricians are seldom interested in estimating a single parameter; economic relationships are usually sufficiently complex as to require more than one parameter, and because these parameters occur in the same relationship, better estimates of these parameters can be obtained if they are estimated together (i.e., the influence of one explaining variable is more accurately captured if the influence of the other explaining variables is simultaneously accounted for). As a result, β seldom refers to a single parameter value; it almost always refers to a set of parameter values, individually called $\beta_1, \beta_2, \ldots, \beta_k$ where k is the number of different parameters in the set. β is then referred to as a vector and is written as

$$\beta = \begin{bmatrix} \beta_1 \\ \beta_2 \\ \vdots \\ \beta_k \end{bmatrix}.$$

In any particular application, an estimate of β will be a set of numbers. For example, if three parameters are being estimated (i.e., if the dimension of β is three), β might be estimated as

$$\begin{bmatrix} 0.8 \\ 1.2 \\ -4.6 \end{bmatrix}.$$

In general, econometric theory focuses not on the estimate itself, but on the *estimator* – the formula or 'recipe' by which the data are transformed into an actual estimate. The reason for this is that the justification of an estimate computed from a particular sample rests on a justification of the estimation method (the estimator). The econometrician has no way of knowing the actual values of the disturbances inherent in a sample of data; depending on these disturbances, an estimate calculated from that sample could be quite inaccurate. It is therefore impossible to justify the estimate itself. However, it may be the case that the econometrician can justify the estimator by showing, for example, that the estimator 'usually' produces an estimate that is 'quite close' to the true parameter value regardless of the particular sample chosen. (The meaning of this sentence is discussed at length in the next chapter.) Thus an estimate of β from a particular sample is defended by justifying the estimator.

Because attention is focused on estimators of β, a convenient way of denoting those estimators is required. An easy way of doing this is to place a mark over the β or a superscript on it. Thus $\hat{\beta}$ (beta-hat) and β^* (beta-star) are often used to denote estimators of beta. One estimator, the ordinary least squares (OLS) estimator, is very popular in econometrics; the notation β^{OLS} is used throughout this book to represent it. Alternative estimators are denoted by $\hat{\beta}$, β^*, or something similar.

1.4 Good and Preferred Estimators

Any fool can produce an estimator of β, since literally an infinite number of them exists; i.e., there exists an infinite number of different ways in which a sample of data can be used to produce an estimate of β, all but a few of these ways producing 'bad' estimates. What distinguishes an econometrician is the ability to produce 'good' estimators, which in turn produce 'good' estimates. One of these 'good' estimators could be chosen as the 'best' or 'preferred' estimator and be used to generate the 'preferred' estimate of β. What further distinguishes an econometrician is his ability to provide 'good' estimators in a variety of different estimating contexts. The set of 'good' estimators (and the choice of 'preferred' estimator) is not the same in all estimating problems. In fact, a 'good' estimator in one estimating situation could be a 'bad' estimator in another situation.

The study of econometrics revolves around how to generate a 'good' or the 'preferred' estimator in a given estimating situation. But before the 'how to' can be explained, the meaning of 'good' and 'preferred' must be made clear. This takes the discussion into the subjective realm: the meaning of 'good' or 'preferred' estimator depends upon the subjective values of the person doing the estimating. The best the econometrician can do under these circumstances is to recognize the more popular criteria used in this regard and generate estimators that meet one or more of these criteria. Estimators meeting certain of these critera could be called 'good' estimators. The ultimate choice of the 'preferred' estimator, however, lies in the hands of the person doing the estimating, for it is his or her value judgements that determine which of these criteria is the most important. This value judgement may well be influenced by the purpose for which the estimate is sought, in addition to the subjective prejudices of the individual.

Clearly, our investigation of the subject of econometrics can go no further until the possible criteria for a 'good' estimator are discussed. This is the purpose of the next chapter.

General Notes

1.1   What is Econometrics?

- The term 'econometrics' first came into prominence with the formation in the early 1930s of the Econometric Society and the founding of the journal *Econometrica*. The introduction of Dowling and Glahe (1970) surveys briefly the landmark publications related to econometrics. Hendry (1980) notes that the word econometrics should not be confused with 'economystics', 'economic-tricks', or 'icon-ometrics'.

- Brunner (1973), Rubner (1970) and Streissler (1970) are good sources of cynical views of econometrics. More comments appear in this book in section 8.2 on errors in variables and chapter 15 on prediction. Fair (1973) and Fromm and Schink (1973) are examples of studies defending the use of sophisticated econometric techniques. The use of econometrics in the policy context has been hampered by the (inexplicable?) operation of 'Goodhart's Law' (1978), namely that all econometric models break down when used for policy.

- Some critics of econometrics believe that economic data is not powerful enough to test and choose among theories, and that, as a result, econometrics has shifted from being a tool for testing theories to being a tool for exhibiting/displaying theories. They claim that good economic theory is stronger than the data, and thus must be imposed on the data, contrary to the original intent of econometrics.

- Critics might choose to paraphrase the Malinvaud quote as 'The art of drawing a crooked line from an unproved assumption to a foregone conclusion'. The importance of a proper understanding of econometric techniques in the face of a potential inferiority of econometrics to inspired economic theorizing is captured nicely by Samuelson (1965) p. 9: 'Even if a scientific regularity were less accurate than the intuitive hunches of a virtuoso, the fact that it can be put into operation by thousands of people who are not virtuosos gives it a transcendental importance.' This guide is designed for those of us who are not virtuosos!

- There exist several books addressed to the empirical applications dimension of econometrics. Examples are Bridge (1971). Chang (1984), Cramer (1971), Desai (1976), Hebden (1983), Mayes (1981), Pindyck and Rubinfeld (1981), Wallis (1979) and Wynn and Holden (1974). Evans (1969) is also useful in this regard. In addition, the econometric theory texts of Gujarati (1978), Intriligator (1978), Koutsoyiannis (1977) and Maddala (1977) all contain numerous examples of empirical applications. Zellner (1968) contains many well-known articles addressed to this empirical dimension of econometrics.

1.2   The Disturbance Term

- The error term associated with a relationship need not necessarily be additive, as it is in the example cited. For some nonlinear functions it is often convenient to specify the error term in a multiplicative form, for example, as noted later in chapter 5. In other instances it may be appropriate to build the stochastic element into the relationship by specifying the parameters to be random variables rather than constants. (This is called the random-coefficients model.) These are usually treated as special topics in econometrics.

- Econometricians usually do not know the actual form of the economic relationship being studied and consequently commit a specification error when formulating the estimation problem, either by omitting variables that should be included or by adopting an incorrect functional form. In these cases the econometrician often views the disturbance term as incorporating this specification error in addition to the other types of error cited. Following this operational procedure creates an error term with unusual properties; estimation under these circumstances is discussed under the heading of specification error (chapter 5).

- Estimation of parameter values is not the only purpose of econometrics. Two other major themes can be identified: testing of hypotheses and economic forecasting. Because both these problems are intimately related to the estimation of parameter values, it is not misleading to characterize econometrics as being primarily concerned with parameter estimation.

- In terms of the throwing-darts-at-a-target analogy, characterizing disturbance terms refers to describing the nature of the misses: are the darts distributed uniformly around the bull's eye? Is the average miss large or small? Does the average miss depend on who is throwing the darts? Is a miss to the right likely to be followed by another miss to the right? In later chapters the statistical specification of these characteristics and the related terminology (such as 'homoskedasticity' and 'autocorrelated errors') are explained in considerable detail.

1.3 Estimates and Estimators

- An estimator is simply an algebraic function of a potential sample of data; once the sample is drawn, this function creates an actual numerical estimate.

- Chapter 2 discusses in detail the means whereby an estimator is 'justified' and compared with alternative estimators.

1.4 Good and Preferred Estimators

- The terminology 'preferred' estimator is used instead of the term 'best' estimator because the latter has a specific meaning in econometrics. This is explained in chapter 2.

2. Criteria for Estimators

2.1 Introduction

Chapter 1 posed the question, What is a 'good' estimator? The aim of this chapter is to answer that question by describing a number of criteria that econometricians feel are measures of 'goodness'. These criteria are discussed under the following headings:

(1) Computational cost
(2) Least squares
(3) Highest R^2
(4) Unbiasedness
(5) Best unbiased
(6) Mean square error
(7) Asymptotic properties
(8) Maximum likelihood

Since econometrics can be characterized as a search for estimators satisfying one or more of these criteria, care is taken in the discussion of these criteria to ensure that the reader understands fully the meaning of the different criteria and the terminology associated with them. Many fundamental ideas of econometrics, critical to the question, What's econometrics all about? are presented in this chapter.

2.2 Computational Cost

To anyone, but particularly to economists, the extra benefit associated with choosing one estimator over another must be compared with its extra cost, where cost refers to expenditure of both money and effort. Thus, the computational ease and cost of using one estimator rather than another must be taken into account whenever selecting an estimator. Fortunately, the existence and ready availability of high-speed computers, along with standard packaged routines for most of the popular estimators, has made computational cost very low. As a result, this criterion does not play as strong a role as it once did. Its influence is now felt only when dealing with two kinds of estimators. One is the case of an atypical estimation procedure for which there does not exist a readily available packaged computer program and for which the cost of programming is high. The second is an estimation method for which the cost of running a packaged program is high because it needs large quantities of computer time; the so-called systems methods of simultaneous equation estimation, involving the simultaneous estimation of an entire set of βs, fall into this latter category.

2.3 Least Squares

For any set of values of the parameters characterizing a relationship, estimated values of the dependent variable (the variable being explained) can be calculated using the values of the independent variables (the explaining variables) in the data set. These estimated values (called $\hat{y}$) of the dependent variable can be subtracted from the actual values (y) of the dependent variable in the data set to produce what are called the *residuals* ($y - \hat{y}$). These residuals could be thought of as estimates of the unknown disturbances inherent in the data set. This is illustrated in Fig. 2.1. The line labelled $\hat{y}$ is the estimated relationship corresponding to a specific set of values of the unknown parameters. The dots represent actual observations on the dependent variable y and the independent variable x. Each observation is a certain vertical distance away from the estimated line, as pictured by the double-ended arrows. The lengths of these double-ended arrows measure the residuals. A different set of specific values of the parameters would create a different estimating line and thus a different set of residuals.

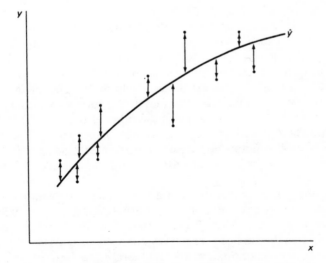

Fig. 2.1   Minimizing the sum of squared residuals

It seems natural to ask that a 'good' estimator be one that generates a set of estimates of the parameters that makes these residuals 'small'. Controversy arises, however, over the appropriate definition of 'small'. Although it is agreed that the estimator should be chosen to minimize a weighted sum of all these residuals, full agreement as to what the weights should be does not exist. For example, those feeling that all residuals should be weighted equally advocate choosing the estimator that minimizes the sum of the absolute values of these residuals. Those feeling that large residuals should be avoided advocate weighting larger residuals more heavily by choosing the estimator that minimizes the sum of the squared values of these residuals. Those worried about misplaced decimals and other data errors advocate placing a constant (sometimes zero) weight on the squared values of particularly large residuals. Those concerned only with whether or not a residual is bigger than some specified value suggest placing a zero weight on residuals smaller than this critical value and a weight equal to the inverse of the residual on residuals larger than this value. Clearly a large number of alternative definitions could be proposed, each with appealing features.

By far the most popular of these definitions of 'small' is the minimization of the sum of squared residuals. The estimator generating the set of values of the parameters that minimizes the sum of squared residuals is called the *ordinary least squares* estimator. It is referred to as the OLS estimator and is denoted by β^{OLS} in this book. This estimator is probably the most popular estimator among researchers doing empirical work. The reason for this popularity, however, does *not* stem from the fact that it makes the residuals 'small' by minimizing the sum of squared residuals. Many econometricians are leery of this criterion because minimizing the sum of squared residuals does not say anything specific about the relationship of the estimator to the true parameter value β that it is estimating. In fact, it is possible to be too successful in minimizing the sum of squared residuals, accounting for so many unique features of that *particular sample* that the estimator loses its general validity, in the sense that, were that estimator applied to a new sample, poor estimates would result. The great popularity of the OLS estimator comes from the fact that in some estimating problems (but not all!) it scores well on some of the other criteria, described below, that are thought to be of greater importance. A secondary reason for its popularity is its computational ease; all computer packages include the OLS estimator for linear relationships, and many have routines for nonlinear cases.

Because the OLS estimator is used so much in econometrics, the characteristics of this estimator in different estimating problems are explored very thoroughly by all econometrics texts. The OLS estimator *always* minimizes the sum of squared residuals; but it does *not* always meet other criteria that econometricians feel are more important. As will become clear in the next chapter, the subject of econometrics can be characterized as an attempt to find alternative estimators to the OLS estimator for situations in which the OLS estimator does not meet the estimating criterion considered to be of greatest importance in the problem at hand.

2.4 Highest R^2

A statistic that appears frequently in econometrics is the coefficient of determination, R^2. It is supposed to represent the proportion of the variation in the dependent variable 'explained' by variation in the independent variables. It does this in a meaningful sense in the case of a linear relationship estimated by OLS. In this case it happens that the sum of squared deviations of the dependent variable about its mean (the 'total' variation in the dependent variable) can be broken into two parts, called the 'explained' variation (the sum of squared deviations of the estimated values of the dependent variable around their mean) and the 'unexplained' variation (the sum of squared residuals). R^2 is measured either as the ratio of the 'explained' variation to the 'total' variation or, equivalently, as 1 minus the ratio of the 'unexplained' variation to the 'total' variation, and thus represents the percentage of variation in the dependent variable 'explained' by variation in the independent variables.

Because the OLS estimator minimizes the sum of squared residuals (the 'unexplained' variation), it automatically maximizes R^2. Thus maximization of R^2, as a criterion for an estimator, is formally identical to the least squares criterion, and as such it really does not deserve a separate section in this chapter. It is given a separate section for two reasons. The first is that the formal identity between the highest R^2 criterion and the least squares criterion is worthy of emphasis. And the second is to distinguish clearly the difference between applying R^2 as a criterion in the context of searching for a 'good' estimator when the functional form and included independent variables are known, as is the case in the present discussion, and using R^2 to help determine the proper functional form and the appropriate independent variables to be included. This latter use of R^2 (and its misuse) are discussed later in the book (in sections 4.5 and 5.2).

2.5 Unbiasedness

Suppose we perform the conceptual experiment of taking what is called a *repeated* sample: keeping the values of the independent variables unchanged, we obtain new observations for the dependent variable by drawing a new set of disturbances. This could be repeated, say, 2000 times, obtaining 2000 of these repeated samples. For each of these repeated samples we could use an estimator β^* to calculate an estimate of β.

Because the samples differ, these 2000 estimates will not be the same. The manner in which these estimates are distributed is called the *sampling distribution* of β^*. This is illustrated for the one-dimensional case in Fig. 2.2, where the sampling distribution of the estimator is labelled $f(\beta^*)$. It is simply the probability density function of β^*, approximated by using the 2000 estimates of β to construct a histogram, which in turn is used to approximate the relative frequencies of different estimates of β from the estimator β^*. The sampling distribution of an alternative estimator, $\hat{\beta}$, is also shown in Fig. 2.2.

This concept of a sampling distribution, the distribution of estimates produced by an estimator in repeated sampling, is crucial to an understanding of econometrics. Most estimators are adopted because their sampling distributions have 'good' properties; the criteria discussed in this and the following three sections are directly concerned with the nature of an estimator's sampling distribution.

The first of these properties is unbiasedness. An estimator β^* is said to be an *unbiased* estimator of β if the mean of its sampling distribution is equal to β, i.e., if the average value of β^* in repeated sampling is β. The mean of the sampling distribution of β^* is called the expected value of β^* and is written $E\beta^*$; the bias of β^* is the difference between $E\beta^*$ and β. In Fig. 2.2, β^* is seen to be unbiased, whereas $\hat{\beta}$ has a bias of size $(E\hat{\beta} - \beta)$. The property of unbiasedness does not mean that $\beta^* = \beta$; it says only that, if we could undertake repeated sampling an infinite number of times, we would get the correct estimate 'on the average'.

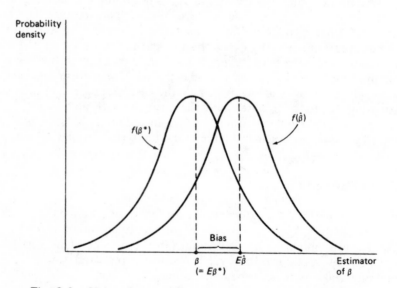

Fig. 2.2   Using the sampling distribution to illustrate bias

The OLS criterion can be applied with no information concerning how the data were generated. This is not the case for the unbiasedness criterion (and all other criteria related to the sampling distribution), since this knowledge is required to construct the sampling distribution. Econometricians have therefore developed a standard set of assumptions (discussed in chapter 3) concerning the way in which observations are generated. The general, but not the specific, way in which the disturbances are distributed is an important component of this. These assumptions are sufficient to allow the basic nature of the sampling distribution of many estimators to be calculated, either by mathematical means (part of the technical skill of an econometrician) or, failing that, by an empirical means called a Monte Carlo study, discussed in section 2.10.

Although the mean of a distribution is not necessarily the ideal measure of its location (the median or mode in some circumstances might be considered superior), most econometricians consider unbiasedness a desirable property for an estimator to have. This preference for an unbiased estimator stems from the *hope* that a particular estimate (i.e., from the sample at hand) will be close to the mean of the estimator's sampling distribution. Having to justify a particular estimate on a 'hope' is not especially satisfactory, however. As a result, econometricians have recognized that being centred over the parameter to be estimated is only *one* good property that the sampling distribution of an estimator can have. The variance of the sampling distribution, discussed next, is also of great importance.

2.6 Best Unbiased

In some econometric problems it is impossible to find an unbiased estimator. But whenever one unbiased estimator can be found, it is usually the case that a large number of other unbiased estimators can also be found. In this circumstance the unbiased estimator whose sampling distribution has the smallest variance is considered the most desirable of these unbiased estimators; it is called the *best unbiased* estimator, or the most *efficient* estimator among all unbiased estimators. Why it is considered the most desirable of all unbiased estimators is easy to visualize. In Fig. 2.3 the sampling distributions of two unbiased estimators are drawn. The sampling distribution of the estimator $\hat{\beta}$, denoted $f(\hat{\beta})$, is drawn 'flatter' or 'wider' than the sampling distribution of β^*, reflecting the larger variance of $\hat{\beta}$. Although both estimators would produce estimates in repeated samples whose average would be β, the estimates from $\hat{\beta}$ would range more widely and thus would be less desirable. A researcher using $\hat{\beta}$ would be less certain that his/her estimate was close to β than would a researcher using β^*.

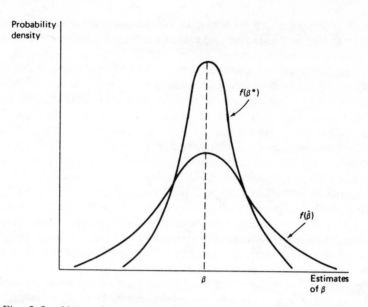

Fig. 2.3   Using the sampling distribution to illustrate efficiency

Sometimes reference is made to a criterion called 'minimum variance'. This criterion, by itself, is meaningless. Consider the estimator $\beta^* = 5.2$ (i.e., whenever a sample is taken, estimate β by 5.2, ignoring the sample). This estimator has a variance of zero, the smallest possible variance, but no one would use this estimator because it performs so poorly on other criteria such as unbiasedness. (It is interesting to note, however, that it performs exceptionally well on the computational cost criterion!) Thus, whenever the minimum variance, or 'efficiency', criterion is mentioned, there must exist some additional constraint, such as unbiasedness, accompanying that criterion. When the additional constraint accompanying the minimum variance criterion is that the estimators under consideration be unbiased, the estimator is referred to as the *best unbiased* estimator. Unfortunately, in many cases it is impossible to determine mathematically which estimator, of all unbiased estimators, has the smallest variance. Because of this problem, econometricians frequently add the further restriction that the estimator be *linear*, i.e., that it be a linear function of the errors. This reduces the task of finding the efficient estimator to mathematically manageable proportions. An estimator that is linear, unbiased and has minimum variance among all linear unbiased estimators is called the *best linear unbiased estimator* (BLUE). The BLUE is very popular among econometricians.

This discussion of minimum variance or efficiency has been implicitly undertaken in the context of a unidimensional estimator, i.e., the case in which β is a single number rather than a vector containing several numbers. In the multidimensional case the variance of β̂ becomes a matrix called the variance–covariance matrix of β̂. This creates special problems in determining which estimator has the smallest variance. The technical notes to this section discuss this further.

2.7 Mean Square Error (MSE)

Using the best unbiased criterion allows unbiasedness to play an extremely strong role in determining the choice of an estimator, since only unbiased estimators are considered. It may well be the case that, by restricting attention to only unbiased estimators, we are ignoring estimators that are only slightly biased but have considerably lower variances. This phenomenon is illustrated in Fig. 2.4. The sampling distribution of β̂, the best unbiased estimator is labelled $f(\hat{\beta})$. β^* is a biased estimator with sampling distribution $f(\beta^*)$. It is apparent from Fig. 2.4 that, although $f(\beta^*)$ is not centred over β, reflecting the bias of β^*, it is 'narrower' than $f(\hat{\beta})$, indicating a smaller variance. It should be clear from the diagram that most researchers would probably choose the biased estimator β^* in preference to the best unbiased estimator β̂.

This trade-off between low bias and low variance is formalized by using as a criterion the minimization of a weighted average of the bias and the

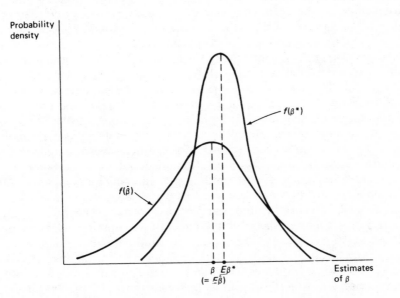

Fig. 2.4 MSE trades off bias and variance

variance (i.e., choosing the estimator that minimizes this weighted average). This is not a viable formalization, however, because the bias could be negative. One way to correct for this is to use the absolute value of the bias; a more popular way is to use its square. When the estimator is chosen so as to minimize a weighted average of the variance and the square of the bias, the estimator is said to be chosen on the *weighted square error* criterion. When the weights are equal, the criterion is the popular mean square error (MSE) criterion. The popularity of the mean square error criterion comes from an alternative derivation of this criterion: it happens that the expected value of a loss function consisting of the square of the difference between β and its estimate (i.e., the square of the estimation error) is the same as the sum of the variance and the squared bias. Minimization of the expected value of this loss function makes good intuitive sense as a criterion for choosing an estimator.

In practice, the MSE criterion is not usually adopted unless the best unbiased criterion is unable to produce estimates with small variances. The problem of multicollinearity, discussed in chapter 10, is an example of such a situation.

2.8   Asymptotic Properties

The estimator properties discussed in sections 2.5, 2.6 and 2.7 above relate to the nature of an estimator's sampling distribution. An unbiased estimator, for example, is one whose sampling distribution is centred over the true value of the parameter being estimated. These properties do not depend on the size of the sample of data at hand: an unbiased estimator, for example, is unbiased in both small and large samples. In many econometric problems, however, it is impossible to find estimators possessing these desirable sampling distribution properties in small samples. When this happens, as it frequently does, econometricians justify an estimator on the basis of its *asymptotic* properties – the nature of the estimator's sampling distribution in extremely large samples.

The sampling distribution of most estimators changes as the sample size changes. The sample mean statistic, for example, has a sampling distribution that is centred over the population mean but whose variance becomes smaller as the sample size becomes larger. In many cases it happens that a biased estimator becomes less and less biased as the sample size becomes larger and larger – as the sample size becomes larger its sampling distribution changes, such that the mean of its sampling distribution shifts closer to the true value of the parameter being estimated. Econometricians have formalized their study of these phenomena by structuring the concept of a *limiting* or *asymptotic distribution* and defining desirable asymptotic or 'large-sample' properties of an estimator in terms of the character of its limiting distribution.

Consider the sequence of sampling distributions of an estimator $\hat{\beta}$, formed by calculating the sampling distribution of $\hat{\beta}$ for successively larger sample sizes. If the distributions in this sequence become more and more similar in form to some specific distribution (such as a normal distribution) as the sample size becomes extremely large, this specific distribution is called the *limiting* or *asymptotic distribution* of $\hat{\beta}$. Two basic estimator properties are defined in terms of the limiting distribution.

(1) If this limiting distribution of $\hat{\beta}$ tends to become concentrated on a particular value k as the sample size approaches infinity, k is said to be the *probability limit* of $\hat{\beta}$ and is written plim $\hat{\beta} = k$; if plim $\hat{\beta} = \beta$, then $\hat{\beta}$ is said to be *consistent*.

(2) The variance of the limiting distribution of $\hat{\beta}$ is called the asymptotic variance of $\hat{\beta}$; if $\hat{\beta}$ is consistent and its asymptotic variance is smaller than the asymptotic variance of all other consistent estimators, $\hat{\beta}$ is said to be *asymptotically efficient*.

A third, and weaker, asymptotic property that is often encountered relates to an estimator's asymptotic expectation. Rather than being defined in terms of the character of the limiting distribution, however, it is defined in terms of the limit of the expectation of $\hat{\beta}$. The *asymptotic expectation* of $\hat{\beta}$ is defined as the limit of $E(\hat{\beta})$ as the sample size goes to infinity; if this asymptotic expectation is equal to β, then $\hat{\beta}$ is said to be *asymptotically unbiased*.

There exists considerable confusion concerning the exact definitions of these three asymptotic properties, their interrelationships and means of undertaking calculations related to them. Several technical notes to this section attempt to clarify these problems. For our intents and purposes, however, we can usefully conceptualize asymptotic unbiasedness as being the large-sample equivalent of unbiasedness. Similarly, consistency can be crudely conceptualized as the large-sample equivalent of the minimum mean square error property, since a consistent estimator can be (loosely speaking) thought of as having, in the limit, zero bias and a zero variance. Asymptotic efficiency is the large-sample equivalent of best unbiasedness: the variance of an asymptotically efficient estimator goes to zero faster than the variance of any other consistent estimator.

Fig. 2.5 illustrates the basic appeal of asymptotic properties. For sample size 20, the sampling distribution of β^* is shown as $f(\beta^*)_{20}$. Since this sampling distribution is not centred over β, the estimator β^* is biased. As shown in Fig. 2.5, however, as the sample size increases to 40, then 70 and then 100, the sampling distribution of β^* shifts so as to be more closely centred over β (i.e., it becomes less biased), and it becomes less spread out (i.e., its variance becomes smaller). If β^* were consistent, as the sample size increased to infinity the sampling distribution would shrink in width to a single vertical line, of infinite height, placed exactly at the point β.

It must be emphasized that these asymptotic criteria are only employed in situations in which estimators with the traditional desirable small-sample

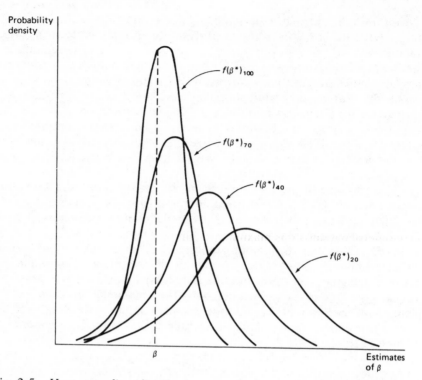

Fig. 2.5 *How sampling distribution can change as the sample size grows*

properties, such as unbiasedness, best unbiasedness and minimum mean square error, cannot be found. Since econometricians quite often must work with small samples, defending estimators on the basis of their asymptotic properties is legitimate only if it is the case that estimators with desirable asymptotic properties have more desirable small-sample properties than do estimators without desirable asymptotic properties. Monte Carlo studies have shown that in general this supposition is warranted.

2.9 Maximum Likelihood

The maximum likelihood principle of estimation is based on the idea that the sample of data at hand is more likely to have come from a 'real world' characterized by one particular set of parameter values than from a 'real world' characterized by any other set of parameter values. The maximum likelihood estimate (MLE) of a vector of parameter values β is simply the particular vector β^{MLE} which gives the greatest probability of obtaining the observed data.

This idea is illustrated in Fig. 2.6. Each of the dots represents an observation on x drawn at random from a population with mean μ and variance σ^2. Pair A of parameter values, μ^A and $(\sigma^2)^A$, gives rise in Fig. 2.6 to the probability density function A for x, while the pair B, μ^B and $(\sigma^2)^B$, gives rise to probability density function B. Inspection of the diagram should reveal that the probability of having obtained the sample in question if the parameter values were μ^A and $(\sigma^2)^A$ is very low compared with the probability of having obtained the sample if the parameter values were μ^B and $(\sigma^2)^B$. On the maximum likelihood principle, pair B is preferred to pair A as an estimate of μ and σ^2. The maximum likelihood estimate is the particular pair of values μ^{MLE} and $(\sigma^2)^{MLE}$ that creates the greatest probability of having obtained the sample in question; i.e., no other pair of values would be preferred to this maximum likelihood pair, in the sense that pair B is preferred to pair A. The means by which the econometrician finds this maximum likelihood estimate is discussed briefly in the technical notes to this section.

In addition to its intuitive appeal, the maximum likelihood estimator has several desirable asymptotic properties. It is asymptotically unbiased, it is consistent, it is asymptotically efficient, and it is distributed asymptotically normally. Its only major theoretical drawback is that in order to calculate the MLE the econometrician must assume a *specific* (e.g., normal) distribution for the error term. Most econometricians seem willing to do this.

These properties make maximum likelihood estimation very appealing for situations in which it is impossible to find estimators with desirable small-sample properties, a situation that arises all too often in practice. In spite of this, however, until recently maximum likelihood estimation has not been popular, mainly because of high computational cost. Considerable algebraic manipulation is required before estimation, and most types

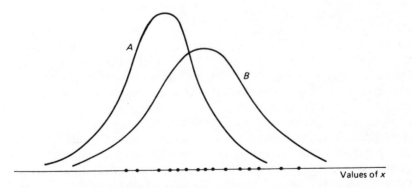

Fig. 2.6 Maximum likelihood estimation

of MLE problems require substantial input preparation for available computer packages. But econometricians' attitude towards MLEs has changed recently, for several reasons. Advances in computers and related software have lessened the computational burden. Many interesting estimation problems have been solved through the use of MLE techniques, rendering this approach more useful (and in the process advertising its properties more widely). And instructors have been teaching students the theoretical aspects of MLE techniques, enabling them to be more comfortable with the algebraic manipulations it requires.

2.10   Monte Carlo Studies

A Monte Carlo study is a simulation exercise designed to shed light on the small-sample properties of competing estimators for a given estimating problem. They are called upon whenever, for that particular problem, there exist potentially attractive estimators whose small-sample properties cannot be derived theoretically. Estimators with unknown small-sample properties are continually being proposed in the econometric literature, so Monte Carlo studies have become quite common, especially now that computer technology has made their undertaking quite cheap. This is one good reason for having a good understanding of this technique. A more important reason is that a thorough understanding of Monte Carlo studies guarantees an understanding of the repeated sample and sampling distribution concepts, crucial to an understanding of econometrics.

The general idea behind a Monte Carlo study is to (1) model the data-generating process, (2) generate several sets of artificial data, (3) employ these data and an estimator to create several estimates, and (4) use these estimates to gauge the sampling distribution properties of that estimator. This is illustrated in Fig. 2.7. These four steps are described below.

(1)   *Model the data-generating process*

Simulation of the process thought to be generating the real-world data for the problem at hand requires building a model for the computer to mimic the data-generating process, including its stochastic component(s). For example, it could be specified that N (the sample size) values of X, Z and an error term generate N values of Y according to $Y = \beta_1 + \beta_2 X + \beta_3 Z + \varepsilon$, where the β_i are specific, known numbers, the N values of X and Z are given, exogenous, observations on explanatory variables, and the N values of ε are drawn randomly from a normal distribution with mean zero and known variance σ^2. (Computers are capable of generating such random error terms.) Any special features thought to characterize the problem at hand must be built into this model. For example, if $\beta_2 = \beta_3^{-1}$ then the

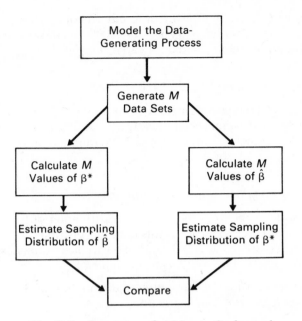

Fig. 2.7   Structure of a Monte Carlo study

values of β_2 and β_3 must be chosen such that this is the case. Or if the variance σ^2 varies from observation to observation, depending on the value of Z, then the error terms must be adjusted accordingly. An important feature of the study is that all of the (usually unknown) parameter values are *known* to the person conducting the study (because this person chooses these values).

(2) *Create sets of data*

With a model of the data-generating process built into the computer, artificial data can be created. The key to doing this is the stochastic element of the data-generating process. A sample of size N is created by obtaining N values of the stochastic variable ε and then using these values, in conjunction with the rest of the model, to generate N values of Y. This yields one complete sample of size N, namely N observations on each of Y, X and Z, corresponding to the particular set of N error terms drawn. Note that this artificially generated set of sample data could be viewed as an *example* of real-world data that a researcher would be faced with when dealing with the kind of estimation problem this model represents. Note especially that the set of data obtained depends crucially on the particular set of error terms drawn. A different set of error terms would create a different data set *for the same problem*. Several of these examples of data sets could be created by drawing different sets of N error terms. Suppose this is done, say, 2000 times, generating 2000 sets of sample data, each of sample size N. These are called repeated samples.

(3) *Calculate estimates*

Each of the 2000 repeated samples can be used as data for an estimator $\hat{\beta}_3$, say, creating 2000 estimates $\hat{\beta}_{3i}$ ($i = 1, 2, \ldots, 2000$) of the parameter β_3. These 2000 estimates can be viewed as random 'drawings' from the sampling distribution of $\hat{\beta}_3$.

(4) *Estimate sampling distribution properties*

These 2000 drawings from the sampling distribution of $\hat{\beta}_3$ can be used as data to estimate the properties of this sampling distribution. The properties of most interest are its expected value and variance, estimates of which can be used to estimate bias and mean square error.

(a) The *expected value* of the sampling distribution of $\hat{\beta}_3$ is estimated by the average of the 2000 estimates:

$$\text{estimated expected value} = \bar{\hat{\beta}} = \left(\sum_{i=1}^{2000} \hat{\beta}_{3i} \right)/2000.$$

(b) The *bias* of $\hat{\beta}_3$ is estimated by subtracting the known true value of β_3 from the average:

$$\text{estimated bias} = \bar{\hat{\beta}}_3 - \beta_3 \ .$$

(c) The variance of the sampling distribution of $\hat{\beta}_3$ is estimated by using the traditional formula for estimating variance:

$$\text{estimated variance} = \sum_{i=1}^{2000} (\hat{\beta}_{3i} - \bar{\hat{\beta}}_3)^2/1999.$$

(d) The mean square error of $\hat{\beta}_3$ is estimated by the average of the squared differences between $\hat{\beta}_3$ and the true value of β_3:

$$\text{estimated MSE} = \sum_{i=1}^{2000} (\hat{\beta}_{3i} - \beta_3)^2/2000.$$

At stage 3 above an alternative estimator β_3^* could also have been used to calculate 2000 estimates, corresponding to β_3^*. If so, the properties of the sampling distribution of β_3^* could also be estimated and then compared with those of the sampling distribution of $\hat{\beta}_3$. (Here $\hat{\beta}_3$ could be, for example, the ordinary least squares estimator and β_3^* any competing estimator such as an instrumental variable estimator, the least absolute error estimator or a generalized least squares estimator. These estimators are discussed in later chapters.) On the basis of this comparison, the person conducting the Monte Carlo study may be in a position to recommend one estimator in preference to another for the sample size N.

2.11 Adding Up

Because in most estimating situations there does not exist a 'super-estimator' that is better than all other estimators on all or even most of these (or other) criteria, the ultimate choice of estimator is made by forming an 'overall judgement' of the desirableness of each available estimator by combining the degree to which an estimator meets each of these criteria with a subjective (on the part of the econometrician) evaluation of the importance of each of these criteria. Sometimes an econometrician will hold a particular criterion in very high esteem and this will determine the estimator chosen (if an estimator meeting this criterion can be found). More typically, other criteria also play a role in the econometrician's choice of estimator, so that, for example, only estimators with reasonable computational cost are considered. Among these major criteria, most attention seems to be paid to the best unbiased criterion, with occasional deference to the mean square error criterion in estimating situations in which all unbiased estimators have variances that are considered too large. If estimators meeting these criteria cannot be found, as is often the case, asymptotic criteria are adopted.

A major skill of econometricians is the ability to determine estimator properties with regard to the criteria discussed in this chapter. This is done either through theoretical derivations using mathematics, part of the technical expertise of the econometrician, or through Monte Carlo studies. To derive estimator properties by either of these means, the mechanism generating the observations must be known; changing the way in which the observations are generated creates a new estimating problem, in which old estimators may have new properties and for which new estimators may have to be developed.

The OLS estimator has a special place in all this. When faced with any estimating problem, the econometric theorist usually tests the OLS estimator first, determining whether or not it has desirable properties. As seen in the next chapter, in some circumstances it does have desirable properties and is chosen as the 'preferred' estimator, but in many other circumstances it does not have desirable properties and a replacement must be found. The econometrician must investigate the circumstances under which the OLS estimate is desirable, and suggest alternative estimators for situations in which the OLS estimator is not acceptable. The next chapter explains how the econometrician orders this investigation.

General Notes

2.2   Computational Cost

• Computational cost has been reduced significantly by the development of extensive computer software for econometricians. For mainframes, RAPE, SHAZAM, TROLL and TSP are popular, and for micros, RATS and a micro-version of SHAZAM are available. All these packages are very comprehensive, encompassing most of the econometric techniques discussed in textbooks. For applications they do not cover, in most cases specialized programs exist. These packages should only be used by those well versed in econometric theory, however. Misleading or even erroneous results can easily be produced if these packages are used without a full understanding of the circumstances in which they are applicable, their inherent assumptions and the nature of their output; sound research cannot be produced merely by feeding data to a computer and saying SHAZAM.

• Problems with the accuracy of computer calculations are ignored in practice, but can be considerable. See Aigner (1971), pp. 99–101, and Rhodes (1975). Quandt (1983) is a survey of computational problems and methods in econometrics.

2.3   Least Squares

• Experiments have shown that OLS estimates tend to correspond to the average of laymen's 'freehand' attempts to fit a line to a scatter of data. See Mosteller *et al.* (1981).

• In Fig. 2.1 the residuals were measured as the vertical distances from the observations to the estimated line. A natural alternative to this vertical measure is the orthogonal measure – the distance from the observation to the estimating line along a line perpendicular to the estimating line. This infrequently seen alternative is discussed in Malinvaud (1966) pp. 7–11; it is sometimes used when measurement errors plague the data, as discussed in section 8.2.

• When residuals are squared, large residuals become relatively larger, implying that, when the sum of squared residuals is minimized, extra care is taken to avoid large residuals. An implication of this is that very large residuals have an extraordinarily strong influence on the parameter estimates, since when a very large number is squared it becomes an *extremely* large number. This is in turn means that OLS estimates are quite sensitive to 'statistical outliers', observations that are abnormal for some special reason such as an error in gathering data, a mistake in key-punching or an unusual circumstance associated with a particular observation, such as an earthquake or an accountant's 'extraordinary item'. Most of the alternative systems of weighting the residuals to form a function to be minimized are designed to reduce or avoid this influence of outliers.

• Estimators that are not sensitive to outliers are called *robust* estimators. More generally, a robust estimator is one whose desirable properties are insensitive to departures from the assumptions under which it is derived: it offers protection against certain fairly general model failures while preserving high efficiency in well-behaved situations.

• The most common robust estimator is the MAD (mean absolute deviation), LAR (least absolute residual) or LAE (least absolute error) estimator. This estimator minimizes the sum of the absolute values of the residuals. It can be obtained as the solution to a linear programming problem. Although some direct comparisons with OLS have shown it to be superior for forecasting and superior in the presence of fat-tailed distributions, not much is known about the properties of this estimator. Even less is known about other robust estimators. Taylor (1974) and Narula and Wellington (1982) have good surveys of LAR estimation. Maddala (1977) pp. 308–14 has a good textbook exposition of robust methods. Koenker (1982) is an advanced survey.

- Koenker and Basset (1978) suggest a promising generalization of LAR using regression quantiles. The θth regression quantile ($0<\theta<1$) is defined as any solution to the minimization problem

$$\min_{b} \left\{ \sum_{A} \theta |y_t - x_t b| + \sum_{B} (1 - \theta) |y_t - x_t b| \right\}$$

where $A(B)$ consists of all values of θ for which the residual ($y_t - x_t b$) is positive (negative). Clearly, when $\theta = \frac{1}{2}$ this produces the LAR estimator. It is suggested that β be estimated by a weighted average of selected regression quantiles. The most prominent of these are the *Gatswirth*, in which the $\frac{1}{3}$, $\frac{1}{2}$ and $\frac{2}{3}$ regression quantiles are weighted 0.3, 0.4 and 0.3, and the *trimean*, in which the $\frac{1}{4}$, $\frac{1}{2}$ and $\frac{3}{4}$ regression quantiles are weighted 0.25, 0.5 and 0.25. A related suggestion is the trimmed least squares estimator. Calculate, say, the 0.05 and 0.95 regression quantiles, discard all observations below the former and above the latter, and use the remaining observations to estimate β via OLS. Judge *et al* (1985) pp. 834–9 have a good exposition.

- When account is taken of other criteria discussed later in this chapter (such as mean square error), the extent to which OLS outperforms (or is outperformed by) these alternative 'robust' estimators depends on the nature of the distribution of the disturbances. In particular, disturbances whose distributions have thick tails decrease the relative performance of the OLS estimator.

- Closely related to an outlier is an observation containing an unusual value of the explanatory variable(s). Either phenomenon can have a substantial impact on a regression analysis, in which case this observation is called an *influential observation*. Such an observation is detected by examining the extent to which the fit of the regression or the values of the estimated coefficients change whenever that observation is omitted. Belsley *et al* (1980) chapter 2 and Krasker *et al*. (1983) discuss this at some length. Detection of such observations allows the researcher to examine carefully whether they arose because of some kind of data error or whether they could represent valuable information. Krasker *et al*. (1983) suggest that estimation in this context be undertaken by a technique called *bounded influence regression*, in which these observations are down-weighted in the regression according to how influential they are.

- This discussion of detecting influential observations suggests that perhaps in general more effort should be expended in looking at the data themselves rather than at summary statistics which can mask important features of that data. This is one of the foundations of EDA, *exploratory data analysis*. This approach to statistics emphasizes that a researcher should begin his or her analyses by looking at the data, on the grounds that the more familiar one is with one's data the more effectively they can be used to develop, test and refine theory. Exploratory data analysts believe in the *inter-ocular trauma test*: keep looking at the data until the answer hits you between the eyes! They use a variety of novel ways of displaying data visually, such as the stem and leaf and the box and whisker diagrams. For an excellent exposition of this approach see Hartwig and Dearing (1979).

2.4 Highest R^2

- R^2 is called the coefficient of determination. It is the square of the correlation coefficient between y and its OLS estimate $\hat{y}$.

- The total variation of the dependent variable y about its mean, $\Sigma(y - \bar{y})^2$, is called *SST* (the total sum of squares); the 'explained' variation, the sum of squared deviations of the estimated values of the dependent variable about their mean, $\Sigma(\hat{y} - \bar{y})^2$ is called *SSR* (the regression sum of squares); and the 'unexplained' variation, the sum of squared residuals, is called *SSE* (the error sum of squares). R^2 is then given by *SSR/SST* or by $1 - (SSE/SST)$.

- What is a high R^2? There is no generally accepted answer to this question. In dealing with time-series data, very high R^2s are not unusual, due to common trends. Ames and Reiter (1961) found, for example, that on average the R^2 of a relationship between a randomly chosen variable and its own value lagged one period is about 0.7, and that an R^2 in excess of 0.5 could be obtained by selecting an economic time series and regressing it against two to six other randomly selected economic time series. For cross-sectional data, typical R^2s are not nearly so high.

- The OLS estimator maximizes R^2. Since the R^2 measure is used as an index of how well an estimator 'fits' the sample data, the OLS estimator is often called the 'best-fitting' estimator. A high R^2 is often called a 'good fit'.

- Because the R^2 and OLS criteria are formally identical, objections to the latter apply to the former. The most frequently voiced of these is that searching for a good fit is likely to generate parameter estimates tailored to the particular sample at hand rather than to the underlying 'real world'. Further, a high R^2 is not necessary for 'good' estimates; R^2 could be low because of a high variance of the disturbance terms, and our estimate of β could be 'good' on other criteria, such as those discussed later in this chapter.

- The neat breakdown of the total variation into the 'explained' and 'unexplained' variations that allows meaningful interpretation of the R^2 statistic is valid only under three conditions. First, the estimator in question must be the OLS estimator. Second, the relationship being estimated must be linear. Thus the R^2 statistic only gives the percentage of the variation in the dependent variable explained *linearly* by variation in the independent variables. And third, the linear relationship being estimated must include a constant, or intercept, term. The formulae for R^2 can still be used to calculate an R^2 for estimators other than the OLS estimator, for nonlinear cases and for cases in which the intercept term is omitted; it can no longer have the same meaning, however, and could possibly lie outside the 0–1 interval. The zero intercept case is discussed at length in Aigner (1971) pp. 85–90. An alternative R^2 measure, in which the variations in y and $\hat{y}$ are measured as deviations from zero rather than their means, is suggested.

- Running a regression without an intercept is the most common way of obtaining an R^2 outside the 0–1 range. To see how this could happen, draw a scatter of points in (x,y) space with an estimated OLS line such that there is a substantial intercept. Now draw in the OLS line that would be estimated if it were forced to go through the origin. In both cases *SST* is identical (because the same observations are used). But in the second case the *SSE* and the *SSR* could be gigantic, because the $\hat{e}$s and the $(\hat{y} - \bar{y})$s could be huge. Thus if R^2 is calculated as $1 - SSE/SST$, a negative number could result; if it is calculated as SSR/SST, a number greater than one could result.

- R^2 is sensitive to the range of variation of the dependent variable, so that comparisons of R^2s must be undertaken with care. The favourite example used to illustrate this is the case of the consumption function versus the savings function. If savings is defined as income less consumption, income will do exactly as well in explaining variations in consumption as in explaining variations in saving, in the sense that the sum of squared residuals, the unexplained variation, will be exactly the same for each case. But in *percentage* terms, the unexplained variation will be a higher percentage of the variation in saving than of the variation in consumption because the latter are larger numbers. Thus the R^2 in the savings function case will be lower than in the consumption function case. This reflects the result that the expected value of R^2 is approximately equal to $\beta^2 V/(\beta^2 V + \sigma^2)$ where V is $\Sigma(x - \bar{x})^2$.

- In general, econometricians are interested in obtaining 'good' parameter estimates where 'good' is not defined in terms of R^2. Consequently the measure R^2 is not of much importance in econometrics. Unfortunately, however, many practitioners act as though it is important; because of this, the meaning and role of R^2 is discussed at some length throughout this book. Section 4.5 and its general notes extend the discussion of this section. Comments are offered in the general notes of other sections when appropriate. For example, one should be aware that R^2 from two equations with different dependent variables should not be compared, and that adding dummy variables (to capture seasonal influences, for example) can inflate R^2.

2.5 Unbiasedness

- Problems in the use and interpretation of the unbiasedness criterion arise in contexts in which it is illegitimate even to conceptualize the independent variables as being fixed in repeated samples, since that criterion requires that the independent variables be fixed in repeated samples. Examples, such as cases in which the independent variables are themselves random variables, are not uncommon in econometrics. See chapters 8 and 9.

- In contrast to the OLS and R^2 criteria, the unbiasedness criterion (and the other criteria related to the sampling distribution) say something specific about the relationship of the estimator to β, the parameter being estimated.

- Many econometricians are not impressed with the unbiasedness criterion, as our later discussion of the mean square error criterion will attest. Savage (1954) p. 244 goes so far as to say: 'A serious reason to prefer unbiased estimates seems never to have been proposed.' This feeling probably stems from the fact that it is possible to have an 'unlucky' sample and thus a bad estimate, with only cold comfort from the knowledge that, had all possible samples of that size been taken, the correct estimate would have been hit on average. This is especially the case whenever a crucial outcome, such as in the case of a matter of life or death, or a decision to undertake a huge capital expenditure, hinges on a single correct estimate. None the less, unbiasedness has enjoyed remarkable popularity among practitioners. Part of the reason for this may be due to the emotive content of the terminology: who can stand up in public and state that they prefer *biased* estimators?

2.6 Best Unbiased

- The BLUE is simply the linear unbiased estimator that minimizes the variance of $\hat{\beta}$, i.e., minimizes the expected value of the square of the deviation of $\hat{\beta}$ from its expected value β. Minimizing the square of this deviation is not the only alternative. Some researchers might prefer to minimize the expectation of the absolute value of this deviation, for reasons similar to those given for the least absolute error estimator discussed in the notes to section 2.3. See, for example, Kadiyala (1972).

- The efficiency property can be sensitive to sample size. An estimator that is efficient for one sample size may not be for another. This is particularly the case when small samples are compared with very large samples.

- Linear estimators are not suitable for all estimating problems. For example, in estimating the variance σ^2 of the disturbance term, quadratic estimators are more appropriate. The traditional formula $SSE/(T - K)$, where T is the number of observations and K is the number of explanatory variables (including a constant), is under general conditions the best quadratic unbiased estimator of σ^2. Note that this formula is sometimes written as $SSE/(T - K - 1)$. Use of this version occurs when K, the number of explanatory variables, does not include the constant (intercept) term.

- Although in many instances it is mathematically impossible to determine the best unbiased estimator (as opposed to the best *linear* unbiased estimator), this is not the case if the *specific* distribution is known. In this instance a lower bound, called the *Cramer–Rao lower bound,* for the variance (or variance–covariance matrix) of unbiased estimators can be calculated. Furthermore, if this lower bound is attained (which is not always the case), it is attained by a transformation of the maximum likelihood estimator (see section 2.9) that creates an unbiased estimator. See Kane (1968) pp. 187–8 for a discussion of the univariate case, and Kmenta (1971) pp. 159–60 for a discussion of the multivariate case. As an example, consider the sample mean statistic $\bar{X}$. Its variance, σ^2/T, is equal to the Cramer–Rao lower bound if the parent population is normal. Thus $\bar{X}$ is the best unbiased estimator of the mean of a normal population.

2.7 Mean Square Error

- Preference for the mean square error criterion over the unbiasedness criterion often hinges on the use to which the estimate is put. As an example of this, consider a man betting on horse races. If he is buying 'win' tickets, he will want an unbiased estimate of the winning horse, but if he is buying 'show' tickets it is not important that his horse wins the race (only that his horse finishes among the first three), so he will be willing to use a slightly biased estimator of the winning horse if it has a smaller variance.

- The difference between the variance of an estimator and its MSE is that the variance measures the dispersion of the estimator around its mean whereas the

MSE measures its dispersion around the true value of the parameter being estimated. For unbiased estimators they are identical.

- Biased estimators with smaller variances than unbiased estimators are easy to find. For example, if $\hat{\beta}$ is an unbiased estimator with variance $V(\hat{\beta})$, then $0.9\hat{\beta}$ is a biased estimator with variance $0.81V(\hat{\beta})$. As a more relevant example, consider the fact that, although $SSE/(T - K)$ is the best quadratic unbiased estimator of σ^2, as noted in section 2.6, it can be shown that among quadratic estimators the MSE estimator of σ^2 is $SSE/(T - K + 2)$.

- The MSE estimator has not been as popular as the best unbiased estimator because of the mathematical difficulties in its derivation. Furthermore, when it can be derived its formula often involves unknown coefficients (the value of β), making its application impossible. Monte Carlo studies have shown that approximating the estimator by using OLS estimates of the unknown parameters can sometimes circumvent this problem.

- Both the best unbiased and the MSE criteria rest heavily on the use of the quadratic loss function. Although this type of loss function has the disadvantage of being symmetrical, it has the advantage of being mathematically convenient and a reasonable approximation to more complicated loss functions.

2.8 Asymptotic Properties

- How large does the sample size have to be for estimators to display their asymptotic properties? The answer to this crucial question depends on the characteristics of the problem at hand. Goldfeld and Quandt (1972) p. 277 report an example in which a sample size of 30 is sufficiently large and an example in which a sample of 200 is required. They also note that large sample sizes are needed if interest focuses on estimation of estimator variances rather than on estimation of coefficients.

- An extremely appealing feature of probability limits (see the Technical Notes) is that the probability limit of a nonlinear function of an estimator is the nonlinear function of the probability limit of the estimator, a property that does not hold true for expectations. Thus, plim $g(\hat{\beta}) = g(\text{plim } \hat{\beta})$ but $Eg(\hat{\beta}) \neq g(E\hat{\beta})$, when g is a nonlinear function. As a specific example, consider the problem of estimating $1/\beta$. Even if $\hat{\beta}$ is an unbiased estimator of β, $1/\hat{\beta}$ is *not* an unbiased estimator of $1/\beta$; but if $\hat{\beta}$ is a consistent estimator of β, $1/\hat{\beta}$ will be a consistent estimator of $1/\beta$.

    It is this property that makes possible the algebraic derivation of asymptotic properties of many estimators in contexts in which the small-sample properties of these estimators cannot be deduced. Econometricians should not allow this attractive feature of asymptotic criteria to steer them away from examining the small-sample properties of alternative estimators, however.

2.9 Maximum Likelihood

- Note that β^{MLE} is *not*, as is sometimes carelessly stated, the most probable value of β; the most probable value of β is β itself. (Only in a Bayesian interpretation, discussed later in this book, would the former statement be meaningful.) β^{MLE} is simply the value of β that maximizes the probability of drawing the sample actually obtained.

- The asymptotic variance of the MLE is usually equal to the Cramer–Rao lower bound, the lowest asymptotic variance that a consistent estimator can have. This is why the MLE is asymptotically efficient. Consequently, the variance (not just the asymptotic variance) of the MLE is estimated by an estimate of the Cramer–Rao lower bound. The formula for the Cramer–Rao lower bound is given in the technical notes to this section.

- Despite the fact that β^{MLE} is sometimes a biased estimator of β (although asymptotically unbiased), often a simple adjustment can be found that creates an unbiased estimator, and this unbiased estimator can be shown to be best unbiased (with no linearity requirement) through the relationship between the maximum likelihood estimator and the Cramer–Rao lower bound. For example, the maximum likelihood estimator of the variance of a random variable x is given by the formula

$$\sum_{i=1}^{T} (x_i - \bar{x})^2 / T$$

which is a biased (but asymptotically unbiased) estimator of the true variance. By multiplying this expression by $T/(T - 1)$, this estimator can be transformed into a best unbiased estimator.

- Maximum likelihood estimators have an invariance property similar to that of consistent estimators. The maximum likelihood estimator of a nonlinear function of a parameter is the nonlinear function of the maximum likelihood estimator of that parameter: $[g(\beta)]^{MLE} = g(\beta^{MLE})$ where g is a nonlinear function. This greatly simplifies the algebraic derivations of maximum likelihood estimators, making adoption of this criterion more attractive.

- Goldfeld and Quandt (1972) conclude that the maximum likelihood technique performs well in a wide variety of applications and for relatively small sample sizes. It is particularly evident, from reading their book, that the maximum likelihood technique is well-suited to estimation involving nonlinearities and unusual estimation problems. Even in 1972 they did not feel that the computational costs of MLE were prohibitive.

- Application of the maximum likelihood technique requires that the econometrician assume a specific distribution for the error term. The normal distribution is invariably chosen for this purpose, usually on the grounds that the error term consists of the sum of a large number of random shocks and thus, by the Central Limit Theorem, can be considered to be approximately normally distributed. (See Bartels, 1977, for a warning on the use of this argument.) A more compelling reason is that the normal distribution is relatively easy to work with. See the general notes to chapter 4 for further discussion.

- Kmenta (1971) pp. 174–82 has a clear discussion of maximum likelihood estimation. A good brief exposition is in Kane (1968) pp. 177–80. Valavanis (1959) pp. 23–6, an econometrics text subtitled 'An Introduction to Maximum Likelihood Methods', has an interesting account of the meaning of the maximum likelihood technique.

2.10   Monte Carlo Studies

- The Monte Carlo technique can be used to examine test statistics as well as parameter estimators. For example, a test statistic could be examined to see how closely its sampling distribution matches, say, a chi-square. In this context interest would undoubtedly focus on determining its size (type I error for a given critical value) and power, particularly as compared with alternative test statistics.

- Examples of and advice on Monte Carlo methods can be found in Smith (1973). Hendry (1984) is a more advanced reference.

2.11 Adding Up

- Other, less prominent, criteria exist for selecting point estimates, some examples of which follow.
  (a) *Admissibility* An estimator is said to be admissible (with respect to some criterion) if, for at least one value of the unknown β, it cannot be beaten on that criterion by any other estimator.
  (b) *Minimax* A minimax estimator is one that minimizes the maximum loss, usually measured as MSE, generated by competing estimators as the unknown β varies through its possible values.
  (c) *Robustness* An estimator is said to be robust if its desirable properties are not sensitive to violations of the conditions under which it is optimal. In general, a robust estimator is applicable to a wide variety of situations, and is relatively unaffected by a small number of bad data values. See the general notes to section 2.3 above.
  (d) *MELO* In the Bayesian approach to statistics (see chapter 12), a decision-theoretic approach is taken to estimation; an estimate is chosen such that it minimizes an expected loss function and is called the MELO (minimum expected loss) estimator. Under general conditions, if a quadratic loss function is adopted the mean of the posterior distribution of β is chosen as the point estimate of β and this has been interpreted in the non-Bayesian approach as corresponding to minimization of average risk. (Risk is the sum of the MSEs of the individual elements of the estimator of the vector β.) See Zellner (1978).
  (e) *Analogy Principle* Parameters are estimated by sample statistics that have the same property in the sample as the parameters do in the population. See chapter 2 of Goldberger (1968b) for an interpretation of the OLS estimator in these terms. This approach is sometimes called the *method of moments* because it implies that a moment of the population distribution will be estimated by the corresponding moment of the sample.

- Two good general references covering in more detail the material presented in this chapter are Kmenta (1971) pp. 8–15, 154–86, and Kane (1968) chapter 8.

Technical Notes

2.5 Unbiasedness

- The expected value of a variable x is defined formally as $Ex = \int xf(x)dx$ where f is the probability density function (sampling distribution) of x. Thus $E(x)$ could be viewed as a weighted average of all possible values of x where the weights are proportional to the heights of the density function (sampling distribution) of x.

2.6   Best Unbiased

- In our discussion of unbiasedness, no confusion could arise from β being multidimensional: an estimator's expected value is either equal to β (in every dimension) or it is not. But in the case of the variance of an estimator, confusion could arise. An estimator β^* that is k-dimensional really consists of k different estimators, one for each dimension of β. These k different estimators all have their own variances. If all k of the variances associated with the estimator β^* are smaller than their respective counterparts of the estimator $\hat{\beta}$, then it is clear that the variance of β^* can be considered smaller than the variance of $\hat{\beta}$. For example, if β is two-dimensional, consisting of two separate parameters β_1 and β_2

$$\left(\text{i.e., } \beta = \begin{bmatrix} \beta_1 \\ \beta_2 \end{bmatrix} \right),$$

an estimator β^* would consist of two estimators β_1^* and β_2^*. If β^* were an unbiased estimator of β, β_1^* would be an unbiased estimator of β_1 and β_2^* would be an unbiased estimator of β_2. The estimators β_1^* and β_2^* would each have variances. Suppose their variances were 3.1 and 7.4, respectively. Now suppose $\hat{\beta}$, consisting of $\hat{\beta}_1$ and $\hat{\beta}_2$, is another unbiased estimator, where $\hat{\beta}_1$ and $\hat{\beta}_2$ have variances 5.6 and 8.3, respectively. In this example, since the variance of β_1^* is less than the variance of $\hat{\beta}_1$ and the variance of β_2^* is less than the variance of $\hat{\beta}_2$, it is clear that the 'variance' of β^* is less than the variance of $\hat{\beta}$. But what if the variance of $\hat{\beta}_2$ were 6.3 instead of 8.3? Then it is *not* clear which 'variance' is smallest.

- An additional complication exists in comparing the variances of estimators of a multidimensional β. There may exist a non-zero covariance between the estimators of the separate components of β. For example, a positive covariance between $\hat{\beta}_1$ and $\hat{\beta}_2$ implies that, whenever $\hat{\beta}_1$ overestimates β_1, there is a tendency for $\hat{\beta}_2$ to overestimate β_2, making the complete estimate of β worse than would be the case were this covariance zero. Comparison of the 'variances' of multidimensional estimators should therefore somehow account for this covariance phenomenon.

- The 'variance' of a multidimensional estimator is called a variance–covariance matrix. If β^* is an estimator of a k-dimensional β, then the variance–covariance matrix of β^*, denoted by $V(\beta^*)$, is defined as a $k \times k$ matrix (a table with k entries in each direction) containing the variances of the k elements of β^* along the diagonal and the covariances in the off-diagonal positions. Thus,

$$V(\beta^*) = \begin{bmatrix} V(\beta_1^*), & C(\beta_1^*, \beta_2^*), & \dots, & C(\beta_1^*, \beta_k^*) \\ & V(\beta_2^*) & & \\ & & \ddots & \\ & & & V(\beta_k^*) \end{bmatrix}$$

where $V(\beta_k^*)$ is the variance of the kth element of β^* and $C(\beta_1^*, \beta_2^*)$ is the covariance between β_1^* and β_2^*. All this variance–covariance matrix does is array the relevant variances and covariances in a table. Once this is done, the econometrician can draw on mathematicians' knowledge of matrix algebra to suggest ways in which the variance–covariance matrix of one unbiased estimator could be considered 'smaller' than the variance–covariance matrix of another unbiased estimator.

- Consider four alternative ways of measuring smallness among variance–covariance matrices, all accomplished by transforming the matrices into single numbers and then comparing those numbers:
  (1) choose the unbiased estimator whose variance–covariance matrix has the smallest *trace* (sum of diagonal elements);
  (2) choose the unbiased estimator whose variance–covariance matrix has the smallest *determinant*;

(3) choose the unbiased estimator for which any given linear combination of its elements has the smallest variance;

(4) choose the unbiased estimator whose variance–covariance matrix minimizes a loss function consisting of a weighted sum of the individual variances and covariances.

This last criterion seems sensible: a researcher can weight the variances and covariances according to the importance he or she subjectively feels their minimization should be given in choosing an estimator. It happens that in the context of an unbiased estimator this loss function can be expressed in an alternative form, as the expected value of a quadratic function of the difference between the estimate and the true parameter value; i.e., $E(\hat{\beta} - \beta)(\hat{\beta} - \beta)'$. This alternative interpretation also makes good intuitive sense as a choice criterion for use in the estimating context.

If the weights in the loss function described above are chosen so as to make it impossible for the loss function to become negative (a reasonable request, since it is supposed to be a *loss* function), then a very fortunate thing occurs. Under these circumstances all four of these criteria lead to the same choice of estimator. What is more, this result does *not* depend on the particular weights used in the loss function.

Although these four ways of defining a smallest matrix are reasonably straightforward, econometricians have chosen, for mathematical reasons, to use as their definition an equivalent but conceptually more difficult idea. This fifth rule says, choose the unbiased estimator whose variance–covariance matrix, when subtracted from the variance–covariance matrix of any other unbiased estimator, leaves a non-negative definite matrix. (A matrix A is non-negative definite if the quadratic function formed by using the elements of A as parameters ($x'Ax$) takes on only non-negative values for all non-zero vectors x).

Proofs of the equivalence of these five selection rules can be constructed by consulting Rothenberg (1973) p. 8, Theil (1971) p. 121, and Goldberger (1964) p. 38.

• A special case of the loss function is revealing. Suppose we choose the weighting such that the variance of any one element of the estimator has a very heavy weight, with all other weights negligible. This implies that each of the elements of the estimator with the 'smallest' variance–covariance matrix has individual minimum variance. (Thus, the example given earlier of one estimator with individual variances 3.1 and 7.4 and another with variances 5.6 and 6.3 is unfair; these two estimators could be combined into a new estimator with variances 3.1 and 6.3.) This special case also indicates that in general covariances play no role in determining the best estimator.

2.7 Mean Square Error

• In the multivariate context the MSE criterion can be interpreted in terms of the 'smallest' (as defined in the technical notes to section 2.6) MSE matrix. This matrix, given by the formula $E(\hat{\beta} - \beta)(\hat{\beta} - \beta)'$, is a natural matrix generalization of the MSE criterion. In practice, however, this generalization is shunned in favour of *risk*, the sum of the MSEs of all the individual components of $\hat{\beta}$.

2.8 Asymptotic Properties

• As the sample size increases, the sampling distribution of an estimator can change its basic mathematical form, as well as its mean and variance. If an estimator's limiting distribution is normal, it is said to be *asymptotically normally distributed*. According to the *Central Limit Theorem*, the sample mean statistic for samples from any population with finite mean and variance is distributed asymptotically normally.

• plim $\hat{\beta} = k$ means that the sampling distribution of $\hat{\beta}$ collapses on the value k as the sample size T approaches infinity (i.e., the sampling distribution of $\hat{\beta}$ approaches a degenerate distribution with all the probability concentrated at the value k). This 'convergence in probability' of $\hat{\beta}$ to k is usually written more formally as

$$\text{plim } \hat{\beta} = k \text{ if } \lim_{T \to \infty} \text{ prob } (|\hat{\beta} - k| < \delta) = 1$$

where δ is any arbitrarily small positive number. Roughly translated, this means that by increasing the sample size indefinitely we can be almost certain of making $\hat{\beta}$ lie as close as we wish to k.

- A formal definition of consistency would be as follows: an estimator $\hat{\beta}$ of β is consistent if the probability that $\hat{\beta}$ differs in absolute value from β by less than some pre-assigned positive number δ (however small) can be made as close to 1 as desired by choosing a suitably large sample size.

- The probability limit and the asymptotic expectation of an estimator are not necessarily the same. Consider the example in which Prob $(\hat{\beta} = \beta) = 1 - 1/T$ and Prob $(\hat{\beta} = T) = 1/T$ where T is the sample size. It is easily seen that plim $\hat{\beta} = \beta$ but that

$$\lim_{T \to \infty} E(\hat{\beta}) = \beta + 1.$$

(Furthermore,

$$\lim_{T \to \infty} V(\hat{\beta}) = \infty .)$$

- It is not unusual for the mean of the limiting distribution of $\hat{\beta}$ to exist without the expected value (and thus the asymptotic expectation) of $\hat{\beta}$ existing. For example, consider the statistic $1/\bar{X}$. Because of the (remote) possibility that $\bar{X} = 0$, the expected value and variance of this statistic do not exist; its limiting distribution does exist (with mean $1/\mu$ and variance $\sigma^2/T\mu^4$), however, and its probability limit can be calculated as $1/\mu$. (Here $\bar{X}$ is the mean of a sample drawn randomly from a population with mean μ and variance σ^2.)

- Sometimes an estimator is defined to be consistent if (1) it is asymptotically unbiased, and (2) its asymptotic variance goes to zero as the sample size approaches infinity. (This definition is at times stated in terms of the limit of the mean square error of $\hat{\beta}$ being zero.) Although this is a *sufficient* condition for $\hat{\beta}$ to be consistent, it is *not* a necessary condition, and thus should not be used as a definition of consistency. This is illustrated by the two preceding examples.

- The asymptotic variance cannot be calculated by taking the limit of the estimator's variance as the sample size goes to infinity, because this limit is often zero. Although strictly speaking this asymptotic variance should be computed by calculating the variance of the asymptotic distribution, operationally what is usually done is to perform the following calculation:

$$\text{Asy. Var } \hat{\beta} = \frac{1}{T} \lim_{T \to \infty} T V(\hat{\beta}).$$

- There do exist estimators that are asymptotically unbiased but not consistent. Consider the estimator of the population mean μ defined by

$$\hat{\mu} = \tfrac{1}{2}x_1 + \frac{1}{2(T-1)} \sum_{i=2}^{T} x_i .$$

Since

$$\lim_{T \to \infty} E \hat{\mu} = \mu,$$

then $\hat{\mu}$ is asymptotically unbiased. But plim $\hat{\mu} = \tfrac{1}{2}x_1 + \tfrac{1}{2}\mu$. Note that the asymptotic variance of $\hat{\mu}$ is $\sigma^2/4 + \sigma^2/4T$, which does not go to zero as the sample size T goes to infinity. (Here σ^2 is the variance of x.)

- The comments and examples given above note definite differences between probability limits and asymptotic expectations. Because probability limits are much easier to evaluate and work with, econometricians often ignore these differences and equate asymptotic expectations to probability limits. This is legitimate only if both the asymptotic expectation and the probability limit exist, and if

$$\lim_{T \to \infty} V(\hat{\beta}) = 0.$$

- Kmenta (1971) pp. 162–71 has a clear discussion of asymptotic properties. Other good discussions can be found in Maddala (1977) pp. 148–51 and in Johnston (1984) pp. 268–74. Advanced references are White (1984) and Greenberg and Webster (1983).

- The reason for the important result that $E\,g(x) \neq g(Ex)$ for g nonlinear is illustrated in Fig. 2.8. On the horizontal axis are measured values of $\hat{\beta}$, the sampling distribution of which is portrayed by $pdf(\hat{\beta})$, with values of $g(\hat{\beta})$ measured on the vertical axis. Values A and B of $\hat{\beta}$, equidistant from $E\hat{\beta}$, are traced to give $g(A)$ and $g(B)$. Note that $g(B)$ is much farther from $g(E\hat{\beta})$ than is $g(A)$: high values of $\hat{\beta}$ lead to values of $g(\hat{\beta})$ considerably above $g(E\hat{\beta})$, but low values of $\hat{\beta}$ lead to values of $g(\hat{\beta})$ only slightly below $g(E\hat{\beta})$. Consequently the sampling distribution of $g(\hat{\beta})$ is asymmetric, as shown by $pdf[g(\hat{\beta})]$, and in this example the expected value of $g(\hat{\beta})$ lies above $g(E\hat{\beta})$.

  If g were a linear function, the asymmetry portrayed in Fig. 2.8 would not arise and thus we would have $Eg(\hat{\beta}) = g(E\hat{\beta})$. For g nonlinear, however, this result does not hold.

  Suppose now that we allow the sample size to become very large, and suppose that plim $\hat{\beta}$ exists and is equal to $E\hat{\beta}$ in Fig. 2.8. As the sample size becomes very large, the sampling distribution $pdf(\hat{\beta})$ begins to collapse on plim $\hat{\beta}$; i.e., its variance becomes very, very

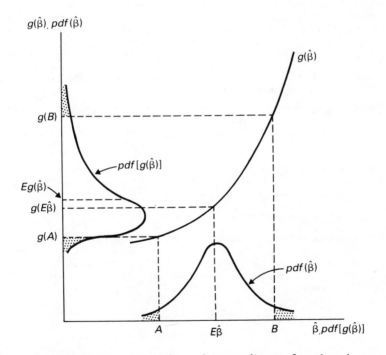

Fig. 2.8 Why the expected value of a nonlinear function is not the nonlinear function of the expected value

small. The points A and B are no longer relevant since values near them now occur with negligible probability. Only values of $\hat{\beta}$ very, very close to plim $\hat{\beta}$ are relevant; such values when traced through $g(\hat{\beta})$ are very, very close to $g(\text{plim } \hat{\beta})$. Clearly, the distribution of $g(\hat{\beta})$ collapses on $g(\text{plim } \hat{\beta})$ as the distribution of $\hat{\beta}$ collapses on plim $\hat{\beta}$. Thus plim $g(\hat{\beta}) = g(\text{plim } \hat{\beta})$.

- An approximate correction factor can be estimated to reduce the small-sample bias discussed here. For example, suppose an estimate $\hat{\beta}$ of β is distributed normally with mean β and variance $V(\hat{\beta})$. Then exp $(\hat{\beta})$ is distributed log-normally with mean exp $[\beta + \frac{1}{2}V(\beta)]$, suggesting that exp (β) could be estimated by exp $[\hat{\beta} - \frac{1}{2}V(\hat{\beta})]$ which, although biased, should have less bias than exp $(\hat{\beta})$. If in this same example the original error were not distributed normally, so that $\hat{\beta}$ was not distributed normally, a Taylor series expansion could be used to deduce an appropriate correction factor. Expand exp $(\hat{\beta})$ around $E\,\hat{\beta} = \beta$ to get

$$\exp (\hat{\beta}) = \exp (\beta) + (\hat{\beta} - \beta) \exp (\beta) + \frac{1}{2}(\hat{\beta} - \beta)^2 \exp (\beta)$$

plus higher-order terms which are neglected. Taking the expected value of both sides produces

$$E \exp (\hat{\beta}) = \exp \beta[1 + \frac{1}{2}V(\hat{\beta})]$$

suggesting that exp β could be estimated by

$$\exp (\hat{\beta}) [1 + \frac{1}{2}\hat{V}(\hat{\beta})]^{-1}.$$

For discussion and examples of these kind of adjustments, see Miller (1984), Kennedy (1981a, 1983) and Goldberger (1968a).

- When g is a linear function, the variance of $g(\hat{\beta})$ is given by the square of the slope of g times the variance of $\hat{\beta}$; i.e., $V(ax) = a^2V(x)$. When g is a nonlinear function its variance is more difficult to calculate. As noted above in the context of Fig. 2.8, when the sample size becomes very large only values of $\hat{\beta}$ very, very close to plim $\hat{\beta}$ are relevant, and in this range a linear approximation to $g(\hat{\beta})$ is adequate. The slope of such a linear approximation is given by the first derivative of g with respect to $\hat{\beta}$. Thus the asymptotic variance of $g(\hat{\beta})$ is often calculated as the square of this first derivative times the asymptotic variance of $\hat{\beta}$, with this first derivative evaluated at $\hat{\beta} = \text{plim } \hat{\beta}$.

- The multivariate analogue of the formula above for the asymptotic variance of $g(\hat{\beta})$ is

$$\left(\frac{\partial g}{\partial \hat{\beta}}\right)' V(\hat{\beta}) \left(\frac{\partial g}{\partial \hat{\beta}}\right).$$

Most practitioners use an estimate of this formula as an estimate of the variance of $g(\hat{\beta})$, rather than attempting to derive some approximation to its small-sample variance (through using a Taylor series expansion).

2.9 Maximum Likelihood

- The mechanics of finding a maximum likelihood estimator are explained in most econometrics texts. Because of the importance that maximum likelihood estimation is gaining in the econometric literature, an alternative description is presented here. Consider a typical econometric problem of trying to find the maximum likelihood estimator of the vector

$$\beta = \begin{bmatrix} \beta_1 \\ \beta_2 \\ \beta_3 \end{bmatrix}$$

in the relationship $y = \beta_1 + \beta_2 x + \beta_3 z + \varepsilon$ where T observations on y, x and z are available.

(1) The first step is to specify the nature of the distribution of the disturbance term ε. Suppose the disturbances are identically and independently distributed with probability density function $f(\varepsilon)$. For example, it could be postulated that ε is distributed normally with mean zero and variance σ^2, so that

$$f(\varepsilon) = (2\pi\sigma^2)^{-1/2} \exp\{-\varepsilon^2/2\sigma^2\}.$$

(2) The second step is to rewrite the given relationship as $\varepsilon = y - \beta_1 - \beta_2 x - \beta_3 z$ so that for the ith value of ε we have

$$f(\varepsilon_i) = (2\pi\sigma^2)^{-1/2} \exp\left\{-\frac{1}{2\sigma^2}(y_i - \beta_1 - \beta_2 x_i - \beta_3 z_i)^2\right\}.$$

(3) The third step is to form the *likelihood function*, the formula for the joint probability distribution of the sample, i.e., a formula proportional to the probability of drawing the particular error terms inherent in this sample. If the error terms are independent of each other, this is given by the product of all the $f(\varepsilon)$s, one for each of the T sample observations. For the example at hand, this creates the likelihood function

$$L = (2\pi\sigma^2)^{-T/2} \exp\left\{-\frac{1}{2\sigma^2}\sum_{i=1}^{T}(y_i - \beta_1 - \beta_2 x_i - \beta_3 z_i)^2\right\}$$

a complicated function of the sample data and the unknown parameters β_1, β_2 and β_3, plus any unknown parameters inherent in the probability density function f – in this case σ^2.

(4) The fourth step is to find the set of values of the unknown parameters (β_1, β_2, β_3 and σ^2), as functions of the sample data, that maximize this likelihood function. Since the parameter values that maximize L also maximize ℓnL, and the latter task is easier, attention usually focuses on the log-likelihood function. In this example,

$$\ell nL = -\frac{T}{2}\ell n(2\pi\sigma^2) - \frac{1}{2\sigma^2}\sum_{i=1}^{T}(y_i - \beta_1 - \beta_2 x_i - \beta_3 z_i)^2.$$

In some simple cases, such as this one, the maximizing values of this function (i.e., the MLEs) can be found using standard algebraic maximizing techniques. In most cases, however, a numerical search technique (described in section 5.3) must be employed to find the MLE.

There are two circumstances in which the technique presented above is incorrect.

(1) *Density of y not equal to density of ε*   We have observations on y, not ε. Thus, the likelihood function should be structured from the density of y, not the density of ε. The technique described above implicitly assumes that the density of y, $f(y)$, is identical to $f(\varepsilon)$, the density of ε, but this is not necessarily the case. The probability of obtaining a value of ε in the small range $d\varepsilon$ is given by $f(\varepsilon)\,d\varepsilon$; this implies an equivalent probability for y of $f(y)|dy|$ where $f(y)$ is the density function of y and $|dy|$ is the absolute value of the range of y values corresponding to $d\varepsilon$. Thus, because $f(\varepsilon)\,d\varepsilon = f(y)|dy|$, we can calculate $f(y)$ as $f(\varepsilon)\,|d\varepsilon/dy|$.

In the example given above $f(y)$ and $f(\varepsilon)$ are identical since $|d\varepsilon/dy|$ is one. But suppose our example were such that we had

$$y^\lambda = \beta_0 + \beta_1 x + \beta_2 z + \varepsilon$$

where λ is some (known or unknown) parameter. In this case,

$$f(y_i) = \lambda\, y_i^{\lambda-1}\, f(\varepsilon_i)$$

and the likelihood function would become

$$L = \lambda^T \prod_{i=1}^{T} y_i^{\lambda-1}\, Q$$

where Q is the likelihood function of the original example, with each y_i raised to the power λ.

(2) *Observations not independent*   In the examples above, the observations were independent of one another so that the density values for each observation could simply be multiplied together to obtain the likelihood function. When the observations are not independent, for example if a lagged value of the regressand appears as a regressor, or if the errors are autocorrelated, an alternative means of finding the likelihood function must be employed. There are two ways of handling this problem.

(a) *Using a multivariate density*   A multivariate density function gives the density of an entire vector of ε rather than of just one element of that vector (i.e., it gives the 'probability' of obtaining the entire set of ε_i). For example, the multivariate normal density function for the vector ε is given (in matrix terminology) by the formula

$$f(\varepsilon) = (2\pi\sigma^2)^{-T/2} \left|\det \Omega\right|^{-1/2} \exp\left\{\frac{1}{-2\sigma^2} \varepsilon'\Omega^{-1}\varepsilon\right\}$$

where $\sigma^2\Omega$ is the variance–covariance matrix of the vector ε. This formula itself can serve as the likelihood function (i.e., there is no need to multiply a set of densities together since this formula has implicitly already done that, as well as taking account of interdependencies among the data). Note that this formula gives the density of the vector ε, not the vector y. Since what is required is the density of y, a multivariate adjustment factor equivalent to the univariate $|d\varepsilon/dy|$ used earlier is necessary. This adjustment factor is $|\det d\varepsilon/dy|$ where $d\varepsilon/dy$ is a matrix containing in its ijth position the derivative of the ith observation of ε with respect to the jth observation of y. It is called the *Jacobian* of the transformation from ε to y. Watts (1973) has a good explanation of the Jacobian.

(b) *Using a transformation*   It may be possible to transform the variables of the problem so as to be able to work with errors that are independent. For example, suppose we have

$$y = \beta_1 + \beta_2 x + \beta_3 z + \varepsilon$$

but ε is such that $\varepsilon_t = \rho\varepsilon_{t-1} + u_t$ where u_t is a normally distributed error with mean zero and variance σ_u^2. The εs are not independent of one another, so the density for the vector ε cannot be formed by multiplying together all the individual densities; the multivariate density formula given earlier must be used, where Ω is a function of ρ and σ^2 is a function of ρ and σ_u^2. But the u errors are distributed independently, so the density of the u vector can be formed by multiplying together all the individual u_t densities. Some algebraic manipulation allows u_t to be expressed as

$$u_t = (y_t - \rho y_{t-1}) - \beta_1(1 - \rho) - \beta_2(x_t - \rho x_{t-1}) - \beta_3(z_t - \rho z_{t-1}).$$

(There is a special transformation for u_1; see the technical notes to section 7.3 where autocorrelated errors are discussed.) The density of the y vector, and thus the required likelihood function, is then calculated as the density of the u vector times the Jacobian of the transformation from u to y. In the example at hand, this second method turns out to be easier, since the first method (using a multivariate density function) requires that the determinant of Ω be calculated, a difficult task.

• Working through examples in the literature of the application of these techniques is the best way to become comfortable with them and to become aware of the uses to which MLEs can be put. To this end see Beach and MacKinnon (1978a), Savin and White (1978), Lahiri and Egy (1981), Spitzer (1982), Seaks and Layson (1983), and Layson and Seaks (1984).

• The likelihood function is identical to the joint probability density function of the given sample. It is given a different name (i.e., the name 'likelihood') to denote the fact that in this context it is to be *interpreted* as a function of the parameter values (since it is to be maximized with respect to those parameter values) rather than, as is usually the case, being interpreted as a function of the sample data.

- The Cramer–Rao lower bound is a matrix given by the formula

$$- \left[E \, \frac{\partial^2 \ell n \, L}{\partial \theta^2} \right]^{-1}$$

where θ is the vector of unknown parameters (including σ^2) for the MLE estimates of which the Cramer–Rao lower bound is the asymptotic variance–covariance matrix. Its estimation is accomplished by inserting the MLE estimates of the unknown parameters. The inverse of the Cramer–Rao lower bound is called the *information matrix*.

- If the disturbances were distributed normally, the MLE estimator of σ^2 is SSE/T. Drawing on similar examples reported in preceding sections, we see that estimation of the variance of a normally distributed population can be computed as $SSE/(T-1)$, SSE/T or $SSE/(T+1)$ which are, respectively, the best unbiased estimator, the MLE, and the minimum MSE estimator. Here SSE is $\Sigma(x-\bar{x})^2$.

- When the error term is distributed with a double exponential density function, the maximum likelihood estimator is the MAD (minimum absolute deviation) estimator.

3. The Classical Linear Regression Model

3.1 Textbooks as Catalogues

In chapter 2 we learned that many of the estimating criteria held in high regard by econometricians (such as best unbiasedness and minimum mean square error) are characteristics of an estimator's sampling distribution. These characteristics cannot be determined unless a set of repeated samples can be taken or hypothesized; to take or hypothesize these repeated samples, knowledge of the way in which the observations are generated is necessary. Unfortunately, an estimator does not have the same characteristics for all ways in which the observations can be generated. This means that in some estimating situations a particular estimator has desirable properties but in other estimating situations it does *not* have desirable properties. Because there is no 'superestimator' having desirable properties in all situations, for each estimating problem (i.e., for each different way in which the observations can be generated) the econometrician must determine anew which estimator is preferred. An econometrics textbook can be characterized as a catalogue of which estimators are most desirable in what estimating situations. Thus, a researcher facing a particular estimating problem simply turns to the catalogue to determine which estimator is most appropriate for him or her to employ in that situation. The purpose of this chapter is to explain how this catalogue is structured.

The cataloguing process described above is centred around a standard estimating situation referred to as the *classical linear regression model* (CLR model). It happens that in this standard situation the OLS estimator is considered the optimal estimator. This model consists of five assumptions concerning the way in which the data are generated. By changing these assumptions in one way or another, different estimating situations are created, in many of which the OLS estimator is no longer considered to be the optimal estimator. Most econometric problems can be characterized as situations in which one (or more) of these five assumptions is violated in a particular way. The catalogue works in a straightforward way: the estimating situation is modelled in the general mould of the CLR model and then the researcher pinpoints the way in which this situation differs from the standard situation as described by the CLR model (i.e., finds out which assumption of the CLR model is violated in this problem); he or she then turns to the textbook (catalogue) to see whether the OLS estimator retains its desirable properties, and if not what alternative estimator should be used. Because econometricians often are not certain of whether the estimating situation they face is one in which an assumption of the CLR model is violated, the catalogue also includes a listing of techniques useful in testing whether or not the CLR model assumptions are violated.

3.2 The Five Assumptions

The CLR model consists of five basic assumptions about the way in which the observations are generated.

(1) The *first assumption* of the CLR model is that the dependent variable can be calculated as a linear function of a specific set of independent variables, plus a disturbance term. The unknown coefficients of this linear function form the vector β and are assumed to be constants. Several violations of this assumption, called specification errors, are discussed in chapter 5:

(a) *wrong regressors* – the omission of relevant independent variables or the inclusion of irrelevant independent variables;
(b) *nonlinearity* – when the relationship between the dependent and independent variables is not linear;
(c) *changing parameters* – when the parameters (β) do not remain constant during the period in which data was collected.

(2) The *second assumption* of the CLR model is that the expected value of the disturbance term is zero; i.e., the mean of the distribution from which the disturbance term is drawn is zero. Violation of this assumption leads to the *biased intercept* problem, discussed in chapter 6.

(3) The *third assumption* of the CLR model is that the disturbance terms all have the same variance and are not correlated with one another. Two major econometric problems, as discussed in chapter 7, are associated with violations of this assumption:

(a) *heteroskedasticity* – when the disturbances do not all have the same variance:
(b) *autocorrelated errors* – when the disturbances are correlated with one another.

(4) The *fourth assumption* of the CLR model is that the observations on the independent variable can be considered fixed in repeated samples; i.e., it is possible to repeat the sample with the same independent variables. Three important econometric problems, discussed in chapters 8 and 9, correspond to violations of this assumption:

(a) *errors in variables* – errors in measuring the independent variables;
(b) *autoregression* – using a lagged value of the dependent variable as an independent variable;

(c) *simultaneous equation estimation* – situations in which the dependent variables are determined by the simultaneous interaction of several relationships.

(5) The *fifth assumption* of the CLR model is that the number of observations is greater than the number of independent variables and that there are no linear relationships between the independent variables. Although this is viewed as an assumption for the general case, for a specific case it can easily be checked, so that it need not be assumed. The problem of *multicollinearity* (two or more independent variables being approximately linearly related in the sample data) is associated with this assumption. This is discussed in chapter 10.

All this is summarized in Table 3.1, which presents these five assumptions of the CLR model, shows the appearance they take when dressed in mathematical notation, and lists the econometric problems most closely associated with violations of these assumptions. Later chapters in this book comment on the meaning and significance of these assumptions, note implications of their violation for the OLS estimator, discuss ways of determining whether or not they are violated, and suggest new estimators appropriate to situations in which one of these assumptions must be replaced by an alternative assumption. Before moving on to this, however, more must be said about the character of the OLS estimator in the context of the CLR model, because of the central role it plays in the econometrician's 'catalogue'.

3.3   The OLS Estimator in the CLR Model

The central role of the OLS estimator in the econometrician's catalogue is that of a standard against which all other estimators are compared. The reason for this is that the OLS estimator is extraordinarily popular. This popularity stems from the fact that, in the context of the CLR model, the OLS estimator has a large number of desirable properties, making it the overwhelming choice for the 'optimal' estimator when the estimating problem is accurately characterized by the CLR model. This is best illustrated by looking at the eight criteria listed in chapter 2 and determining how the OLS estimator rates on these criteria in the context of the CLR model.

(1) *Computational cost*   Because of the popularity of the OLS estimator, many packaged computer routines exist, as do standard short-cut means of hand computation. Whenever the functional form being estimated is linear, as it is in the CLR model, the OLS estimator involves very little computational cost.

(2) *Least squares*   Because the OLS estimator is designed to minimize the sum of squared residuals, it is automatically 'optimal' on this criterion.

TABLE 3.1

Assumption	Mathematical expression		Violations	Chapter in which discussed
	Univariate	*Multivariate*		
(1) Dependent variable a linear function of a specific set of independent variables, plus a disturbance	$y_t = \beta_0 + \beta_1 x_t + \varepsilon_t,$ $t = 1,\ldots,T$	$Y = X\beta + \varepsilon$	Wrong regressors Nonlinearity Changing parameters	5
(2) Expected value of disturbance term is zero	$E\varepsilon_t = 0$, for all t	$E\varepsilon = 0$	Biased intercept	6
(3) Disturbances have uniform variance and are uncorrelated	$E\varepsilon_t\varepsilon_r = 0,\ t \neq r$	$E\varepsilon\varepsilon' = \sigma^2 I$	Heteroskedasticity Autocorrelated errors	7
(4) Observations on independent variables can be considered fixed in repeated samples	x_t fixed in repeated samples	X fixed in repeated samples	Errors in variables Autoregression Simultaneous equations	8 9
(5) No exact linear relationships between independent variables and more observations than independent variables	$\displaystyle\sum_{t=1}^{T}(x_t - \bar{x})^2 \neq 0$	Rank of $X = K \leq T$	Multicollinearity	10

Explanatory note: The mathematical terminology is explained in the technical notes to this section. The notation is as follows: Y is a vector of observations on the dependent variables; X is a matrix of observations on the independent variables; ε is a vector of disturbances; σ^2 is the variance of the disturbances; I is the identity matrix; K is the number of independent variables; T is the number of observations.

(3) *Highest R^2*   Because the OLS estimator is optimal on the least squares criterion, it will automatically be optimal on the highest R^2 criterion.

(4) *Unbiasedness*   The assumptions of the CLR model can be used to show that the OLS estimator β^{OLS} is an unbiased estimator of β.

(5) *Best unbiasedness*   In the CLR model β^{OLS} is a linear estimator; i.e., it can be written as a linear function of the errors. As noted earlier, it is unbiased. Among all linear unbiased estimators of β, it can be shown (in the context of the CLR model) to have the 'smallest' variance–covariance matrix. Thus the OLS estimator is the BLUE in the CLR model. If we add the additional assumption that the disturbances are distributed normally (creating the CNLR model – the *classical normal linear regression model*), it can be shown that the OLS estimator is the best unbiased estimator (i.e., best among *all* unbiased estimators, not just linear unbiased estimators).

(6) *Mean square error*   It is not the case that the OLS estimator is the minimum mean square error estimator in the CLR model. Even among linear estimators, it is possible that a substantial reduction in variance can be obtained by adopting a slightly biased estimator. This is the OLS estimator's weakest point; chapters 10 and 11 discuss several estimators whose appeal lies in the possibility that they may beat OLS on the MSE criterion.

(7) *Asymptotic criteria*   Because the OLS estimator in the CLR model is unbiased, it is also unbiased in samples of infinite size and thus is asymptotically unbiased. It can also be shown that the variance–covariance matrix of β^{OLS} goes to zero as the sample size goes to infinity, so that β^{OLS} is also a consistent estimator of β. Further, in the CNLR model it is asymptotically efficient.

(8) *Maximum likelihood*   It is impossible to calculate the maximum likelihood estimator given the assumptions of the CLR model, because these assumptions do not specify the functional form of the distribution of the disturbance terms. However, if the disturbances are assumed to be distributed normally (the CNLR model), it turns out that β^{MLE} is identical to β^{OLS}.

Thus, whenever the estimating situation can be characterized by the CLR model, the OLS estimator meets practically all of the criteria econometricians consider relevant. It is no wonder, then, that this estimator has become so popular. It is in fact *too* popular; it is often used, without justification, in estimating situations that are not accurately represented by the CLR model. If some of the CLR model assumptions do not hold, many of the desirable properties of the OLS estimator no longer hold. If the OLS estimator does not have the properties that are thought to be of most importance, an alternative estimator must be found. Before moving to this aspect of our examination of econometrics, however, we spend a chapter discussing some concepts of and problems in inference, to provide a foundation for later chapters.

General Notes

3.1 Textbooks as Catalogues

- The econometricians' catalogue is not viewed favourably by all. Consider the opinion of Worswick (1972) p. 79: '[Econometricians] are not, it seems to me, engaged in forging tools to arrange and measure actual facts so much as making a marvellous array of pretend-tools which would perform wonders if ever a set of facts should turn up in the right form.'

- Bibby and Toutenberg (1977) pp. 72–3 note that the CLR model, what they call the GLM (general linear model), can be a trap, a snare and a delusion. They quote Whitehead as saying: 'Seek simplicity ... and distrust it', and go on to explain how use of the linear model can change in undesirable ways the nature of the debate on the phenomenon being examined in the study in question. For example, casting the problem in the mould of the CLR model narrows the question by restricting its terms of reference to a particular model based on a particular set of data; it trivializes the question by focusing attention on apparently meaningful yet potentially trivial questions concerning the values of unknown regression coefficients; and it technicalizes the debate, obscuring the real questions at hand, by turning attention to technical statistical matters capable of being understood only by experts.

    They warn users of the GLM by noting that 'it certainly eliminates the complexities of hardheaded thought, especially since so many computer programs exist. For the soft-headed analyst who doesn't want to think too much, an off-the-peg computer package is simplicity itself, especially if it cuts through a mass of complicated data and provides a few easily reportable coefficients. Occam's razor has been used to justify worse barbarities: but razors are dangerous things and should be used carefully.'

- If more than one of the CLR model assumptions is violated at the same time, econometricians often find themselves in trouble because their catalogues usually tell them what to do if only *one* of the CLR model assumptions is violated. Much recent econometric research examines situations in which two assumptions of the CLR model are violated simultaneously. These situations will be discussed when appropriate.

3.3 The OLS Estimator in the CLR Model

- The process whereby the OLS estimator is applied to the data at hand is usually referred to by the terminology 'running a regression'. The dependent variable (the 'regressand') is said to be 'regressed' on the independent variables ('the regressors') to produce the OLS estimates. This terminology comes from a pioneering empirical study in which it was found that the mean height of children born of parents of a given height tends to 'regress' or move towards the population average height. See Maddala (1977) pp. 97–101 for further comment on this and for discussion of the meaning and interpretation of regression analysis. Critics note that the New Standard Dictionary defines regression as 'The diversion of psychic energy ... into channels of fantasy'.

- The result that the OLS estimator in the CLR model is the BLUE is often referred to as the *Gauss–Markov* theorem.

- The formula for the OLS estimator of a specific element of the β vector usually involves observations on *all* the independent variables (as well as observations on the dependent variable), not just observations on the independent variable corresponding to that particular element of β. This is because, to obtain an accurate estimate of the influence of one independent variable on the dependent variable, the simultaneous influence of other independent variables on the dependent variable must be taken into account. Doing this ensures that the jth element of β^{OLS} reflects the influence of the jth independent variable on the dependent variable, holding all the other independent variables constant. Similarly, the formula for the variance of an element of β^{OLS} also usually involves observations on all the independent variables.

- Because the OLS estimator is so popular, and because it so often plays a role in the formulation of alternative estimators, it is important that its mechanical properties be well understood. The most effective way of expositing these characteristics is through the use of a Venn diagram called the Ballentine. Suppose the CLR model applies, with Y determined by X and an error term. In Fig. 3.1 the circle Y represents variation in the dependent variable Y and the circle X represents variation in the independent variable X. The overlap of X with Y, the blue area, represents variation that Y and X have in common in the sense that this variation in Y can be explained by X via an OLS regression. The blue area reflects information employed by the estimating procedure in estimating the slope coefficient β_x; the larger this area, the more information is used to form the estimate and thus the smaller is its variance.

  Now consider Fig. 3.2, in which a Ballentine for a case of two explanatory variables, X and Z, is portrayed (i.e., now Y is determined by both X and Z). In general, the X and Z circles will overlap, reflecting some collinearity between the two; this is shown in Fig. 3.2 by the red-plus-orange area. If Y were regressed on X alone, information in the blue-plus-red area would be used to estimate β_x, and if Y were regressed on Z alone, information in the green-plus-red area would be used to estimate β_z. What happens, though, if Y is regressed on X and Z together?

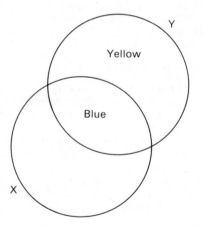

Fig. 3.1   Defining the Ballentine Venn diagram

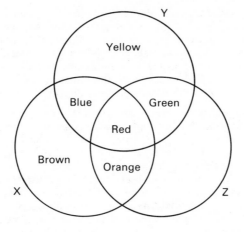

Fig. 3.2 Interpreting multiple regression with the Ballentine

In the multiple regression of Y on X and Z together, the OLS estimator uses the information in the blue area to estimate β_x and the information in the green area to estimate β_z, *discarding the information in the red area.* The information in the blue area corresponds to variation in Y that matches up uniquely with variation in X; using this information should therefore produce an unbiased estimate of β_x. Similarly, information in the green area corresponds to variation in Y that matches up uniquely with variation in Z; using this information should produce an unbiased estimate of β_z. The information in the red area is not used because it reflects variation in Y that is determined by variation in *both* X and Z, the relative contributions of which are not *a priori* known. In the blue area, for example, variation in Y is all due to variation in X, so matching up this variation in Y with variation in X should allow accurate estimation of β_x. But in the red area, matching up these variations will be misleading because not all variation in Y is due to variation in X.

- Notice that regressing Y on X and Z together creates unbiased estimates of β_x and β_z whereas regressing Y on X and Z separately creates biased estimates of β_x and β_z because this latter method uses the red area. But notice also that, because the former method discards the red area, it uses less information to produce its slope coefficient estimates and thus these estimates will have larger variances. As is invariably the case in econometrics, the price of obtaining unbiased estimates is higher variances.

- Whenever X and Z are orthogonal to one another (have zero collinearity) they do not overlap as in Fig. 3.2 and the red area disappears. Because there is no red area in this case, regressing Y on X alone or on Z alone produces the same estimates of β_x and β_z as if Y were regressed on X and Z together. Thus, although in general the OLS estimate of a specific element of the β vector involves observations on *all* the regressors, in the case of orthogonal regressors it involves observations on only one regressor (the one for which it is the slope coefficient estimate).

- Whenever X and Z are highly collinear and therefore overlap a lot, the blue and green areas become very small, implying that when Y is regressed on X and Z together very little information is used to estimate β_x and β_z. This causes the variances of these estimates to be very large. Thus, the impact of multicollinearity is to raise the variances of the OLS estimates. Perfect collinearity causes the X and Z circles to overlap completely; the blue and green areas disappear and estimation is impossible. Multicollinearity is discussed at length in chapter 10.

- In Fig. 3.1 the blue area represents the variation in Y explained by X. Thus, R^2 is given as the ratio of the blue area to the entire Y circle. In Fig. 3.2 the blue-plus-red-plus-green area represents the variation in Y explained by X and Z together. (Note that the red area is discarded only for the purpose of estimating the coefficients, not for predicting Y; once the coefficients are estimated, all variation in X and Z is used to predict Y.) Thus, the R^2 resulting from the multiple regression is given by the ratio of the blue-plus-red-plus-green area to the entire Y circle. Notice that there is no way of allocating portions of the total R^2 to X and Z because the red area variation is explained by *both*, in a way that cannot be disentangled. Only if X and Z are orthogonal, and the red area disappears, can the total R^2 be allocated unequivocally to X and Z separately.

- The yellow area represents variation in Y attributable to the error term, and thus the magnitude of the yellow area represents the magnitude of σ^2, the variance of the error term. This implies, for example, that if, in the context of Fig. 3.2, Y had been regressed on only X, omitting Z, σ^2 would be estimated by the yellow-plus-green area, an overestimate.

- The Ballentine was named, by its originators Cohen and Cohen (1975), after a brand of US beer whose logo resembles Fig. 3.2. Their use of the Ballentine was confined to the exposition of various concepts related to R^2. Kennedy (1981b) extended its use to the exposition of other aspects of regression. A limitation of the Ballentine is that it is necessary in certain cases for the red area to represent a negative quantity. (Suppose the two explanatory variables X and Z each have positive coefficients, but in the data X and Z are negatively correlated: X alone could do a poor job of explaining variation in Y because, for example, the impact of a high value of X is offset by a low value of Z.) This suggests that the explanations offered above are lacking and should be revised; for example, the result that regressing on X alone reduces the variance of its coefficient estimate should be explained in terms of this regression incorporating a greater range of variation of X (i.e., the entire X circle as opposed to just the blue-plus-brown area). This problem notwithstanding, the interpretation advanced earlier is retained in this book, on the grounds that the benefits of its illustrative power outweigh the danger that it will lead to error. The Ballentine is used here as a metaphoric device illustrating some regression results; it should not be given meaning beyond that.

Technical Notes

3.2 The Five Assumptions

- The regression model $y = g(x_1, \ldots, x_k) + \varepsilon$ is really a specification of how the conditional means $E(y|x_1, \ldots, x_k)$ are related to each other through x. The population regression function is written as $E(y|x_1, \ldots, x_k) = g(x)$; it describes how the average or expected value of y varies with x. Suppose g is a linear function so that the regression function is $y = \beta_1 + \beta_2 x_2 + \beta_3 x_3 + \ldots + \beta_k x_k + \varepsilon$. Each element of β^{OLS} (β_4^{OLS}, for example) is an estimate of the effect on the conditional expectation of y of a unit change in x_4, with all other x held constant.

- In the CLR model, the regression model is specified as $y = \beta_1 + \beta_2 x_2 + \ldots + \beta_k x_k +$ disturbance, a formula that can be writen down T times, once for each set of observations on the dependent and independent variables. This gives a large stack of equations, which can be consolidated via matrix notation as $Y = X\beta + \varepsilon$. Here Y is a vector containing the T observations on the dependent variable y; X is a matrix consisting of K columns, each column being a vector of T observations on one of the independent variables; and ε is a vector containing the T unknown disturbances.

3.3 The OLS Estimator in the CLR Model

- The general formula for the OLS estimator β^{OLS} is $(X'X)^{-1}X'Y$. For the simple regression function $y = \beta_2 x_2 + \varepsilon$, this produces the formula $\Sigma x_2 y / \Sigma x_2^2$ for β_2^{OLS} where the summation is over the T observations. For the simple regression function $y = \beta_1 + \beta_2 x_2 + \varepsilon$, it produces the formula

$$\Sigma(x_2 - \bar{x}_2)y/\Sigma(x_2 - \bar{x}_2)^2 \quad \text{or} \quad \Sigma(x_2 - \bar{x}_2)(y - \bar{y})/\Sigma(x_2 - \bar{x}_2)^2$$

for β_2^{OLS}. As more regressors are added these formulae become more complicated.

- The OLS slope coefficient estimates remain unchanged when calculated with observations expressed as deviations about their respective means. This fact is often used to simplify algebraic manipulations.

- The formula for the variance–covariance matrix β^{OLS} is $\sigma^2(X'X)^{-1}$ where σ^2 is the variance of the disturbance term. For the simple case in which the regression function is $y = \beta_1 + \beta_2 x_2$ this gives the formula $\sigma^2/\Sigma(x_2 - \bar{x}_2)^2$ for the variance of β_2^{OLS}. Note that, if the variation in the regressor values is substantial, the denominator of this expression will be large, tending to make the variance of β^{OLS} small.

- The variance–covariance matrix of β^{OLS} is usually unknown because σ^2 is usually unknown. It is estimated by $s^2(X'X)^{-1}$ where s^2 is an estimator of σ^2. The estimator s^2 is usually given by the formula $\hat{\varepsilon}'\hat{\varepsilon}(T - K) = \Sigma\hat{\varepsilon}_i^2/(T - K)$ where $\hat{\varepsilon}$ is the estimate of the disturbance vector, calculated as $(Y - \hat{Y})$ where $\hat{Y}$ is $X\beta^{\mathrm{OLS}}$. In the CLR model s^2 is the best quadratic unbiased estimator of σ^2; in the CNLR model it is best unbiased.

- By discarding the red area in Fig. 3.2, the OLS formula ensures that its estimates of the influence of one independent variable are calculated while controlling for the simultaneous influence of the other independent variables, i.e., the interpretation of, say, the jth element of β^{OLS} is as an estimate of the influence of the jth explanatory variable, holding all other explanatory variables constant. That the red area is discarded can be emphasized by noting that the OLS estimate of, say, β_x can be calculated from either the regression of Y on X and Z together or the regression of Y on X 'residualized' with respect to Z (i.e., with the influence of Z removed). In Fig. 3.2, if we were to regress X on Z we would be able to explain the red-plus-orange area; the residuals from this regression, the blue-plus-brown area, is called X residualized for Z. Now suppose that Y is regressed on X residualized for Z. The overlap of the Y circle with the blue-plus-brown area is the blue area, so exactly the same information is used to estimate β_x in this method as is used when Y is regressed on X and Z together, resulting in an identical estimate of β_x.

Notice further that, if Y were also residualized for Z, producing the yellow-plus-blue area, regressing the residualized Y on the residualized X would also produce the same estimate of β_x since their overlap is the blue area. An important implication of this result is that, for example, running a regression on data from which a linear time trend has been removed will produce exactly the same coefficient estimates as when a linear time trend is included among the regressors in a regression run on raw data. As another example, consider the removal of a linear seasonal influence; running a regression on linearly deseasonalized data will produce exactly the same coefficient estimates as if the linear seasonal influence were included as an extra regressor in a regression run on raw data.

- A variant of OLS called *stepwise regression* is to be avoided. It consists of regressing Y on each explanatory variable separately and keeping the regression with the highest R^2. This determines the estimate of the slope coefficient of that regression's explanatory variable. Then the residuals from this regression are used as the dependent variable in a new search using the remaining explanatory variables and the procedure is repeated. Suppose that, for the example of Fig. 3.2, the regression of Y on X produced a higher R^2 than the regression of Y on Z. Then the estimate of β_x would be formed using the information in the blue-plus-red area. Note that this estimate is biased.

- The Ballentine can be used to illustrate several variants of R^2. Consider, for example, the simple R^2 between Y and Z in Fig. 3.2. If the area of the Y circle is normalized to be unity, this simple R^2, denoted R^2_{yz}, is given by the red plus green area. The *partial R^2* between Y and Z is defined as reflecting the influence of Z on Y *after* accounting for the influence of X. It is measured by obtaining the R^2 from the regression of Y corrected for X on Z corrected for X, and is denoted $R^2_{yz \cdot x}$. Our earlier use of the Ballentine makes it easy to deduce that in Fig. 3.2 it is given as the green area divided by the yellow-plus-green area. The reader might like to verify that it is given by the formula

$$R^2_{yz \cdot x} = (R^2 - R^2_{yz})/(1 - R^2_{yx}).$$

4. Interval Estimation and Hypothesis Testing

4.1 Introduction

In addition to estimating parameters, econometricians often wish to construct confidence intervals for their estimates and test hypotheses concerning parameters. To strengthen the perspective from which violations of the CLR model are viewed in the following chapters, this chapter provides a brief discussion of these principles of inference in the context of traditional applications found in econometrics.

Using the CLR model itself, nothing can be said on this subject. However, if the CLR model is extended by assuming the disturbances are distributed normally, forming the classical normal linear regression model (CNLR model), discussion of inference problems such as interval estimation and hypothesis testing can proceed. When the disturbances are normally distributed, statistical tables (found at the back of many textbooks) giving critical values for the normal and its associated distributions such as the t distribution and the F distribution, can be employed to aid in testing hypotheses and creating interval estimates. This chapter is therefore conducted in the context of the CNLR model. (Distributions other than the normal distribution could be assumed for this purpose, but are seldom employed.)

4.2 The Unidimensional Case

Hypothesis tests on and interval estimates of single parameters are straightforward applications of techniques familiar to all students of elementary statistics. In the CNLR model the OLS estimator β^{OLS} generates estimates that are distributed joint-normally in repeated samples. This means that $\beta_1^{OLS}, \beta_2^{OLS}, \ldots, \beta_k^{OLS}$ are all connected to one another (through their covariances). In particular, this means that β_3^{OLS}, say, is distributed normally with mean β_3 (since the OLS estimator is unbiased) and variance $V(\beta_3^{OLS})$ equal to the third diagonal element of the variance–covariance matrix of β^{OLS}. The square root of $V(\beta_3^{OLS})$ is the standard deviation of β_3^{OLS}. Using the normal table and this standard deviation, interval estimates can be constructed and hypotheses can be tested.

A major drawback to this procedure is that the variance–covariance matrix of β^{OLS} is not usually known (because σ^2, the variance of the disturbances, which appears in the formula for this variance–covariance matrix, is not usually known). Estimating σ^2 by s^2, as discussed in the technical notes to section 3.4, allows an estimate of this matrix to be created. The square root of the third diagonal element of this matrix is the standard error of β_3^{OLS}, an estimate of the standard deviation of β_3^{OLS}. With this estimate the t-table can be used in place of the normal table to test hypotheses or construct interval estimates.

The use of such t tests, as they are called, is so common that most packaged computer programs designed to compute the OLS estimators (designed to run OLS regressions) have included in their output a number called the t statistic for each parameter estimate. This gives the value of the parameter estimate divided by its estimated standard deviation (the standard error). This value can be compared directly to critical values in the t-table to test the hypothesis that that parameter is equal to zero. In some research reports, this t statistic is printed in parentheses underneath the parameter estimates, creating some confusion because sometimes the standard errors appear in this position. (A negative number in parentheses would have to be a t value, so that this would indicate that these numbers were t values rather than standard errors.)

4.3   The Multidimensional Case

Suppose that a researcher wanted to test the joint hypothesis that, say, the fourth and fifth elements of β are equal to 1.0 and 2.0, respectively. That is, he wishes to test the hypothesis that the subvector

$$\begin{bmatrix} \beta_4 \\ \beta_5 \end{bmatrix}$$

is equal to the vector

$$\begin{bmatrix} 1.0 \\ 2.0 \end{bmatrix}.$$

This is a different question from the two separate questions of whether β_4 is equal to 1.0 and whether β_5 is equal to 2.0. It is possible, for example, to accept the hypothesis that β_4 is equal to 1.0 and also to accept the hypothesis that β_5 is equal to 2.0, but to *reject* the joint hypothesis that

$$\begin{bmatrix} \beta_4 \\ \beta_5 \end{bmatrix}$$

is equal to

$$\begin{bmatrix} 1.0 \\ 2.0 \end{bmatrix}.$$

The purpose of this section is to explain this phenomenon and discuss the manner in which hypothesis tests are undertaken in the multidimensional context.

This explanation is best begun by referring to the special case of testing all the parameters (except the intercept) simultaneously against the zero vector; i.e., under what circumstances can it be claimed that the entire set of independent variables, taken as a set, has no ability to explain variation in the dependent variable? If the independent variables, as a set of explanatory variables, have no ability to explain variation in the dependent variable, then all the parameters associated with these independent variables must be zero; except for the intercept term (which explains no variation regardless of its value), β equals the zero vector.

Recall the discussion in section 2.4 of the R^2 statistic. There it was noted that the 'variation' in the dependent variable (measured as the sum of squared deviations of the dependent variable around its mean) was equal to the sum of the 'explained' variation (the sum of squared deviations of the estimated values of the dependent variable around their mean) and the 'unexplained' variation (the sum of squared residuals). It makes intuitive sense to specify that the set of independent variables has no explanatory power if the 'explained' variation is small in the sample relative to the 'unexplained' variation. If the 'explained' variation were not substantially larger than the 'unexplained' variation, one could not claim that the independent variables had any more explanatory power than the disturbances and thus one would be forced to conclude that the vector of coefficients of all the independent variables is equal to zero. This suggests forming the ratio of the 'explained' variation to the 'unexplained' variation. The 'explained' variation must, however, be corrected for the fact that a larger number of independent variables, simply because there are more of them, will *ceteris paribus* 'explain' more variation in the dependent variable than will a smaller number of independent variables. The 'unexplained' variation must undergo a similar correction. When the numerator and the denominator of this ratio are divided by their respective degrees of freedom, an F statistic is created, the critical values for which can be found in an F-table. Should this ratio exceed a chosen critical value, the 'explained' variation is significantly high relative to the 'unexplained' variation and the independent variables can, as a set, be said to influence the dependent variable.

It is now easy to guess how one would test the hypothesis that some subset of β, say the fourth and fifth elements of β, is equal to a zero vector. Regress the dependent variable on the independent variables, omitting the fourth and fifth independent variables, and calculate the 'explained' variation. Then regress the dependent variable on all the independent variables and again calculate the 'explained' variation. The second 'explained' variation will be larger than the first. This is because the OLS estimator, by minimizing the sum of squared residuals (the 'unexplained' variation), is maximizing its mirror image the 'explained' variation. In the first case this maximization was undertaken under the constraint that the two excluded variables could not help; removing this constraint can only make the maximization more successful. If the fourth and fifth independent variables do indeed influence the dependent variable, their addition should significantly increase the 'explained' variation. A significant increase in the 'explained' variation is an increase that is high relative to the variation attributable to the disturbances, the 'unexplained' variation. This suggests forming the ratio of the 'additional explained' variation to the 'unexplained' variation. Dividing each by their respective degrees of freedom produces another F statistic. Should this statistic be higher than a chosen critical value from an F-table, the addition to the 'explained' variation due to adding the extra independent variables is significantly greater than the 'unexplained' variation (attributable to the disturbances) and thus the extra independent variables, as a set, can be considered to be determinants of the dependent variable; their coefficients cannot both be said to be zero.

The idea behind the method of testing the vector

$$\begin{bmatrix} \beta_4 \\ \beta_5 \end{bmatrix}$$

against

$$\begin{bmatrix} 1.0 \\ 2.0 \end{bmatrix}$$

should by now be clear. First, run the regression constraining β_4^{OLS} to be 1.0 and β_5^{OLS} to be 2.0, and then run it unconstrained. If the 'explained' variation increases by only a little (relative to the 'unexplained' variation) the hypothesis is accepted. This is formalized by taking the ratio of the 'additional explained' variation (divided by its degrees of freedom) to the 'unexplained' variation (divided by its degrees of freedom) to create an F statistic. (See the general notes to this section.)

Interval estimation in the multidimensional case is best illustrated by a two-dimensional example. Suppose that the sub-vector

$$\begin{bmatrix} \beta_4 \\ \beta_5 \end{bmatrix}$$

is of interest. The OLS estimate of this sub-vector is shown as the point in the centre of the rectangle in Fig. 4.1. Using the *t*-table and the square root of the fourth diagonal term in the estimated variance–covariance matrix of β^{OLS}, a 95% confidence interval can be constructed for β_4. This is shown in Fig. 4.1 as the interval from *A* to *B*; β_4^{OLS} lies half way between *A* and *B*. Similarly, a 95% confidence interval can be constructed for β_5; it is shown in Fig. 4.1 as the interval from *C* to *D* and is drawn larger than the interval *AB* to reflect an assumed larger standard error for β_5^{OLS}.

An interval estimate for the sub-vector

$$\begin{bmatrix} \beta_4 \\ \beta_5 \end{bmatrix}$$

is a *region* or area that, when constructed in repeated samples, covers the true value (β_4, β_5) in, say, 95% of the samples. Furthermore, this region should for an efficient estimate be the smallest such region possible. A natural region to choose for this purpose is the rectangle formed by the individual interval estimates, as shown in Fig. 4.1. If β_4^{OLS} and β_5^{OLS} have zero covariance, then in repeated sampling rectangles calculated in this

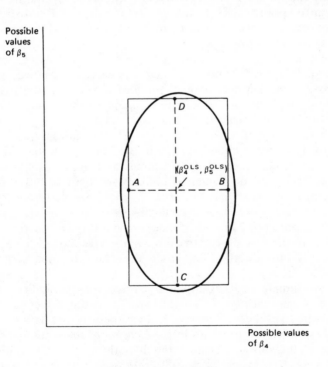

Fig. 4.1   A confidence region with zero covariance

fashion will cover the unknown point (β_4, β_5) in $0.95 \times 0.95 = 90.25\%$ of the samples. (In repeated samples the probability is 0.95 that the β_4 confidence interval covers β_4, as is the probability that the β_5 confidence interval covers β_5; thus the probability for both β_4 and β_5 to be covered simultaneously is 0.95×0.95.)

Evidently, this rectangle is not 'big' enough to serve as a 95% joint confidence interval. Where should it be enlarged? Because the region must be kept as small as possible, the enlargement must come in those parts that have the greatest chance of covering (β_4, β_5) in repeated samples. The corners of the rectangle will cover (β_4, β_5) in a repeated sample whenever β_4^{OLS} and β_5^{OLS} are simultaneously a long way from their mean values of β_4 and β_5. The probability in repeated samples of having these two unlikely events occur simultaneously is very small. Thus the areas just outside the rectangle near the points A, B, C and D are more likely to cover (β_4, β_5) in repeated samples than are areas just outside the corners of the rectangle: the rectangle should be made bigger near the points A, B, C, and D. Further thought suggests that the areas just outside the points A, B, C, and D are more likely, in repeated samples, to cover (β_4, β_5) than the areas just *inside* the corners of the rectangle. Thus the total region could be made smaller by chopping a lot of area off the corners and extending slightly the areas near the points A, B, C, and D. In fact, the last F statistic described earlier allows the econometrician to derive the confidence region as an ellipse, as shown in Fig. 4.1.

The ellipse in Fig. 4.1 represents the case of zero covariance between β_4^{OLS} and β_5^{OLS}. If β_4^{OLS} and β_5^{OLS} have a positive covariance (an estimate of this covariance is found in either the fourth column and fifth row or the fifth column and fourth row of the estimate of the variance–covariance matrix of β^{OLS}), whenever β_4^{OLS} is an overestimate of β_4, β_5^{OLS} is likely to be an overestimate of β_5, and whenever β_4^{OLS} is an underestimate of β_4, β_5^{OLS} is likely to be an underestimate of β_5. This means that the area near the top right-hand corner of the rectangle and the area near the bottom left-hand corner are no longer as unlikely to cover (β_4, β_5) in repeated samples; it also means that the areas near the top left-hand corner and bottom right-hand corner are even less likely to cover (β_4, β_5). In this case the ellipse representing the confidence region is tilted to the right, as shown in Fig. 4.2. In the case of negative covariance between β_4^{OLS} and β_5^{OLS}, the ellipse is tilted to the left. In all cases, the ellipse remains centred on the point $(\beta_4^{OLS}, \beta_5^{OLS})$.

This two-dimensional example illustrates the possibility, mentioned earlier, of accepting two individual hypotheses but rejecting the corresponding joint hypothesis. Suppose the hypothesis is that $\beta_4 = 0$ and $\beta_5 = 0$, and suppose the point $(0,0)$ lies inside a corner of the rectangle in Fig. 4.1, but outside the ellipse. Testing the hypothesis $\beta_4 = 0$ using a t test concludes that β_4 is insignificantly different from zero (because the interval AB contains zero), and testing the hypothesis $\beta_5 = 0$ concludes that β_5 is

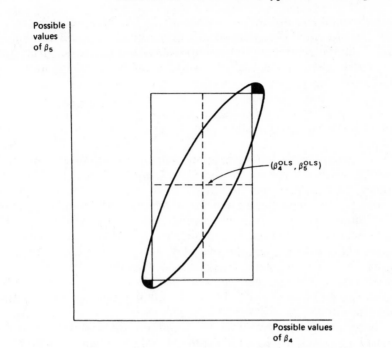

Fig. 4.2   A confidence region with positive covariance

insignificantly different from zero (because the interval *CD* contains zero). But testing the joint hypothesis

$$\begin{bmatrix} \beta_4 \\ \beta_5 \end{bmatrix} = \begin{bmatrix} 0 \\ 0 \end{bmatrix},$$

using an *F* test, concludes that

$$\begin{bmatrix} \beta_4 \\ \beta_5 \end{bmatrix}$$

is significantly different from the zero vector because (0, 0) lies outside the ellipse. In this example one can confidently say that *at least one* of the two variables has a significant influence on the dependent variable, but one cannot with confidence assign that influence to either of the variables individually. The typical circumstance in which this comes about is in the case of multicollinearity (see chapter 10), in which independent variables are related so that it is difficult to tell which of the variables deserves credit for explaining variation in the dependent variable. Fig. 4.2 is representative of the multicollinearity case.

In three dimensions the confidence region becomes a confidence volume and is represented diagrammatically by an ellipsoid. In higher dimensions diagrammatic representation is impossible, but the hypersurface corresponding to a critical value of the F statistic can be called a multidimensional ellipsoid.

4.4   LR, W and LM Statistics

The F test discussed above is applicable whenever we are testing linear restrictions in the context of the CNLR model. Whenever the problem cannot be cast into this mould – for example, if the restrictions are nonlinear, the model is nonlinear in the parameters or the errors are distributed non-normally – this procedure is inappropriate and is usually replaced by one of three asymptotically equivalent tests. These are the *likelihood ratio* (LR) test, the *Wald* (W) test, and the *Lagrange multiplier* (LM) test. The test statistics associated with these tests have unknown small-sample distributions, but are each distributed asymptotically as a chi-square (χ^2) with degrees of freedom equal to the number of restrictions being tested.

These three test statistics are based on three different rationales. Consider Fig. 4.3, in which the log-likelihood (lnL) function is graphed as a function of β, the parameter being estimated. β^{MLE} is, by definition, the value of β at which lnL attains its maximum. Suppose the restriction being tested is written as $g(\beta) = 0$, satisfied at the value β_R^{MLE} where the function $g(\beta)$ cuts the horizontal axis:

(1) *The LR test*   If the restriction is true, then lnL_R, the maximized value of lnL imposing the restriction, should not be *significantly* less than lnL_{max}, the unrestricted maximum value of lnL. The LR test tests whether $(lnL_R - lnL_{max})$ is significantly different from zero.
(2) *The W test*   If the restriction $g(\beta) = 0$ is true, then $g(\beta^{MLE})$ should not be *significantly* different from zero. The W test tests whether β^{MLE} (the unrestricted estimate of β) violates the restriction by a significant amount.
(3) *The LM test*   The log-likelihood function lnL is maximized at point A where the slope of lnL with respect to β is zero. If the restriction is true, then the slope of lnL at point B should not be *significantly* different from zero. The LM test tests whether the slope of lnL, evaluated at the restricted estimate, is significantly different from zero.

When faced with three statistics with identical asymptotic properties, econometricians would usually choose among them on the basis of their small-sample properties, as determined by Monte Carlo studies. In this case, however, it happens that computational cost plays a dominant role in this respect. To calculate the LR statistic, both the restricted and the

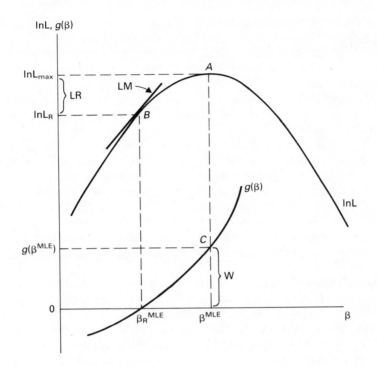

Fig. 4.3 Explaining the LR, W and LM statistics

unrestricted estimates of β must be calculated. If neither is difficult to compute, then the LR test is computationally the most attractive of the three tests. To calculate the W statistic only the unrestricted estimate is required; if the restricted but not the unrestricted estimate is difficult to compute, owing to a nonlinear restriction, for example, the W test is computationally the most attractive. To calculate the LM statistic, only the restricted estimate is required; if the unrestricted but not the restricted estimate is difficult to compute – for example, when imposing the restriction transforms a nonlinear functional form into a linear functional form – the LM test is the most attractive.

4.5 R^2 Again

The coefficient of determination, R^2, was discussed briefly in section 2.4. Its use (and abuse) in econometrics is so common, particularly in the context of hypothesis testing, that further discussion of this statistic is warranted.

It is noted in the general notes to section 4.3 that the *F* test could be interpreted in terms of R^2 and changes in R^2. Whether or not a set of extra independent variables belongs in a relationship depends on whether or not, by adding the extra regressors, the R^2 statistic increases significantly. This suggests that, when one is trying to determine which independent variable should be included in a relationship, one should search for the highest R^2.

This rule would lead to the choice of a relationship with too many regressors (independent variables) in it, because the addition of a regressor cannot cause the R^2 statistic to fall (for the same reason that the addition of a regressor cannot cause the minimized sum of squared residuals to become larger – minimizing without the restriction that the extra regressor must be ignored gives at least as low a minimand as when the restriction is imposed). Correcting the R^2 statistic for degrees of freedom solves this problem. The R^2 statistic adjusted to account for degrees of freedom is called the 'adjusted R^2' or '$\bar{R}^2$' and is now reported by most packaged computer regression programs, and by practically all researchers, in place of the unadjusted R^2.

Adding another regressor changes the degrees of freedom associated with the measures that make up the R^2 statistic. If an additional regressor accounts for very little of the unexplained variation in the dependent variable, $\bar{R}^2$ falls (whereas R^2 rises). Thus, only if $\bar{R}^2$ rises should an extra variable be seriously considered for inclusion in the set of independent variables. This suggests that econometricians should search for the 'best' set of independent variables by determining which potential set of independent variables produces the highest $\bar{R}^2$. This procedure is valid only in the sense that the 'correct set' of independent variables will produce, on average in repeated samples, a higher $\bar{R}^2$ than will any 'incorrect' set of independent variables.

Another common use of the R^2 statistic is in the context of measuring the relative importance of different independent variables in determining the dependent variable. Textbooks present several ways of decomposing the R^2 statistic into component parts, each component being identified with one independent variable and used as a measure of the relative importance of that independent variable in the regression. Unfortunately, none of these partitions of R^2 is meaningful unless it happens that the independent variables are uncorrelated with one another in the sample at hand. (This happens only by experimental design or by extraordinary luck, economists almost never being in a position to effect either.) In the typical case in which the independent variables are correlated in the sample, these suggested partitionings are not meaningful because: (a) they can no longer be legitimately allocated to the independent variables; (b) they no longer add up to R^2; or (c) they do add up to R^2 but contain negative as well as positive terms.

The main reason for this can be explained as follows. Suppose there are only two independent variables, and they are correlated in the sample.

Two correlated variables can be thought of as having, between them, three sorts of variation: variation unique to the first variable, variation unique to the second variable and variation common to both variables. (When the variables are uncorrelated, this third type of variation does not exist.) Each of the three types of variation in this set of two variables 'explains' some of the variation in the dependent variable. The basic problem is that no one can agree how to divide the explanatory power of the common variation between the two independent variables. If the dependent variable is regressed on both independent variables, the resulting R^2 reflects the explanatory power of all three types of independent variable variation. If the dependent variable is regressed on only one independent variable, variation unique to the other variable is removed and the resulting R^2 reflects the explanatory power of the other two types of independent variable variation. Thus, if one independent variable is removed, the remaining variable gets credit for *all* of the common variation. If the second independent variable were reinstated and the resulting increase in R^2 were used to measure the influence of this second variable, this variable would get credit for *none* of the common variation. Thus it would be illegitimate to measure the influence of an independent variable either by its R^2 in a regression of the dependent variable on only that independent variable, or by the addition to R^2 when that independent variable is added to a set of regressors. This latter measure clearly depends on the order in which the independent variables are added. Such procedures, and others like them, can only be used when the independent variables are uncorrelated in the sample. The use of breakdowns of the R^2 statistic in this context should be avoided.

General Notes

4.1 Introduction

- It is extremely convenient to assume that errors are distributed normally, but there exists little justification for this assumption. Tiao and Box (1973) p. 13 speculate that 'Belief in universal near-Normality of disturbances may be traced, perhaps, to early feeding on a diet of asymptotic Normality of maximum likelihood and other estimators.' Poincaré is said to have claimed that 'everyone believes in the [Gaussian] law of errors, the experimenters because they think it is a mathematical theorem, the mathematicians because they think it is an empirical fact.' Several tests for normality exist; for a textbook exposition see Maddala (1977) pp. 305–8. See also Judge *et al.* (1985) pp. 822–7. The consequences of non-normality of the fat-tailed kind, implying infinite variance, are quite serious, since hypothesis testing and interval estimation cannot be undertaken meaningfully. Faced with such non-normality, two options exist. First, one can employ robust estimators, as described in the general notes to section 2.3. And second, one can transform the data to create transformed errors that are closer to being normally distributed. For discussion see Maddala (1977) pp. 314–17.

- Testing hypotheses is viewed by some with scorn. Consider for example the remark of Johnson (1971) p. 2: 'The "testing of hypotheses" is frequently merely a euphemism for obtaining plausible numbers to provide ceremonial adequacy for a theory chosen and defended on *a priori* grounds.'

- Sometimes econometricians develop statistics (for testing hypotheses) whose distributions cannot be deduced. In such circumstances a Monte Carlo study is used to determine the appropriate critical values.

- For a number of reasons, tests of significance can sometimes be misleading. A good discussion can be found in Bakan (1966). One of the more interesting problems in this respect is the fact that almost any parameter can be found to be significantly different from zero if the sample size is sufficiently large. (Almost every relevant independent variable will have *some* influence, however small, on a dependent variable; increasing the sample size will reduce the variance and eventually make this influence statistically significant.) Thus, although a researcher wants a large sample size to generate more accurate estimates, too large a sample size might cause difficulties in interpreting the usual tests of significance. Here one must ask if the magnitude of the coefficient in question is large enough for its explanatory variable to have a meaningful (as opposed to 'significant') influence on the dependent variable. This is called the *too-large sample size problem*. It is suggested that the significance level be adjusted downward as the sample size grows; for a formalization see Leamer (1978) pp. 88–9, 104–5. Another interesting dimension of this problem is the question of what significance level should be employed when replicating a study with new data; conclusions must be drawn by considering both sets of data as a unit, not just the new set of data. For discussion see Busche and Kennedy (1984). A third interesting example in this context is the propensity for published studies to contain a disproportionately large number of type I errors; studies with statistically significant results tend to get published, whereas those with insignificant results do not. For comment see Feige (1975). Yet another example that should be mentioned here is pre-test bias, discussed in chapter 11.

- Inferences from a model may be sensitive to the model specification, the validity of which may be in doubt. A *fragility analysis* is recommended to deal with this; it examines the range of inferences resulting from the range of believable model specifications. See Leamer and Leonard (1983) and Leamer (1983a).

- Armstrong (1978) pp. 406–7 advocates the use of the method of multiple hypotheses, in which research is designed to compare two or more reasonable hypotheses, in contrast to the usual advocacy strategy in which a researcher tries to find confirming evidence for a favourite hypothesis. (Econometricians, like artists, tend to fall in love with their models!) It is claimed that the latter procedure biases the way scientists perceive the world, and that scientists employing the former strategy progress more rapidly.

4.3 The Multidimensional Case

- If there are only two observations, a linear function with one independent variable (i.e., two parameters) will fit this data perfectly, *regardless* of what independent variable is used. Adding a third observation will destroy the perfect fit, but the fit will remain quite good, simply because there is effectively only one observation to explain. It is to correct this phenomenon that statistics are adjusted for *degrees of freedom* – the number of 'free' or linearly independent observations used in the calculation of the statistic. For all of the *F* tests cited in this section, the degrees of freedom appropriate for the numerator is the number of parameters whose values are specified by the null hypothesis. The degrees of freedom for the denominator is $T - K$, the number of observations less the number of parameters being estimated. $T - K$ is also the degrees of freedom for the *t* statistic mentioned in section 4.2.

- The degrees of freedom of a statistic is the number of quantities that enter into the calculation of the statistic minus the number of constraints connecting these quantities. For example, the formula used to compute the sample variance involves the sample mean statistic. This places a constraint on the data – given the sample mean, any one data point can be determined by the other $(N - 1)$ data points. Consequently there are in effect only $(N - 1)$ unconstrained observations available to estimate the sample variance; the degrees of freedom of the sample variance statistic is $(N - 1)$.

- The procedure described for constructing an *F* test could be applied to the case of a null hypothesis concerning only one independent variable (rather than two or more independent variables). In this case the *F* test becomes identical to the individual *t* test (as it should, since the square of a *t* statistic is an *F* statistic).

- To run a regression constraining β_4^{OLS} to be 2.0, say, simply subtract 2.0 times the fourth independent variable from the dependent variable to form a new dependent variable and then regress this new dependent variable on the remaining independent variables.

- By dividing both the numerators and the denominators of the *F* statistics cited in this section by the total variation in the dependent variable (*SST*), these *F* statistics could be interpreted in terms of R^2, $1 - R^2$, and ΔR^2 (change in R^2) instead of 'explained', 'unexplained' and 'additional explained' variations. For example, the first *F* statistic discussed was *SSR/SSE* (omitting the degrees of freedom), which could be rewritten as $R^2/(1 - R^2)$. The second *F* statistic discussed was $\Delta SSR/SSE$ (omitting the degrees of freedom), which could then be rewritten as $\Delta R^2/(1 - R^2)$.

- The *F* tests developed in section 4.3 fall into a general form applicable to the testing of any set of linear restrictions. An *F* statistic with R and $T - K$ degrees of freedom can be constructed as:

$$\frac{[SSE \text{ (constrained)} - SSE(\text{unconstrained})]/R}{SSE \text{ (unconstrained)}/(T - K)}$$

where R is the number of restrictions, T is the number of observations, and K is the number of regressors in the unconstrained regression. This general format is useful for developing other *F* tests. See, for example, the technical notes to section 5.4, where the Chow test for testing for the equality of coefficients in two regressions is explained.

- Fig. 4.2 can be used to illustrate another curiosity – the possibility of accepting the hypothesis that

$$\begin{bmatrix} \beta_4 \\ \beta_5 \end{bmatrix} = \begin{bmatrix} 0 \\ 0 \end{bmatrix}$$

on the basis of an F test while rejecting the hypothesis that $\beta_4 = 0$ and the hypothesis that $\beta_5 = 0$ on the basis of individual t tests. This would be the case if, for the sample at hand, the point $(0, 0)$ fell in either of the small shaded areas (in the upper right or lower left) of the ellipse in Fig. 4.2. For a summary discussion of the possible cases that could arise here, along with an example of this seldom-encountered curiosity, see Geary and Leser (1968).

- One application of the F test is in testing for causality. It is usually assumed that movements in the dependent variable are caused by movements in the independent variable(s), but the existence of a relationship between these variables proves neither the existence of causality nor its direction. Using the dictionary meaning of causality, it is impossible to test for causality. Granger developed a special definition of causality which econometricians use in place of the dictionary definition; strictly speaking, econometricians should say 'Granger-cause' in place of 'cause', but usually they do not. A variable x is said to Granger-cause y if prediction of the current value of y is enhanced by using past values of x. This definition is implemented for empirical testing by regressing y on past, current and future values of x; if causality runs one way, from x to y, the set of coefficients of the future values of x should test insignificantly different from the zero vector (via an F test), and the set of coefficients of the past values of x should test significantly different from zero. Before running this regression both data sets are transformed (using the same transformation), so as to eliminate any autocorrelation in the error attached to this regression. (This is required to permit use of the F test; chapter 7 examines the problem of autocorrelated errors.) Great controversy exists over the appropriate way of conducting this transformation and the extent to which the results are sensitive to the transformation chosen. Other criticisms focus on the possibility of expected future values of x affecting the current value of y, and, in general, the lack of full correspondence between Granger-causality and causality. (Consider, for example, the fact that Christmas card sales Granger-cause Christmas!) Bishop (1979) has a concise review and references to the major studies on this topic.

4.4   LR, W and LM Statistics

- For an alternative way of expositing the similarities and differences among the LR, W and LM statistics, see Buse (1982).

- The name of the LM statistic comes from an alternative derivation of this statistic. To maximize subject to restrictions, the Lagrange multiplier technique is usually employed; if the restrictions are not binding, the vector of Lagrange multipliers is zero. Thus, when maximizing the log-likelihood subject to restrictions, if the restrictions are true they should be close to being satisfied by the data and the value of the Lagrange multiplier vector should be close to zero. The validity of the restrictions could therefore be tested by testing the vector of Lagrange multipliers against the zero vector. This produces the LM test.

- Critical values from the χ^2 distribution are used for the LR, W and LM tests, in spite of the fact that in small samples they are not distributed as χ^2. This is a weakness of all three of these tests. Furthermore, it has been shown by Berndt and Savin (1977) that in linear models in small samples the values of these test statistics are such that $W \geq LR \geq LM$ for the same data, testing for the same restrictions. Consequently, it is possible for conflict among these tests to arise in the sense that in small samples a restriction could be accepted on the basis of one test but rejected on the basis of another.

- Because it requires estimation under only the null hypothesis, the LM test is less specific than other tests concerning the precise nature of the alternative hypothesis. This could be viewed as an advantage, since it allows testing to be conducted in the context of a more general alternative hypothesis, or as a disadvantage, since it does not permit the precise nature of an alternative hypothesis to play a role and thereby increase the power of the test. Monte Carlo studies, for example, have shown that this potential drawback is not of great concern.

- For the special case of testing linear restrictions in the CNLR model with σ^2 known, the LR, W and LM tests are equivalent to the F test (which in this circumstance, because σ^2 is known, becomes a χ^2 test). When σ^2 is unknown, see Vandaele (1981) for the relationships among these tests.

4.5 R^2 Again

- $\bar{R}^2$, the adjusted R^2, is derived from an interpretation of R^2 as 1 minus the ratio of the variance of the disturbance term to the variance of the dependent variable (i.e., it is concerned with variances rather than variation). Estimation of these variances involves corrections for degrees of freedom, yielding (after manipulation) the expression

$$\bar{R}^2 = R^2 - \frac{K-1}{T-K}(1-R^2) \quad \text{or} \quad 1 - \frac{T-1}{T-K}(1-R^2)$$

where K is the number of independent variables and T is the number of observations. Armstrong (1978) p. 324 discusses some alternative adjustments to R^2. It is interesting to note that, if the true R^2 is zero (i.e., if there is no relationship between the dependent and independent variables), then the expected value of the unadjusted R^2 is K/T, a value that could be quite large. See Montgomery and Morrison (1973) for the general formula when the true R^2 is not zero.

- Both R^2 and $\bar{R}^2$ are biased but consistent estimators of the 'true' or 'population' coefficient of determination. $\bar{R}^2$ has a smaller bias than R^2, though. An unbiased estimator of the population coefficient of determination has not been developed because the distributions of R^2 and $\bar{R}^2$ are intractable when this population coefficient is non-zero.

- The result that the 'correct' set of independent variables produces a higher $\bar{R}^2$ on average in repeated samples was derived by Theil (1957).

- If adding an independent variable increase $\bar{R}^2$, its t value is greater than unity. See Edwards (1969). Thus the rule of maximizing $\bar{R}^2$ is quite different from the rule of keeping variables only if their t values are significant at the 5% level.

- It is worth reiterating that searching for a high R^2 or a high $\bar{R}^2$ runs the real danger of finding, through perseverance, an equation that fits the data well but is incorrect because it captures accidental features of the particular data set at hand (called 'capitalizing on chance'), rather than the true underlying relationship. This is illustrated in convincing fashion by Mayer (1975) and Bacon (1977).

- Aigner (1971) pp. 101–7 presents a good critical summary of measures used to capture the relative importance of independent variables in determining the dependent variable. He stresses the point that the relative strength of individual regressors should be discussed in a policy context, so that, for example, the impact on the dependent variable per dollar of policy action is what is relevant.

Technical Notes

4.4   LR, W and LM Statistics

- The LR test statistic is computed as $-2 \ln \lambda$ where λ is the *likelihood ratio*, the ratio of the constrained maximum of the likelihood (i.e., under the null hypothesis) to the unconstrained maximum of the likelihood.

- The W statistic is computed using a generalized version of the χ^2 which is useful to know. A sum of J independent, squared standard normal variables is distributed as χ^2 with J degrees of freedom. (This in effect defines a χ^2 distribution in most elementary statistics texts.) Thus, if the J elements θ_j of θ are distributed normally with mean zero, variance σ_j^2 and zero covariance, then $Q = \Sigma^J \theta_j^2 / \sigma_j^2$ is distributed as a χ^2 with J degrees of freedom. This can be written in matrix terminology as $Q = \theta' V^{-1} \theta$ where V is a diagonal matrix with σ_j^2 as its diagonal elements. Generalizing in the obvious way, we obtain $\theta' V^{-1} \theta$ distributed as a χ^2 with J degrees of freedom, where the $J \times 1$ vector θ is distributed multivariate normally with mean zero and variance–covariance matrix V.

   For the W statistic, θ is a vector of $\hat{g}$ of the J restrictions evaluated at β^{MLE}, and V, the variance–covariance matrix of $\hat{g}$, is given by $G'CG$ where G is the $(K \times J)$ matrix of derivatives of $\hat{g}$ with respect to β and C is the Cramer–Rao lower bound, representing the asymptotic variance of β^{MLE}. (Recall the technical notes of section 2.8 for an explanation of why the asymptotic variance of $\hat{g}$ is given by $G'CG$.) Placing hats over G and C to indicate that they are evaluated at β^{MLE}, we obtain $W = \hat{g}'[\hat{G}'\hat{C}\hat{G}]^{-1}\hat{g}$.

- Calculation of the LM statistic can be undertaken by the formula $\hat{d}'\hat{C}\hat{d}$, sometimes referred to as the *score* statistic. $\hat{d}$ is a $K \times 1$ vector of the slopes (first derivatives) of $\ln L$ with respect to β, evaluated at β_R^{MLE} the restricted estimate of β. $\hat{C}$ is an estimate of the Cramer–Rao lower bound. Different ways of estimating the Cramer–Rao lower bound give rise to a variety of LM statistics with identical asymptotic properties but slightly different small-sample properties. For discussion of the various different ways of computing the LM statistic, and an evaluation of their relative merits, see Davidson and MacKinnon (1983).

- If the model in question can be written as $Y = h(x; \beta) + \varepsilon$ where h is either a linear or nonlinear functional form and the ε are distributed independent normally with zero mean and common variance, an auxiliary regression can be employed to facilitate calculation of the LM statistic for a test of some portion of β equal to a specific vector. Consider H, the vector of the K derivatives of h with respect to β. Each element of this vector could be evaluated for each of the N observations, using β_R^{MLE} the restricted estimate of β. This would give a set of N 'observations' on each of the K derivatives. Consider also $\hat{\varepsilon}$, the vector of N residuals resulting from the calculation of β_R^{MLE}. Suppose $\hat{\varepsilon}$ is regressed on the K derivatives in H. Then the product of the resulting R^2 and the sample size N yields the LM statistic: $LM = NR^2$. For a derivation of this, and an instructive example illustrating its application, see Breusch and Pagan (1980) pp. 242–3. Additional examples of the derivation and use of the LM statistic can be found in Godfrey (1978), Breusch and Pagan (1979). Harvey (1981) pp. 167–74 and Tse (1984).

5. Violating Assumption One: Specification Errors

5.1 Introduction

The first assumption of the CLR model states that the dependent variable can be written as a linear function of a specific set of independent variables, plus a disturbance term. In this chapter we discuss 'specification errors': the ways in which this assumption can be violated. First is the case in which the specified set of independent variables omits relevant variables or includes irrelevant variables. Second is the case of a nonlinear functional form. And third is the case in which the parameters did not remain constant during the time period in which the data were collected.

The discussion of this chapter is couched in terms of testing for the 'true' model. In reality, no such 'true' model could ever hope to be found; an investigator is really searching for an 'adequate' (and parsimonious) approximation. What 'adequate' means depends on the purpose of the analysis in question. If what is desired is a forecasting formula, accuracy of prediction is the relevant criterion (see chapter 15). If what is desired is a 'good' estimate of a particular parameter or set of parameters, the correct specification may or may not be the most appropriate. (Omitting a relevant variable, for example, may reduce the mean square error, as noted later.) If what is desired is to determine if the truth is better approximated by, say, a Keynesian rather than a monetarist world, non-nested hypothesis tests may be called for. It seems reasonable to suppose, however, that, whatever the purpose of the analysis in question, knowledge of what best approximates the 'true' data-generating process will help rather than hinder, so that the techniques discussed in this chapter can all be of value.

In recent years the focus of econometrics has shifted to some extent from parameter estimation to model specification/evaluation. A wide variety of specific testing procedures has been developed, but very few general principles have emerged. Three results that seem worthy of classifying as general principles in this regard are noted below:

(1) Specification v. mis-specification

Tests used in searching for the correct specification are of two types: *specification tests*, in which one hunts for an alternative specification that is 'better', and *mis-specification tests*, in which one hunts for ways in which the current specification is inadequate. In general, the former are constructed with some clear alternative hypothesis in mind whereas the latter are not.

A specification search is best undertaken by beginning with a general, unrestricted model and then systematically simplifying it in the light of the sample evidence. This approach (deliberate 'overfitting') is preferred to/has more power than a search beginning with a very simple model and expanding as the data permit (see Harvey, 1981, pp. 183–7). Tests of mis-specification are best undertaken by testing simultaneously for several mis-specifications. By such an 'overtesting' technique one avoids the problem of one type of mis-specification adversely affecting a test for some other type of mis-specification (see Bera and Jarque, 1982). This approach helps deflect the common criticism that specification tests rely for their power on aspects of the maintained hypothesis about which little is known.

(2) *The encompassing principle*

An attractive criterion for undertaking specification searches is the *encompassing principle*: the chosen model should be able to predict the results of estimating on the basis of alternative models. Thus, for example, using the chosen model, one should be able to predict the parameter estimates resulting from running the regression suggested by an alternative model. In this sense the chosen model encompasses the alternative. In essence, the chosen model should account for the results of competing models and explain something new itself. (For discussion see Mizon, 1984).

An extension of the encompassing criterion is to explain why other researchers were led to accept the models they ultimately chose. Such explanations focus on the implicit (self-imposed) constraints that investigators tend to place on themselves concerning the range of specifications entertained, the estimators employed, the data used, the diagnostic tests performed, etc. For an example of this approach, see Davidson *et al.* (1978).

(3) *Fragility analysis*

A researcher's rationale for selecting a particular model specification is never so cogent as to be completely convincing. Consequently it is of interest to ask how the inferences made by a study would be affected if a different model specification were chosen. Addressing this problem thoroughly requires that the range of inferences generated by a range of models be determined, rather than that the single inference implied by a specific model be identified. If the range of models considered is broad enough to be believable and the resulting range of inferences is small enough to be useful, we can conclude that the data at hand yield useful information. If not, we must conclude that inferences from these data are too *fragile* to be useful. For discussion, see Leamer and Leonard (1983) and Leamer (1983a).

5.2 Incorrect Set of Independent Variables

The consequences of using an incorrect set of independent variables fall into two categories. Intuitive explanations for these results are given in the general notes to this section.

(i) *Omission of a relevant independent variable*

(a) In general, the OLS estimates of the coefficients of the remaining variables are biased. If by luck (or experimental design, should the researcher be fortunate enough to have control over the data) the observations on the omitted variable(s) are uncorrelated in the sample with the observations on the other independent variables (i.e., if the omitted variable is orthogonal to the included variables), the slope coefficients will be unbiased; the intercept estimate will retain its bias unless the mean of the observations on the omitted variable is zero.

(b) The estimator of the variance–covariance matrix of β^{OLS} is biased upward, causing inferences concerning these parameters to be inaccurate. This is the case even if the omitted variable is orthogonal to the others.

(ii) *Inclusion of an irrelevant variable*

(a) β^{OLS} and the estimator of its variance–covariance matrix remain unbiased.

(b) Unless the irrelevant variable is orthogonal to the other independent variables, the variance–covariance matrix of β^{OLS} becomes larger; the OLS estimates are not as efficient.

To avoid these problems a researcher usually trys to determine the correct set of explanatory variables. The first and most important ingredient in such a search is economic theory. If economic theory cannot defend the use of a variable as an explanatory variable, it should not be included in the set of potential independent variables. Such theorizing should take place *before* any empirical testing of the appropriateness of potential independent variables; this guards against the adoption of an independent variable just because it happens to 'explain' a significant portion of the variation in the dependent variable in the particular sample at hand.

Once economic theory has provided its input, there are several techniques available to help in the search for the correct set of independent variables.

(1) *R^2, F and t criteria*

A common procedure in determining the appropriate set of regressors is to include a variable if its *t* value is greater than some specified number. In the general notes to section 4.5 we noted that, if this critical t value is unity, this rule corresponds to maximizing $\bar{R}^2$; an obvious alternative critical value is the t value corresponding to testing the variable's coefficient against zero at the 5% level. If we are dealing with the question of inclusion or exclusion of a set of variables, rather than a single variable, the t value noted above must be an F value. Whenever a large number of potential independent variables exists, checking every combination of these variables for their performance on the basis of one of these rules can be very costly computationally. This problem has led to the development of several iterative techniques, with names such as 'forward selection', 'backward elimination' and 'stepwise regression'. These techniques are not all reliable, however, as pointed out in the general notes to this section.

Maximizing an alternative adjusted form of R^2 (i.e., different from $\bar{R}^2$) arises from other approaches based on specific loss functions. For example, the set of variables may be chosen so as to minimize some sort of expected loss associated with prediction errors. These alternative criteria create slightly different trade-offs between goodness of fit (R^2) and parsimony (number of explanatory variables). They may also be interpreted in some cases as giving rise to slightly different critical values of the t or F statistics discussed above.

(2) *Non-nested hypothesis tests*

The criteria discussed in (1) above are model 'selection' or 'discrimination' methods; they are techniques for choosing one model in preference to another. They are not methods of testing for the 'validity' of 'truth' of a model. One model will always be chosen using a model selection method, whereas when testing for the 'truth' of a model one should be able to reject all models. This latter feature is one of the attractive properties of *non-nested hypothesis tests*. Two models are 'separate' or 'non-nested' if one cannot be obtained from the other by imposing a restriction (and thus an F test of the restriction cannot be employed as a specification test). If the specification problem can be structured such that the competing models are non-nested, several non-nested hypothesis tests can be employed. Such tests provide a way of testing the specification of one model against the evidence provided by one or more non-nested alternative models. Unlike many alternative specification testing procedures, they attempt to exploit the supposed 'falsity' of specific alternative models.

Many of these tests result from an artificial nesting procedure, a popular variant of which is the non-nested F test. Suppose there are two theories, H_0 and H_1. According to H_0, the independent variables are X and Z; according to H_1, they are X and W. A general model with X, Z and W as explanatory variables is formed (without any economic rationale!) and then the coefficients of Z and W are each (separately) tested against zero. If Z and W each represent a set of variables rather than a single variable, traditional *F* tests are used for this purpose. (Notice that it is possible via this procedure to reject *both* H_0 and H_1.)

(3) *Extra-sample validation*

Evaluating the performance of the chosen independent variables with data not used to determine the original specification is a good way of checking if the set of independent variables is correct. This approach is particularly useful for guarding against errors caused by fitting a particular sample too closely. One such technique is *cross-validation*. If the sample is large enough, it is split into two sub-samples. Parameters are estimated from the first sub-sample and then the dependent variable values for the second sub-sample are predicted. Using these predictions, an R^2 for the second sample is calculated; if this R^2 is not significantly below the R^2 in the first sub-sample, the specification is said to be satisfactory. In double cross-validation this procedure is repeated, interchanging the roles of the two sub-samples. Once the appropriate set of independent variables is decided upon, estimation is undertaken using all of the data. When the sample size is not large enough to employ this technique, a useful alternative is to set aside one or two observations, estimate using the rest of the observations and then check that the observations set aside fall within a prediction interval. (See chapter 15 on prediction.)

(4) *Hausman tests*

Sometimes two different estimators have identical expectations whenever the model in question is true, but have different expectations whenever this model is false. Hausman tests are based on testing whether or not the estimates from the two estimating procedures differ significantly from one another. For example, regressing on data in levels and regressing on these data in first difference form should produce similar slope coefficient estimates if the model (in levels) is true, but these estimates can be quite different from one another if this model is false.

(5) *RESET*

When a relevant variable is omitted from a model, the 'disturbance' term of the false model incorporates the influence of the omitted variable. If some variable or set of variables *Z* can be used as a proxy for the (unknown) omitted variable(s), a specification error test can be formed by examining *Z*'s relationship to the false model's error term. The RESET (regression specification error test) does this by adding *Z* to the set of regressors and then testing *Z*'s set of coefficient estimates against the zero vector by means of a traditional *F* test.

(6) *Dynamic specification analysis*

When dealing with time-series data, economic theory, which invariably relies on steady-state arguments, often specifies a model capturing long-run behaviour but fails to incorporate features capturing short-run disequilibrium behaviour. Including lagged values of the regressand and regressor(s) as explanatory variables creates a more general model capable of reflecting short-run behaviour. Any such dynamic relationship should be tested, however, to ensure that it embodies the parameter restrictions necessary to ensure that the steady state it implies accords with economic theory. Additional restrictions (e.g., that the coefficients of the lagged variables are all zero) must be shown to be valid if this dynamic model is discarded in favour of a model without lagged variables.

(7) *Diagnostic checking*

A mis-specification usually causes the OLS residuals to exhibit non-randomness of one sort or another, so that tests on these residuals, referred to as *diagnostic checks*, are undertaken to aid in specification searches. Such tests range from an informal visual inspection of the residuals graphed in some order to more formal tests such as tests for normality. Tests for autocorrelation and heteroskedasticity, discussed in chapter 7, are also popular.

5.3   Nonlinearity

The first assumption of the CLR model specifies that the functional form of the relationship to be estimated is linear. Running an OLS regression when this is not true is clearly unsatisfactory, since parameter estimates not only are biased but also are without meaning except in so far as the linear functional form can be interpreted as an approximation to a nonlinear functional form. The OLS estimation procedure must be revised to handle a nonlinear functional form. These revisions fall into two categories.

(1) *Transformations*

If by transforming one or more variables a nonlinear function can be translated into a linear function in the transformed variables, OLS estimation procedures can be applied to transformed data. These transformations are of two types.

(a) *Transforming only independent variables*   If, for example, the nonlinear functional form is

$$y = a + bx + cx^2 + \varepsilon$$

a linear function

$$y = a + bx + cz + \varepsilon$$

can be created by structuring a new independent variable z whose observations are the squares of the observations on x. This is an example of an equation nonlinear in variables but linear in parameters. The dependent variable y can be regressed on the independent variables x and z using β^{OLS} to estimate the parameters. The OLS estimator has its CLR model properties, the R^2 statistic retains its traditional properties, and the standard hypothesis tests are valid.

(b) *Transforming the entire equation* When transforming only independent variables cannot create a linear functional form, it is sometimes possible to create a linear function in transformed variables by transforming the entire equation. If, for example, the nonlinear function is the Cobb–Douglas production function (with a multiplicative disturbance)

$$Y = AK^{\alpha}L^{\gamma}\varepsilon$$

then transforming the entire equation by taking natural logarithms of both sides creates

$$\ln Y = \ln A + \alpha \ln K + \gamma \ln L + \ln \varepsilon$$

or

$$Y^* = A^* + \alpha K^* + \gamma L^* + \varepsilon^*,$$

a linear function in the transformed variables Y^*, K^* and L^*. If this new relationship meets the CLR model assumptions, which econometricians usually assume is the case, the OLS estimates from a regression using these transformed variables have their traditional desirable properties.

(2) *Computer-assisted numerical techniques*

Some nonlinear functions cannot be transformed into a linear form. The CES production function is an example of this, as is the Cobb–Douglas function with an additive, rather than a multiplicative, disturbance. In these cases econometricians turn to either nonlinear least squares or maximum likelihood methods, both of which require computer search procedures. In nonlinear least squares the computer uses an iterative technique to find those values of the parameters in the relationship that cause the sum of squared residuals to be minimized. It starts with approximate guesses of the parameter values and computes the residuals and then the sum of squared residuals; next, it changes one of the parameter values slightly, recomputes the residuals and sees if the sum of squared residuals becomes larger or smaller. It keeps changing parameter values in directions that lead to smaller sums of squared residuals until it finds the set of parameter values that, when changed slightly in any direction, causes the sum of squared residuals to rise. These parameter values are the least squares estimates in the nonlinear context. A good initial guess of the parameter values is necessary to ensure that the procedure reaches a global and not a local minimum for the sum of squared residuals. For maximum likelihood estimation a similar computer search technique is used to find parameter values that maximize the likelihood function.

In general, the desirable properties of the OLS estimator in the CLR model do not carry over to the nonlinear least squares estimator. For this reason the maximum likelihood estimator is usually chosen in preference to the nonlinear least squares estimator. The two techniques are identical whenever the dependent variable is determined by a nonlinear function of the independent variables plus a normally distributed, additive disturbance.

Variants of all the methods discussed earlier for selecting/testing for omitted explanatory variables can be used to select/test for functional form. This reflects a weakness of these tests: if a model is rejected on the basis of one of these tests, it is not clear whether it is because of an omitted explanatory variable or an incorrect functional form. Two additional methods can be used to test for functional form.

(a) *Recursive residuals*   The nth recursive residual is the error in predicting the nth observation using parameters estimated from a linear regression employing the first $n-1$ observations. If the true functional form is nonlinear, then, if the data are ordered according to the variable entering nonlinearly, these residuals could become either all positive or all negative, a result that can be exploited to test for nonlinearity.

(b) *General functional forms*   Some functional forms contain particular forms, such as linearity or log-linearity, as special cases corresponding to specific values of a parameter. These particular functional forms can then be tested by testing the estimate of this parameter against these specific values.

5.4   Changing Parameter Values

A common criticism of econometricians concerns their assumption that the parameters are constants. In time-series estimation, changing institutions and social mores have surely caused the parameter values characterizing the economy to change over time, and in cross-section estimation it is surely unrealistic to assume that the parameters for every individual or every region are exactly the same. Although most econometricians usually ignore these criticisms, maintaining that with small sample sizes they are forced to make these simplifying assumptions to obtain estimates of any sort, several techniques are available for addressing this problem.

(1) *Switching regimes*

It may be known that at a particular point in time the economic structure changed. For example, the data of the Canada–USA auto pact might mark a change in parameter values associated with the Canadian or US auto industries. In such a case we need run only two regressions, one for each 'regime'. More often than not, however, the point in time at which the parameter values changed is unknown and must be estimated. If the error variances are the same for both regimes, this can be done by selecting several likely points of change, running pairs of regressions for each and then choosing among these points of change by determining which corresponds to the smallest total sum of squared residuals. (If the error variances cannot be assumed equal, a maximum likelihood technique must be used.) This approach has been extended in several directions:

(a) to accommodate more than two regimes;
(b) to permit continuous switching back and forth, either randomly or according to a critical value of an unknown function of some additional variables;
(c) to eliminate discontinuities, so that the function describing one regime blends into the function describing the next regime over an adjustment period.

(2) *Parameters determined by other variables*

It could be that β is itself determined by variables outside the model. For example, the extent to which a firm reacts to demand changes may depend on government policy parameters such as tax rates. This problem is most easily resolved by substituting the relationship determining β directly into the original estimating function. Thus if we have, for example,

$$y = \beta_1 + \beta_2 x_2 + \varepsilon$$

and β_2, say, is determined as

$$\beta_2 = \alpha_1 + \alpha_2 z_2,$$

we can combine these relationships to get

$$y = \beta_1 + \alpha_1 x_2 + \alpha_2(x_2 z_2) + \varepsilon$$

so that estimation should be undertaken by including the new variable $(x_2 z_2)$ as an additional regressor. If the relationship for β_2 includes an error term, the error term attached to the final estimating question is more complicated, and although the OLS estimator remains unbiased, a maximum likelihood estimating procedure is required for efficiency.

(3) *Random coefficients*

Instead of being determined by specific variables, the parameters may be random variables. This could be viewed as an alternative way of injecting a stochastic element into a relationship, or it could reflect specific recognition of the fact that the parameters being estimated are not the same for every observation. In this case the estimating equation can be rewritten, substituting for the random β its mean plus a disturbance term, to yield a new estimating equation, with a somewhat more complicated error term, in which the parameter to be estimated is the mean value of the random coefficient β. Although OLS estimation of the mean of β is unbiased, the more complicated nature of the error term requires a more sophisticated estimation procedure for efficiency (such as a maximum likelihood method or a weighted least squares technique: see chapter 7). This approach has been extended in two directions:
(a) β is allowed to 'drift' according to a random walk (i.e., β is equated to its value in the previous time-period, plus a disturbance);
(b) β is random and 'drifts', but converges on an unknown fixed value.

General Notes

5.1   Introduction

- The term 'specification error' is sometimes used to refer to violations of any assumption of the CLR model. It is also sometimes used to refer only to the case of omission of a relevant independent variable or inclusion of an irrelevant independent variable. We use the term to refer to any violation of the first assumption of the CLR model.

- It must be kept in mind that rejecting an economic hypothesis couched in terms of a specific model may merely be a rejection of the modeller's detailed parametric specification and not the economic hypothesis of interest.

- Our earlier discussion of outliers (in the general notes to section 2.3) suggested the use of robust estimation methods, some of which discard outliers. In the context of specification, however, outliers can sometimes be of particular value – unusual and surprising facts can generate major advances as generalizations are sought to explain them. For examples and discussion see Zellner (1981).

- Exploratory data analysis, discussed in the general notes to section 2.3, can play a role in specification. For an example see L. S. Mayer (1980).

- Using techniques that adopt specifications on the basis of searches for high R^2 or high t values, is called data-mining, fishing, grubbing or number-crunching. This methodology is described eloquently by Coase: 'if you torture the data long enough, Nature will confess.' In reference to this unjustified (but unfortunately typical) means of specifying relationships, Leamer (1983a) is moved to comment: 'There are two things you are better off not watching in the making: sausages and econometric estimates.'

Peach and Webb (1983) fabricated 50 macroeconomic models at random and discovered that the majority of these models exhibited very high R^2 and t statistics. This casts considerable doubt on the practice of using a high R^2 or high t values to defend a specification, and suggests that practitioners should utilize some of the more relevant specification testing methods exposited in this chapter.

It must be noted, however, that the data-mining methodology does have one positive feature: sometimes such experimentation uncovers empirical regularities that point to errors in theoretical specifications. For example, through data-mining one of my colleagues discovered a result that led him to re-examine the details of the British Columbia stumpage fee system. He discovered that he had overlooked some features of this tax that had an important bearing on the behaviour of the forest industry. Because of this, he was able to develop a much more satisfactory theoretical specification, and thereby to produce better empirical results.

I give John Maynard Keynes (1940) p. 155 the last word on this subject:

> It will be remembered that the seventy translators of the Septuagint were shut up in seventy separate rooms with the Hebrew text and brought out with them, when they emerged, seventy identical translations. Would the same miracle be vouchsafed if seventy multiple correlators were shut up with the same statistical material?

• A potential violation of the first assumption that is not discussed in this chapter is the possibility that the disturbance term is not additive. For example, the disturbance term could enter multiplicatively, so that the dependent variable is determined by forming a linear function of the independent variables, which is then multiplied by a disturbance term. Kmenta (1971) pp. 400–2 shows that an incorrect specification of this nature leads to biased OLS estimates. When dealing with linear functions, econometricians almost always assume that the disturbance term is additive.

5.2   Incorrect Set of Independent Variables

• Rao (1971) and Giles (1973) pp. 9–13 have good discussions of the consequences of omitting a relevant independent variable or including an irrelevant variable.

• Kennedy (1981b) employs the Ballentine to exposit the consequences of omitting a relevant variable or adding an irrelevant variable. In Fig. 5.1 the real world is such that Y is determined by X and Z but the variable (or set of variables) Z is erroneously omitted from the regression. Several results can be noted.

(a)   Since Y is regressed on only X, the blue-plus-red area is used to estimate β_x. But the red area reflects variation in Y due to *both* X and Z, so the resulting estimate of β_x will be biased.

(b)   If Z had been included in the regression, only the blue area would have been used in estimating β_x. Omitting Z thus increases the information used to estimate β_x by the red area, implying that the resulting estimate, although biased, will have a smaller variance. Thus it is possible that by omitting Z the mean square error of the estimate of β_x may be reduced.

(c)   The magnitude of the yellow area reflects the magnitude of σ^2. But when Z is omitted, σ^2 is estimated using the yellow-plus-green area, resulting in an overestimate of σ^2 (i.e., the green area influence of Z is erroneously attributed to the error term). This overestimate of σ^2 causes an over estimate of the variance–covariance matrix of β_x.

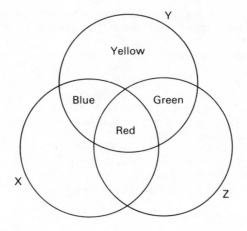

Fig. 5.1   Omitting a relevant variable Z

(d)   If Z is orthogonal to X the red area does not exist, so the bias noted above disappears.

• In Fig. 5.2 the real world is such that Y is determined by X but the irrelevant variable Z is erroneously added to the regression. The overlap of Z with Y comes about virtually entirely because of its collinearity with X; in this case the red area reflects variation in Y explained 100% by X and zero % by Z. The shaded area is negligible in size because only with finite degrees of freedom will Z be able to

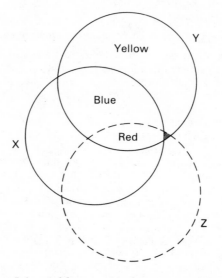

Fig. 5.2   Adding an irrelevant variable Z

explain a small amount of variation in Y independently of X. Using the correct specification, Y is regressed on X and the blue-plus-red area is employed to create an unbiased estimate of β_x. Including Z in the regression implies that only the blue area is used to estimate β_x. Several results follow.

(a)   The blue area reflects variation in Y due entirely to X, so this estimate of β_x is unbiased. Thus, adding an irrelevant variable does not bias coefficient estimates.

(b)   Since the blue area is smaller than the blue-plus-red area, the variance of the estimate of β_x becomes larger; there is a loss in efficiency.

(c)   The usual estimator of σ^2, using the yellow area, remains unbiased because the negligible shaded area is offset by the change in the degrees of freedom. Thus the usual estimator of the variance–covariance matrix of β_x remains unbiased. (It does become bigger, though, as noted in (b) above.)

(d)   If Z is orthogonal to X, the red area disappears and there is no efficiency loss.

- Iterative techniques used to find the set of independent variables meeting some t-test criterion are not always reliable. Consider the 'forward selection' technique, for example. It augments the set of regressors one by one, by selecting the new variable with the highest t value, until no more variables with t values higher than the critical t value can be found. Unfortunately, a variable included in an early step may have its usefulness negated by the inclusion of new variables, whose *joint* influence is more effective in explaining the variation in the dependent variable that the variable included earlier had explained. Only if at each step the iterative procedure pauses and rechecks all the already included variables will this be caught. (Note that it will never be caught if the new variables, whose *joint* influence is more effective than an already included variable, are never included in the set of regressors because their individual t values are too low.) In summary, these methods tend to select sets of variables that are relatively uncorrelated, a result difficult to justify, particularly since, as noted above, omitting a correlated explanatory variable leads to bias in the estimation of the remaining parameters. For a summary discussion of this problem see Maddala (1977) pp. 124–7.

- When using a t or F criterion the too-large sample size phenomenon should be kept in mind.

- Several different ways of trading off goodness of fit and parsimony exist. They vary mainly in the extent to which they adjust R^2 for the degrees of freedom, $\bar{R}^2$ in general having the least adjustment, and are defended on the basis of the loss function on which they rest. The better-known of these are $\bar{R}^2$, Amemiya's prediction criterion PC, Mallows' C_p statistic, and Akaike's information criterion AIC. Amemiya (1980) has an extensive discussion of these criteria, the relationships among them, and their relative merits. See also Judge et al. (1985) chapter 21. Having so many such criteria, differing by so little, creates a dilemma of choice, reflected by Amemiya's comment that 'all the critieria considered are based on a somewhat arbitrary assumption which cannot be fully justified, and that by slightly varying the loss function and the decision strategy one can indefinitely go on inventing new criteria.'

- The feature of non-nested hypothesis tests that all models under consideration may be rejected (or accepted) is discussed at some length by Dastoor (1981).

- The non-nested F test is argued by some to be the best of the non-nested hypothesis tests. However, it is often the case that degrees-of-freedom problems, collinearity problems or nonlinear functional forms cause this test to become unattractive. There are two basic alternatives: the *J* test and its variants, and the Cox test and its variants. For a survey of this literature see MacKinnon (1983); the comments on this paper provide an interesting view of controversies in this area.

- As is made clearer in the technical notes to this section, the *J* test is akin to the *F* test in that it stems from an artificial nesting model. To conduct this test, the dependent variable *Y* is regressed on the explanatory variables of hypothesis H_0, together with $\hat{Y}$, the estimated *Y* from the regression associated with H_1. If $\hat{Y}$ has some explanatory power beyond that contributed by the explanatory variables of H_0, then H_0 cannot be the 'true' model. This question is addressed by using a *t* test to test if the coefficient of $\hat{Y}$ is significantly different from zero; if it is, H_0 is rejected; otherwise, H_0 is accepted. The roles of H_0 and H_1 are reversed and the procedure is repeated to allow H_1 to be either rejected or accepted.

- The rationale behind the Cox test is similar to that of the encompassing principle. H_0 is tested by asking if the 'performance' of H_1 (in particular, the estimate of σ^2 from running the regression associated with H_1) is what would be expected if H_0 were true. If H_1 performs either significantly better or significantly worse than what we would expect if H_0 were true, then H_0 is rejected. Otherwise H_0 is accepted. The roles of H_0 and H_1 are then reversed and the procedure is repeated to test H_1.

- Any method that selects regressors on the basis of a sample statistic such as R^2 is likely to 'capitalize on chance' – select a regressor because of an accidental feature of the particular sample at hand. Cross-validation is designed to overcome this problem. Unfortunately, however, satisfactory methods for predicting the degree of shrinkage in R^2 when moving to the new data are not available, so that no formal statistical tests have been structured to formalize this technique; its use is subjective. Uhl and Eisenberg (1970) examine shrinkage in R^2. Snee (1977) discusses the optimal way to split a sample for cross-validation.

- Leamer (1983b) notes that one form of cross-validation via sample splitting is equivalent to minimizing the sum of squared errors with a penalty for coefficient instability. He suggests that a proper means of accommodating coefficient instability be employed instead. He also shows that cross-validation done by deleting one observation at a time (i.e., using all observations but one to estimate and then predict that missing observation) is inferior to the traditional $\bar{R}^2$ criterion.

- Christ (1966) pp. 546–9 maintains that in time-series with limited data it makes no difference if all the data are used and the results tested for specification or if some data are set aside and predictions are tested.

- Hausman (1978) popularized the concept forming the basis for Hausman tests. His applications were in testing for a violation of assumption 4 of the CLR model, but the idea can be applied to the present context. Two promising examples are the *differencing test* and the *information matrix test*. Plosser, Schwert and White (1982) show that comparing estimates from data in levels with estimates from that same data in differenced form is an attractive specification test. White (1982) has shown that two different ways of calculating the information matrix (and thus the variance–covariance matrix) will in general not yield similar results in the presence of a mis-specification.

• Thursby and Schmidt (1977) suggest that the best variant of RESET is one in which the additional regressors Z are the squares, cubes and fourth powers of the explanatory variables. Thursby (1979, 1981, 1982) has examined how RESET can be combined with a variety of other tests to aid in specification.

• For a good discussion of dynamic specification, see Davidson *et al.* (1978). Autocorrelated errors (discussed at length in chapter 7) can play an important role in this context. A dynamic specification, under certain parameter restrictions, may reduce to a relationship without lagged values but with an autocorrelated error. These parameter restrictions are called common factors; COMFAC analysis is used to investigate this. Note the implication that finding autocorrelated residuals may imply a dynamic mis-specification (rather than an inherently autocorrelated error). COMFAC analysis can also be used to address the question of whether a regression should be run in levels or first differences. Use of first differences implies a special type of common factor; its use should therefore be preceded by an appropriate test. Hendry and Mizon (1978) have a good exposition of COMFAC analysis. See the technical notes for an example illustrating COMFAC analysis. Harvey (1980) has a completely different approach to the levels *v.* first differences question, based on a variant of the sum of squared errors. Layson and Seaks (1984) address the question of whether first differences should be measured in raw terms or percentage terms. It must be stressed, however, that dynamic specification is made more difficult if differenced or seasonally adjusted data are employed.

• Visual inspection of the residuals to verify that they appear to be randomly distributed is an informal technique sometimes used to check for specification error. Ramsey (1969) develops several tests for specification error, based on the idea that the effect of the specification error is to alter the distribution of the residuals from what it would be without specification error. Ramsey and Gilbert (1972) examine these tests via a Monte Carlo study.

5.3 Nonlinearity

• Cassidy (1981) pp. 46–54 has an exposition of how a variety of popular but simple functional forms are estimated.

• Judge *et al.* (1985) Appendix B has a good review of numerical methods used to find maxima/minima of nonlinear functions. See also Gallant (1975) and Quandt (1983).

• The properties of the OLS estimator applied to a situation in which the true functional form is nonlinear can be analysed in terms of omitted relevant variables. A nonlinear function can be restated, via a Taylor series expansion, as a polynomial. Estimating a linear function is in effect omitting the higher-order terms of this polynomial.

• Transforming an equation into a linear form sometimes creates an error term for that linear function that does not meet all of the CLR model assumptions. See chapter 6 for an example.

• A multiplicative error term for some nonlinear functional forms (such as the Cobb–Douglas production function) facilitates the tranformation of the equation to a linear estimating form. It is not obvious, however, that this error term need necessarily be multiplicative. Leech (1975) addresses the problem of testing this error specification.

- A distinct danger in using the highest $\bar{R}^2$ criterion to choose the functional form is that, if the dependent variables are not the same, the R^2 is not directly comparable. For example, the R^2 from a regression of the logarithm of the dependent variable on the logarithms of the independent variables gives the proportion of the variation in the *logarithm* of the dependent variable explained, not the proportion of the variation in the dependent variable itself. Estimated values of the dependent variable must be used to construct a comparable R^2, or some transformation must be applied to the data to assure compatibility. (An example of such a transformation for a popular application is given in Rao and Miller, 1971, pp. 108–9.) Note, however, that Granger and Newbold (1976) suggest that under general conditions this entire problem of the comparability of the R^2s can be ignored. See Haessel (1978) on measuring goodness of fit in nonlinear models.

- Non-nested hypothesis tests can be used to test for functional form. A variant of the *J* test, called the *P* test, seems to be the most attractive way of doing this. A modified *P* test can be used for situations in which the dependent variable is transformed in some of the competing models (see MacKinnon, 1983).

- The DW, or Durbin–Watson, test (see chapter 7) is sometimes used as a test for nonlinearity. However, the results of Thursby (1979) indicate that the RESET test is better than the DW test in detecting a specification error of an omitted variable or incorrect functional form, and furthermore is robust to autocorrelated errors (the phenomenon the DW test is designed to detect).

- An example of selecting the functional form on the basis of the 'randomness' of the residuals is given by Ramsey and Zarembka (1971), who show how the specification error tests developed by Ramsey (1969) can be used to choose among several different functional forms, all of which have very high R^2.

- Recursive residuals are standardized one-step-ahead prediction errors. Suppose the observations are ordered by the size of the explanatory variable and the true relationship is U-shaped. Use, say, the first ten observations to estimate via OLS a linear relationship. When this estimated relationship is employed to predict the eleventh observation, it will probably underpredict because of the U-shaped nonlinearity; the recursive residual for the eleventh observation is this (probably negative) prediction error, standardized by dividing by its variance. To obtain the twelfth recursive residual, the first eleven observations are used to estimate the linear relationship. Doing this will tilt the estimating line up a bit from what it was before, but not nearly by enough to prevent another unprediction; once again, the recursive residual, because of the nonlinearity, is likely to be negative. Thus a string of negative recursive residuals indicates a U-shaped nonlinearity and a string of positive recursive residuals indicates a hill-shaped nonlinearity. Harvey and Collier (1977) advocate the use of recursive residuals to test for nonlinearity.

- Unlike OLS residuals, recursive residuals are homoskedastic (because they are standardized) and are independent of one another (because a recursive residual's own observation is not involved in estimating the prediction line from which it is calculated). These attractive properties have made them a popular alternative to OLS residuals for use in calculating a variety of regression diagnostics. For a good review of their uses in this regard, see Galpin and Hawkins (1984).

- A related way of testing for linearity is to break the data into sub-groups based on the magnitude of the independent variable being tested for nonlinearity and then run separate regressions for each sub-group. If these separate regressions are significantly different from one another, there is good reason to believe the functional form is not linear.

- The most popular general functional form used for testing nonlinearity is that associated with the Box–Cox transformation, in which a variable Z is transformed to $(Z^\lambda - 1)/\lambda$. Since the limit of this as λ approaches zero is ln Z, it is defined to be ln Z when $\lambda = 0$. If all variables in a linear functional form are transformed in this way and then λ is estimated (in conjunction with the other parameters) via a maximum likelihood technique, significance tests can be performed on λ to check for special cases. If $\lambda = 0$, for example, the functional form becomes Cobb–Douglas in nature; if $\lambda = 1$ it is linear. Aigner (1971) pp. 166–9 and Johnston (1984) pp. 61–74 have good discussions of this approach. Spitzer (1982) is a particularly useful reference. Estimating the variance of a Box–Cox estimate can be a problem; see Spitzer (1984).

- The Box–Cox technique has been generalized in several ways to permit testing of functional form simultaneously with testing for other violations of the CNLR model. All of these studies have concluded that there is much to gain (in terms of power) and little to lose from pursuing a policy of 'overtesting' in this respect. For a survey of some of these studies, see Seaks and Layson (1983). The most general of these approaches is that of Bera and Jarque (1982), in which functional form, normality of the error term, heteroskedasticity and autocorrelated errors are tested for simultaneously.

- Although the most popular way of testing for linear and log-linear functional forms is via the Box–Cox technique, there exist other methods with attractive features. Godfrey and Wickens (1981), for example, develop an LM test for this purpose, as well as a test based on a method introduced by Andrews (1971). The former has computational advantages; the latter is exact (as opposed to being justified on asymptotic grounds).

5.4 Changing Parameter Values

- Surveys of regime-switching can be found in Goldfeld and Quandt (1976) chapter 1 and Poirier (1976) chapter 7. In some cases it is reasonable to suppose that a regime change involves a transition period during which the relationship changes smoothly from the old to the new regime. Goldfeld and Quandt model this by using an S-curve (cumulative density); Wilton (1975) uses a polynomial in time. Disequilibrium models are popular examples of continuous regime-switching. If observations are generated by the minimum of the quantities supplied and demanded, for example, then some observations come from a supply curve (one regime) and the other observations come from a demand curve (the other regime). Estimation in this context exploits some kind of an indicator variable; for example, was the most recent price change positive or negative? Work in this area stems from Fair and Jaffee (1972). For surveys see Fomby *et al.* (1984) pp. 567–75 and Quandt (1982).

- Random parameter models create a regression equation with a non-spherical error term (chapter 7 discusses non-spherical errors). Estimation techniques begin by deriving the nature of this non-sphericalness, i.e., the variance–covariance matrix of the regression's error term. Then this is either built into a maximum likelihood estimation procedure or is somehow estimated and employed as input to an EGLS estimator (see chapter 7). Tests for heteroskedasticity (see chapter 7) are often used to test for whether parameters are random. To illustrate these ideas, one of the more popular random coefficient models is discussed in the technical notes. Maddala (1977) chapter 17 has a good textbook exposition of changing parameter models. Johnson (1978) is a useful survey of random coefficient models. Raj and Ullah (1981) exposit the role of varying parameters in most dimensions of econometrics. The role of stochastic parameters in the context of pooling cross-sectional and time-series data is discussed in the general notes of chapter 13.

- Many of the tests discussed earlier for omitted variables and functional form can be used to test for a regime switch, reflecting a disadvantage of these tests (i.e., a negative test result could be due to a structural change rather than, say, a nonlinear functional form). Two tests have become particularly popular for testing for structural change. (For an annotated bibliography see Shaban 1980.)
    (a) *The Chow test*, discussed in the technical notes to this section, is used to test whether or not a parameter or parameters are unchanged from one data set to another. Ashley (1984) suggests an attractive generalization of the Chow test, along with a diagrammatic means of examining the model for structural change.
    (b) *The Cusum of Squares test* uses recursive residuals; it is based on the cumulative sum of squared recursive residuals. Brown, Durbin and Evans (1975) develop this and some related tests. Dufour (1982) is a useful extension.

- *Spline theory*, an approach to the regime-switching problem in which functions are spliced together at points of structural change, is applied to economics by Poirier (1976). Suits *et al.* (1978) have a good exposition. Robb (1980) extends its application to seasonal data.

Technical Notes

5.1 Introduction

- Pagan (1984) suggests a general famework within which most specification tests can be classified. Most tests take the form of investigating whether or not the assumptions made about the moments in the model are compatible with the behaviour of the sample moments, in particular the conditional mean and the conditional variance. He further notes that in most cases this principle is operationalized by means of *variable addition*: extra variables added to the conditional mean or conditional variance should be shown, when tested, to have no influence. One major type of test that cannot be categorized as a variable addition test is a test based on examining changes induced in a model by variable transformation: predicted and actual consequences of the transformation should not differ significantly if the specification is correct.

5.2 Incorrect Set of Independent Variables

- The essence of COMFAC analysis can be illustrated with a specific dynamic model

$$Y_t = \alpha Y_{t-1} + \beta X_t + \gamma X_{t-1} + \varepsilon_t$$

which can be rewritten, using the lag operator L (where $LX_t = X_{t-1}$), as

$$(1 - \alpha L) \, Y_t + \beta[1 + (\gamma/\beta)L] \, X_t + \varepsilon_t \, .$$

If $\alpha = -\gamma/\beta$ the polynomials in L multiplying Y_t and X_t have a common root of α and the terms involving Y_t and X_t have a common factor of $(1 - \alpha L)$. Dividing through by this common factor produces

$$Y_t = \beta X_t + U_t, \text{ where } U_t = \alpha U_{t-1} + \varepsilon_t \, .$$

This illustrates how a dynamic specification could be equivalent to a relationship in levels with an autocorrelated error. If, further, this common factor can be shown to be unity, a model in first differences results.

- The rationale behind the J test is easily seen by structuring the artificial nesting model on which it rests. Suppose there are two competing linear hypotheses: H_0, in which

$$Y = X\beta + \varepsilon_0,$$

and H_1, in which

$$Y = Z\gamma + \varepsilon_1 \, .$$

The artificial nesting model

$$Y = (1 - \lambda) \, X\beta + \lambda Z\gamma + \varepsilon_2$$

is formed, combining H_0 and H_1 with weights $(1 - \lambda)$ and λ, respectively. Clearly, if $\lambda = 0$ then H_0 is the correct specification and if $\lambda = 1$ then H_1 is correct, so a specification test can be formed by testing λ. Regressing Y on X and Z will permit estimation of $(1 - \lambda)\beta$ and $\lambda\gamma$, but not λ. Even this cannot be done if X and Z have a common variable. This dilemma is resolved by the following two-step procedure.
  (a) Regress Y on Z, obtain γ^{OLS} and calculate $\hat{Y} = Z\gamma^{OLS}$, the estimated Y from this regression.
  (b) Regress Y on X and $Z\gamma^{OLS}$ and test the (single) slope coefficient estimate $(\hat{\lambda})$ of $Z\gamma^{OLS}$ against zero by a t test.
This permits H_0 to be either accepted or rejected. The roles of H_0 and H_1 are then reversed and the procedure is repeated to allow H_1 to be either accepted or rejected.

- Kennedy (1984) uses the Ballentine to exposit the relationships between a variety of non-nested hypothesis tests and the common feature they share. Three examples are given below. Fig. 5.3 reflects H_0, a model in which Y is determined by X but not by Z; Fig. 5.4 illustrates H_1, a case in which Y is determined by Z but not X.
  (a) *The F test* Using H_0 as the null hypothesis, the non-nested F test consists first of regressing Y on X and Z^* together, where Z^* is Z with variables common to X and Z removed. (This is necessary to avoid perfect multicollinearity and allow this regression to be run; it causes Z to shrink at the expense of the red and orange areas.) Then the coefficients of Z^* are tested against the zero vector via an F test. In this case, as noted in chapter 4, this test is based on whether or not the sum of squared errors changes significantly when Z^* is added to the regression. The sum of squared errors from regressing Y on just X is represented by the yellow-plus-green area; adding Z^* reduces this to just the yellow area. Thus the F test tests whether or not the green area is significantly large. In Fig. 5.3, when H_0 is true (and thus the green area is very small), the null hypothesis is likely to be accepted, whereas in Fig. 5.4, when H_0 is false, this hypothesis is likely to be rejected.
  (b) *The J test* With H_0 as the null hypothesis, the first step of the J test is to regress Y on Z and obtain the predicted values $\hat{Y}$ of Y, represented by the red-plus-green area. The second step is to regress Y on X and $\hat{Y}$ together and use a t test to test the coefficient estimate of $\hat{Y}$ against zero. The square of this t test is just an F test, so the argument given in (a) above can be used to show that this test, in a different way, tests for a significantly large green area.
  (c) *The Cox test* With H_0 as the null hypothesis, the first step of the Cox test is to estimate the magnitude of σ_1^2 (the variance of the error term associated with H_1)

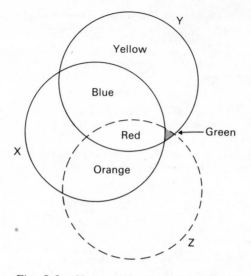

Fig. 5.3 H_0 true; Y *determined by* X

using H_1 by regressing Y on Z. This produces $\hat{\sigma}_1^2$, the size of which is represented by the yellow-plus-blue area. This is to be compared with the value of $\hat{\sigma}_1^2$ that would be expected to be obtained if H_0 were in fact true. Call this value σ_{10}^2. If H_0 were true (Fig. 5.3), Z would be expected to explain the red area, because of its partial collinearity with the true explanatory variable X. (The green area is expected to be negligible in magnitude.) If Z is expected to explain the red area, then σ_{10}^2 is represented by the complement of the red area with respect to Y, the blue-plus-

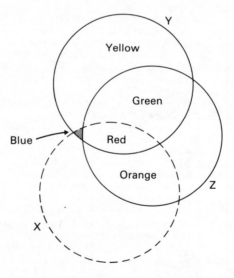

Fig. 5.4 H_1 true; Y *determined by* Z

yellow-plus green area. The difference between $\hat{\sigma}_1^2$ and σ_{10}^2, the green area, will be negligible if H_0 is true (Fig. 5.3), but not if H_1 is false (Fig. 5.4). Thus this method also is essentially testing whether or not the green area is significantly different from zero in size. (As with all other non-nested hypothesis tests, however, the means whereby it measures the green area is slightly different; in this method an estimate of σ_{10}^2 is subtracted from $\hat{\sigma}_1^2$ to estimate the magnitude of the green area.)

5.3 Nonlinearity

- When an entire equation is transformed to produce a linear estimating equation, sometimes a parameter is also transformed. This means that running an OLS regression on the transformed data produces an unbiased estimate of the transformed parameter rather than of the parameter itself. To obtain an estimate of the parameter itself, the unbiased estimate of the transformed parameter is transformed in reverse. Unfortunately, this commonly used technique creates a biased (although consistent if the original estimate was consistent) estimate of the parameter in question. This is because the expected value of a nonlinear function of a variable is *not* equal to the nonlinear function of the expected value of that variable. This problem was discussed in the technical notes to section 2.8, where suggestions for offsetting this bias were made.

  The Cobb–Douglas function discussed in section 5.3 provides an example of this. The intercept of the linear estimating equation is the logarithm of A, where A is the constant term in the original Cobb–Douglas function. Thus, when the OLS estimation procedure is applied to the transformed data, we obtain an unbiased estimate of the logarithm of A rather than of A itself. Taking the antilog of this unbiased estimate produces an estimate of A, but this estimate is biased (but consistent).

5.4 Changing Parameter Values

- The 'Chow' test is the most popular way of testing whether or not the parameter values associated with one data set (say, period 1) are the same as those associated with another data set (say, period 2). There are two versions of this test, both employing the general format (explained in section 4.3 and its general notes) in which an F statistic with R and $T - K$ degrees of freedom is formed as:

$$\frac{[SSE \text{ (constrained)} - SSE \text{ (unconstrained)}]/R}{SSE \text{ (unconstrained)}/(T - K)}$$

where R is the number of restrictions being tested, T is the number of observations and K is the number of regressors (including the intercept) in the unconstrained regression.

Case I Enough observations in the second period to run a separate regression. In this case running two separate regressions allows the parameters to differ between the two time-periods. The unconstrained SSE is thus just the sum of the SSEs from the two separate regressions. Running one regression on all the data (i.e., on both periods' observations) constrains the parameters to be the same in both periods. This regression yields the constrained SSE. The F statistic thus becomes:

$$\frac{[SSE \text{ (constrainted)} - SSE \text{ (unconstrained)}]/K}{SSE \text{ (unconstrained)}/(T_1 + T_2 - 2K)}$$

where K is the number of parameters, T_1 is the number of observations in the first period and T_2 is the number of observations in the second period.

Case II Too few observations in the second period to run a separate regression. In this case T_2 dummy variables (see chapter 13) are formed, one for each observation in the second period. Each dummy has a value of 1 for its particular observation and 0 elsewhere. Regressing on the K independent variables plus the T_2 dummies over the $T_1 + T_2$ observations gives the unrestricted regression, identical to the regression using the K independent variables and T_1 observations. (This identity arises because the coefficient of each dummy variable takes on whatever value is necessary to create a perfect fit, and thus a zero residual, for that observation.)

The restricted version comes from restricting each of the T_2 dummy variable coefficients to be zero, yielding a regression identical to one using the K independent variables and $T_1 + T_2$ observations. The F statistic thus becomes:

$$\frac{[SSE \text{ (constrained)} - SSE \text{ (unconstrained)}]/T_2}{SSE \text{ (unconstrained)}/(T_1 - K)}.$$

This statistic can be shown to be equivalent to testing whether or not the second period's set of observations falls within the prediction confidence interval formed by using the regression from the first period's observations.

This dummy-variable approach for Case II, introduced in the first edition of this book, has been formalized by Dufour (1980).

- An alternative way of structuring the test for Case I above is through the use of dummy variables. This is described in the general notes to chapter 13, where it is shown that this alternative method can easily be modified to structure equality tests for subsets of the parameters, and thus is more useful.

- In the Chow test σ^2 is forced to be the same in both periods in the constrained version but is allowed to differ between periods in the unconstrained version; if σ^2 actually differs between the two periods, the Chow test is no longer suitable. Honda (1982) discusses how to conduct a Chow test (for Case I) when the disturbance variances are unequal; he suggests that a Wald test due to Watt (1979) is the best available. Suppose b_1 and b_2 are the OLS estimates of the vector β from the first and second data sets, respectively, and $s_1^2(X'_1X_1)^{-1}$ and $s_2^2(X'_2X_2)^{-1}$ are their respective variance–covariance estimates. We wish to test $(b_1 - b_2)$ against the zero vector. A Wald test for this takes the form

$$W = (b_1 - b_2)'\, Q^{-1}\, (b_1 - b_2)$$

where Q is the variance–covariance matrix of $(b_1 - b_2)$. In this example Q is easily seen to be estimated by the sum of the estimated variance–covariance matrices of b_1 and b_2.

- The model of Hildreth and Houck (1968) is a popular variant of the random parameter model. Suppose $Y_t = \alpha + \beta_t X_t + \gamma_t Z_t$ with $\beta_t = \beta + u_t$ and $\gamma_t = \gamma + v_t$ where u_t and v_t are errors with means zero and variances σ_u^2 and σ_v^2. In this example, for simplicity, we assume that u and v are independent; in general, we would not expect this to be the case, requiring a more complicated version of the analysis below. Substituting for β_t and γ_t, we get $Y_t = \beta X_t + \gamma Z_t + \varepsilon_t$ where the composite error $\varepsilon_t = X_t u_t + Z_t v_t$ has mean zero and variance $\sigma_t^2 = X_t^2 \sigma_u^2 + Z_t^2 \sigma_v^2$. Two approaches can be taken at this stage. This formula for the variance can be incorporated in the formulation of the likelihood function, and estimation of all unknown parameters can proceed using the maximum likelihood technique. Alternatively, an effort could be made to estimate σ_u^2 and σ_v^2, and thereby σ_t^2, and the EGLS estimation procedure, described in chapter 7, could be employed. One obvious way of estimating σ_u^2 and σ_v^2 is to exploit the relationship $\sigma_t^2 = X_t^2\sigma_v^2 + Z_t^2\sigma_v^2$ by regressing the square of the OLS residual $\hat{\varepsilon}_t^2$ on X_t^2 and Z_t^2. Hildreth and Houck do not do this, preferring an alternative procedure which corrects for the fact that the squared OLS residuals, because of the way in which they are calculated, necessarily bear a relationship to X_t^2 and Z_t^2. This procedure is described briefly below, to give a flavour of the kind of estimation procedures common in this area.

The vector of OLS residuals is given by $\hat{\varepsilon} = M\varepsilon$ where $M = I - W(W'W)^{-1}W'$ and W is the data matrix (in this example a column of ones, a column of X_t and a column of Z_t). Thus $\hat{\varepsilon}_t$, the tth OLS residual, is given by $\hat{\varepsilon}_t = m_{t1}\varepsilon_1 + m_{t2}\varepsilon_2 + \ldots + m_{tT}\varepsilon_T$ where the m_{ti} are the elements of the tth row of M. Squaring and taking expected values gives

$$E\hat{\varepsilon}_t^2 = m_{t1}^2\,\sigma_1^2 + \ldots + m_{tT}^2\,\sigma_T^2$$
$$= (m_{t1}^2 X_1^2 + \ldots + m_{tT}^2 X_T^2)\sigma_u^2 + (m_{t1}^2 Z_1^2 + \ldots m_{tT}^2 Z_T^2)\sigma_v^2.$$

Regressing the squared OLS residuals on the bracketed measures on the right-hand side of this equation produces estimates of σ_u^2 and σ_v^2 which can be used via EGLS (see chapter 7) to produce estimates of α, β and γ. Note that there is no guarantee this regression will produce positive estimates of σ_u^2 and σ_v^2; an inequality restriction must therefore be imposed on this regression.

6.   Violating Assumption Two: Nonzero Expected Disturbance

The second assumption of the CLR model states that the population from which the disturbance is drawn has mean zero. This assumption could be violated if, for example, there were systematically positive or systematically negative errors of measurement in calculating the dependent variable. This problem is most easily analysed if the estimating equation is rearranged by removing the nonzero mean from the error term and adding it to the intercept term. This creates an estimating equation obeying all the CLR model assumptions; in particular, the mean of the new error term is zero. The only problem is that OLS estimation gives an unbiased estimate of the *new* intercept, which is the sum of the original intercept and the mean of the original error term; it is therefore a *biased* estimate of the original intercept (the bias being exactly equal to the mean of the original error term). Thus the only implication of the violation of the second assumption of the CLR model is that the OLS estimate of the intercept is biased; the slope coefficient estimates are unaffected. This biased estimate is often welcomed by the econometrician since for prediction purposes he would want to incorporate the mean of the error term into his prediction.

It must be noted that violation of this assumption cannot always be shrugged off so cavalierly. A nonzero expected disturbance could, for example arise because of an omitted variable. The mean value of this omitted variable, times its coefficient, gives the magnitude of the expected value of the disturbance term of this mis-specified model. The serious econometric problem in this example is not caused by the nonzero expected disturbance. It is caused by the fact that the expected value of the disturbance term is not constant – it varies with the omitted independent variable. This specification error, as discussed in chapter 5, causes OLS estimates in general to be biased.

A similar example arises in the case of a limited dependent variable, discussed in chapter 14. Suppose an observation is included in a sample only if the dependent variable is less than K. For example, data may have been gathered only on people whose income fell below some poverty level K. This means that the data will not contain errors large enough to cause the dependent variable to be greater than K. Thus in this example the right-hand tail of the distribution of the error terms is chopped off (the error comes from a 'truncated' distribution), implying that the expected value of the error term is negative. As discussed at length in the general notes of chapter 14, the expected value of this error term is not only nonzero, it also varies from observation to observation, creating bias in the OLS estimates.

Another example of a case in which having a disturbance with a nonzero expectation can cause trouble is a circumstance in which economic theory has suggested that the constant term in the relationship to be estimated is zero. Regressing without a constant term will produce biased estimates of the other parameters if the error term does not have a zero expectation. Fortunately, in this instance a significance test on the intercept in a preliminary regression run with a constant term can guard against this error.

A fourth instance in which a nonzero expected disturbance could be undesirable is a context in which the researcher is in fact interested in obtaining an accurate estimate of the intercept coefficient. An example of this arises in the case of a nonlinear functional form converted to a linear functional form via a transformation of the entire equation. In this case the disturbance term associated with the original nonlinear functional form must also be transformed, and it is not always the case that this original disturbance, appropriate to the nonlinear functional form, is such as to have a zero expectation when transformed. A popular example of this is the Cobb–Douglas production function, whose nonlinear formulation requires a multiplicative disturbance if the logarithmic transformation is to create a linear estimating form in transformed variables. Now if, as is traditional, the nonlinear function without the disturbance is to represent the expected value of the dependent variable given the independent variables, the expected value of this multiplicative disturbance must be unity. The logarithm of this disturbance, which is the 'disturbance' associated with the linear estimating form, does not have a zero expectation. This means that the OLS estimate of the constant in the linear estimating equation (the logarithm of the original Cobb–Douglas constant) is biased. This creates extra problems (beyond those discussed in the technical notes to section 5.3) in using this estimate to obtain an unbiased estimate of the original Cobb–Douglas constant.

General Notes

- Since the OLS estimation procedure is such as automatically to create residuals whose mean is zero, the only way in which the assumption of zero expected disturbance can be tested is through theoretical means (such as that illustrated by the Cobb–Douglas example).

- The multiplicative error used for the Cobb–Douglas function is usually assumed to be distributed log-normally; this implies that the logarithm of this error is distributed normally. It is interesting to note that assuming that the logarithm of this multiplicative disturbance has zero mean implies that the Cobb–Douglas function without the disturbance represents the *median* (rather than the mean) value of the dependent variable given the independent variables. This example of the Cobb–Douglas production function is discussed at length in Goldberger (1968a).

• The frontier production function is a good example of a nonzero expected error. In this case the production function by definition determines the *maximum* output that can be generated with given inputs. Firms could be less than fully efficient and thus produce inside the production frontier, but they cannot produce more than the output given by this frontier. Consequently, the error term can never be positive. For a survey of estimation in this context, see Forsund *et al.* (1980)

7. Violating Assumption Three: Nonspherical Disturbances

7.1 Introduction

The third assumption of the CLR model is that the disturbances are spherical: they have uniform variance and are not correlated with one another. These characteristics are usually described in terms of the variance–covariance matrix of the disturbance vector. Recall that the variance–covariance matrix of a vector $\hat{\beta}$ of parameter estimates is a matrix with the variances of the individual parameter estimates along the diagonal and the covariances between these individual estimates in the off-diagonal positions. The disturbance vector is simply a vector containing the (unobserved) disturbance terms for the given data set (i.e., if the sample is of size T, the disturbance vector is of length T, containing T 'observations' on the disturbance term). The variance–covariance matrix of the disturbance vector is a matrix with T columns and T rows. The diagonal terms are the variances of the individual disturbances, and the off-diagonal terms are the covariances between them.

Each diagonal term gives the variance of the disturbance associated with one of the sample observations (i.e., the first diagonal term gives the variance of the disturbance associated with the first observation, and the last diagonal term gives the variance of the disturbance associated with the Tth observation). If all these diagonal terms are the same, the disturbances are said to have uniform variance or to be *homoskedastic*. If the diagonal terms are not all the same, the disturbances are said to be *heteroskedastic*; the disturbance term is then thought of as being drawn from a different distribution for each observation. This case of heteroskedasticity is discussed in detail in section 7.3.

Each off-diagonal element of the variance–covariance matrix gives the covariance between the disturbances associated with two of the sample observations (i.e., the element in the second column and the fifth row gives the covariance between the disturbance associated with the second observation and the disturbance associated with the fifth observation). If all these off-diagonal terms are zero, the disturbances are said to be uncorrelated. This means that in repeated samples there is no tendency for the disturbance associated with one observation (corresponding, for example, to one time period or one individual) to be related to the disturbance associated with any other. If the off-diagonal terms are not all

93

zero, the disturbances are said to be *autocorrelated*: the disturbance term for one observation is correlated with the disturbance term for another observation. This case of autocorrelated disturbances is discussed in detail in section 7.4.

If either heteroskedasticity or autocorrelated disturbances are present, assumption 3 of the CLR model is said to be violated. In mathematical terminology, if assumption 3 is satisfied, the variance–covariance matrix of the disturbance vector ε, written as $E\varepsilon\varepsilon'$, is given by $\sigma^2 I$ where σ^2 is the uniform variance of the individual disturbance terms and I is an identity matrix of size T (i.e., a matrix with T rows and T columns, with ones along the diagonal and zeros on the off-diagonal). When assumption 3 is violated, by either heteroskedasticity or autocorrelated errors, the variance–covariance matrix of the disturbance vector does not take this special form, and must be written as a general matrix G. The disturbances in this case are said to be *non-spherical*, and the CLR model in this context is referred to as the *generalized linear regression* model (GLR model).

7.2   Consequences of Violation

If assumption 3 is violated and the variance–covariance matrix of the disturbance vector must be written as a general matrix G, the CLR model becomes the GLR model. There are three major consequences of this for the OLS estimator.

(1) *Efficiency*   In the GLR model, although β^{OLS} remains unbiased, it no longer has minimum variance among all linear unbiased estimators. A different estimator, called the generalized least squares (GLS) estimator, and denoted β^{GLS}, can be shown to be the BLUE. This estimator involves the matrix G in its formulation; by explicitly recognizing the nonsphericalness of the disturbances, it is possible to produce a linear unbiased estimator with a 'smaller' variance–covariance matrix (i.e., a more efficient estimator).

This is accomplished by making use of the information (in the heteroskedasticity case) that some disturbances are likely to be large because their variances are large or the information (in the autocorrelated disturbances case) that when, for example, one disturbance is large and positive then another disturbance is likely to be large and positive. Instead of minimizing the sum of squared residuals (OLS estimation), an appropriately *weighted* sum of squared residuals is minimized. Observations that are expected to have large residuals because the variances of their associated disturbances are known to be large are given a smaller weight. Observations whose residuals are expected to be large because other residuals are large (due to correlation between the disturbances) are also given smaller weights. The GLS procedure thus produces a more efficient estimator by minimizing a weighted sum of squared residuals (hence the name 'generalized least squares') where the weights are determined by the elements of the variance–covariance matrix G of the disturbance vector.

(2) *Estimated variance* In the GLR model the usual formula for the variance–covariance matrix of β^{OLS} is incorrect and therefore the usual estimator of $V(\beta^{OLS})$ is biased. Thus, although β^{OLS} is unbiased in the GLR model, interval estimation and hypothesis testing using β^{OLS} can no longer be trusted in this context. The correct formula for $V(\beta^{OLS})$ in the GLR model involves the matrix G and is quite complicated. Only in some special cases, noted in the technical notes to this section, can it be determined whether the usual estimator of $V(\beta^{OLS})$ is biased upwards or downwards.

(3) *Maximum likelihood* In the GLR model with the additional assumption that the disturbances are distributed joint-normally, β^{OLS} is not the maximum likelihood estimator (as it was in the CNLR model). β^{GLS} turns out to be the maximum likelihood estimator in this context.

These consequences of using β^{OLS} in the GLR model suggest that β^{GLS} be used in this situation. The problem with this proposal is that to calculate β^{GLS} the matrix G must be *known* to a factor of proportionality. In actual estimating situations, of course, G is rarely, if ever, known. Faced with this dilemma, it is tempting simply to forget about β^{GLS} and employ β^{OLS}. (After all, β^{OLS} is unbiased, produces the highest R^2 and has low computational cost.)

Econometricians have not done this, however. Instead they have used the data at hand to estimate G (by $\hat{G}$, say) and then have used $\hat{G}$ in place of the unknown G in the β^{GLS} formula. This creates a new estimator, called the EGLS (estimated GLS) or FGLS (feasible GLS) estimator, denoted here by β^{EGLS}. This new estimator is no longer linear or unbiased, but if $\hat{G}$ is a consistent estimator of G, it can be shown to have desirable asymptotic properties corresponding to the small-sample properties of β^{GLS}. Intuitively it would seem that, because this new estimator at least tries to account for the nonsphericalness of the disturbances, it should produce a better estimate of β than does β^{OLS}. Monte Carlo studies have shown that β^{EGLS} is in many circumstances (described in the general notes to this section) superior to β^{OLS} on the criteria on which β^{GLS} can be shown mathematically to be superior to β^{OLS}. Thus econometricians often adopt β^{EGLS} as the appropriate estimator to employ in a GLR model estimating context.

There remains, however, the problem of estimating G. This is not a trivial problem. The matrix G contains T^2 elements, $\frac{1}{2}T(T+1)$ of which are conceptually different. (The off-diagonal elements below the diagonal are identical to those above the diagonal.) But there are only T observations, implying that it is impossible to estimate the matrix G in its general form. This dilemma is resolved by specifying (assuming) that the nonsphericalness of the disturbances takes a specific form within *one* of the general categories of heteroskedasticity or autocorrelated disturbances. This reduces the problem to one of finding the appropriate specific form, estimating the small number of parameters (usually only one) that characterize that specific form, and then using these estimates to produce the required estimate of G. This approach should become clear in the discussions below of heteroskedasticity and autocorrelated disturbances.

7.3 Heteroskedasticity

One way of resolving the problem of estimating G is to assume that the nonsphericalness is exclusively that of heteroskedasticity, and that this heteroskedasticity bears a particular relationship to a set of known variables, usually chosen to be a single independent variable. This means that the off-diagonal elements of the variance–covariance matrix of the disturbance term are assumed to be zero, but that the diagonal elements are not all equal, varying in size with an independent variable. This is not an unreasonable specification – often, the larger an independent variable, the larger the variance of the associated disturbance. For example, if consumption is a function of the level of income, at higher levels of income (the independent variable) there is a greater scope for the consumer to act on whims and deviate by larger amounts from the specified consumption relationship. In addition, it may also be the case that errors associated with measuring consumption are greater at higher levels of income.

Fig. 7.1 illustrates how this type of heteroskedasticity affects the properties of the OLS estimator. The higher absolute values of the residuals to the right in this graph indicate that there is a positive relationship between the error variance and the independent variable. With this kind of error pattern, a few additional large positive errors near the right in this graph would tilt the OLS regression line considerably. A.

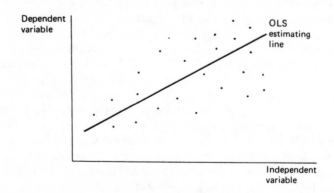

Fig. 7.1   Illustrating heteroskedasticity

few additional large negative errors would tilt it in the opposite direction considerably. In repeated sampling these unusual cases would average out, leaving the OLS estimator unbiased, but the variation of the OLS regression line around its mean will be greater – i.e., the variance of β^{OLS} will be greater. The GLS technique pays less attention to the residuals associated with high-variance observations (by assigning them a low weight in the weighted sum of squared residuals it minimizes) since these observations give a less precise indication of where the true regression line lies. This avoids these large tilts, making the variance of β^{GLS} smaller than that of β^{OLS}.

The usual first step in attacking this problem is to determine whether or not heteroskedasticity actually exists. There are several tests for this, the more prominent of which are discussed below.

(1) *Visual inspection of residuals*

The residuals are plotted on a graph against the independent variable to which it is suspected the disturbance variance is related. (Many econometric computer packages can produce this graph with simple instructions.) If it appears that the absolute magnitudes of the residuals are on average the same regardless of the values of the independent variables, then heteroskedasticity probably does not exist. However, if it appears that the absolute magnitude of the residuals is related to the independent variable (for example, if the residuals are quite small for low values of the independent variable, but noticeably larger for high values of the independent variable), then a more formal check for heteroskedasticity is in order.

(2) *The Goldfeld–Quandt test*

In this test the observations are ordered according to the magnitude of the independent variable thought to be related to the variance of the disturbances. A certain number of central observations are omitted, leaving two equal-sized groups of observations, one group corresponding to low values of the chosen independent variable and the other group corresponding to high values. Separate regressions are run for each of the two groups of observations and the ratio of their sums of squared residuals is formed. This ratio is an F statistic, which should be approximately unity if the disturbances are homoskedastic. A critical value from the F-distribution table can be used to test this hypothesis.

(3) *The Breusch–Pagan test*

This test is relevant for a very wide class of alternative hypotheses, namely that the variance is some function of a linear combination of known variables. An LM test is employed, for which a computationally convenient means of calculation exists (see the technical notes). The generality of this test is both its strength (it does not require prior knowledge of the functional form involved) and its weakness (more powerful tests could be employed if this functional form were known). Tests utilizing specific functional forms are discussed in the general notes.

(4) *The White test*

This test examines whether the error variance is affected by any of the regressors, their squares or their cross-products. The strength of this test is that it tests specifically for whether or not any heteroskedasticity present causes the variance–covariance matrix of the OLS estimator to differ from its usual formula. It also has a computationally convenient formula (see the technical notes).

Once the presence of heteroskedasticity has been confirmed, steps must be taken to calculate β^{EGLS}. The first step in this process is to determine the specific form taken by the heteroskedasticity i.e., find the functional form of the relationship determining the variance. This relationship is then estimated and used to form an estimate of the variance of each disturbance term and thus an estimate of the variance–covariance matrix G of the disturbance term. Using this estimate $(\hat{G})$, the estimator β^{EGLS} can be calculated.

In most applications, however, $\hat{G}$ is not calculated. This is because using $\hat{G}$ to calculate β^{EGLS} is computationally difficult, due primarily to the fact that $\hat{G}$ is usually such a large matrix. Instead, an alternative, and fully equivalent, way of calculating β^{EGLS} is employed. This alternative way involves transforming the original equation to create an estimating relationship, in transformed variables, that has spherical disturbances (i.e., the original disturbance, when transformed, is spherical). Then the OLS estimator is applied to the transformed data, producing the GLS estimator. In the case of heteroskedasticity, the appropriate transformation is obtained by dividing each observation (including the constant unit observation on the intercept term) by the square root of the estimated variance of the disturbance term. An example of this appears in the technical notes to this section.

7.4   Autocorrelated Disturbances

When the off-diagonal elements of the variance–covariance matrix G of the disturbance term are nonzero, the disturbances are said to be auto-correlated. This could arise for several reasons.

(1) *Spatial autocorrelation*   In regional cross-section data, a random shock affecting economic activity in one region may cause economic

activity in an adjacent region to change because of close economic ties between the regions. Shocks due to weather similarities might also tend to cause the error terms between adjacent regions to be related.

(2) *Prolonged influence of shocks* In time-series data, random shocks (disturbances) have effects that often persist over more than one time period. An earthquake, flood, strike or war, for example, will probably affect the economy's operation in periods following the period in which it occurs. Disturbances on a smaller scale could have similar effects.

(3) *Inertia* Owing to inertia or psychological conditioning, past actions often have a strong effect on current actions, so that a positive disturbance in one period is likely to influence activity in succeeding periods.

(4) *Data manipulation* Published data often undergo interpolation or smoothing, procedures that average true disturbances over successive time periods.

(5) *Mis-specification* An omitted relevant independent variable that is autocorrelated will make the disturbance (associated with the mis-specified model) autocorrelated. An incorrect functional form could do the same. In these instances the appropriate procedure to follow is to correct the mis-specification; the correction methods proposed in this chapter cannot be justified if the errors arise in this way.

Since autocorrelated errors arise most frequently in time-series models, for ease of exposition the discussion in the rest of this chapter is couched in terms of time-series data. Furthermore, throughout the rest of this chapter the correlation between the error terms is assumed, in line with most econometric work, to take a specific form called first-order autocorrelation. Econometricians make this assumption because it makes tractable the otherwise impossible task of estimating the very large number of off-diagonal elements of G, the variance–covariance matrix of the disturbance vector. First-order autocorrelation occurs when the disturbance in one time period is a proportion of the disturbance in the previous time period, plus a spherical disturbance. In mathematical terms, this is written as $\varepsilon_t = \rho\varepsilon_{t-1} + u_t$ where ρ (rho), a parameter less than 1 in absolute value, is called the autocorrelation coefficient and u_t is a traditional spherical disturbance.

The consequences for OLS estimation in a situation of positive (i.e., ρ positive) first-order autocorrelation are illustrated in Fig. 7.2. The first error term was arbitrarily chosen to be positive. With positive first-order autocorrelated errors this implies that several succeeding error terms are likely also to be positive, and once the error term becomes negative it is likely to remain negative for a while. Thus the data pattern portrayed is not atypical of the autocorrelated error case if the independent variable is

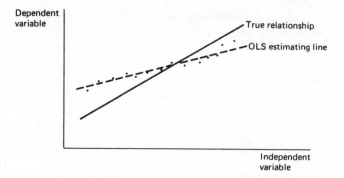

Fig. 7.2   Illustrating autocorrelated errors

growing over time. Fitting an OLS estimating line to these data clearly gives an estimate quite wide of the mark. In repeated samples these poor estimates will average out, since we are as likely to start with a negative error as with a positive one, leaving the OLS estimator unbiased, but the high variation in these estimates will cause the variance of β^{OLS} to be greater than it would have been had the errors been distributed randomly. The GLS technique pays less attention to large residuals that follow large residuals (by assigning them a low weight in the weighted sum of squared residuals it minimizes) since these residuals are likely to be large simply because the preceding residual is large. This causes the GLS estimator to miss the true value by less in situations such as that portrayed on the graph, making the variance of β^{GLS} smaller than that of β^{OLS}. Notice that the OLS estimating line gives a better fit to the data than the true relationship. This reveals why in this context R^2 is overestimated and σ^2 (and the variance of β^{OLS}) is underestimated.

The great appeal of the first-order autocorrelation assumption is that if the disturbance term takes this form all the off-diagonal elements of G can be expressed in terms of ρ so that estimation of a single parameter (ρ) permits estimation of G and allows calculation of β^{EGLS}. A 'good' estimate of ρ will make β^{EGLS} superior to β^{OLS}; a 'poor' estimate of ρ will do the opposite.

Before calculating β^{EGLS}, however, it must first be determined that the disturbances actually are autocorrelated. There are several ways of doing this, the most popular of which, the Durbin–Watson test, is described below; some of the less common tests are described in the general notes to this section.

The Durbin–Watson (D–W) test   Most packaged computer regression programs and most research reports provide the D–W or d statistic in their output. This statistic is calculated from the residuals of an OLS regression and is used to test for first-order autocorrelation. When the parameter ρ of the first-order autocorrelation case is zero (reflecting no autocorrelation) the d statistic is approximately 2.0. The further away the d statistic is from 2.0, the less confident one can be that there is no autocorrelation in the disturbances. Unfortunately, the exact distribution of this d statistic, on the hypothesis of zero autocorrelation, depends on the particular observations on the independent variables (i.e., on the X matrix), so that a table giving critical values of the d statistic is not available. However, it turns out that the actual distribution of the d statistic can be shown to lie between two limiting distributions for which critical values have been tabulated. These limiting distributions, labelled 'lower distribution' and 'upper distribution', are shown in Fig. 7.3. The 95% critical levels are marked off for each distribution and denoted by A, B, C and D. Now suppose the value of the d statistic lies to the left of A. Then, regardless of whether the d statistic for this case is distributed as the lower or upper distribution, or anywhere in between, the hypothesis of no autocorrelation will be rejected. Similarly, if the value of the d statistic lies to the right of D, the hypothesis of no autocorrelation will be rejected, regardless of the actual distribution of the d statistic for this particular estimating problem. Similar reasoning shows that, if the d statistic lies between B and C, the hypothesis of no autocorrelation will be accepted, regardless of the actual distribution of d. It is the cases in which the d statistic falls between A and B or between C and D that cause trouble. Suppose d falls between A and B. If the actual distribution of the d statistic for this problem were the lower distribution, the hypothesis of no autocorrelation would be accepted, but if the actual distribution were the upper distribution, it would be rejected. Since the actual distribution is unknown, the D–W test in this case must be considered inconclusive. The existence of these two inconclusive regions is the most serious weakness of the D–W test. (Some solutions to this inconclusiveness are discussed in the general notes to this section.)

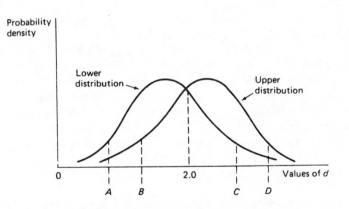

Fig. 7.3 The Durbin–Watson statistic

Another weakness is that the test is biased towards acceptance of the hypothesis of no autocorrelation if a lagged value of the dependent variable is included among the regressors. (This case is discussed further in section 8.3.)

Once the presence of first-order autocorrelation has been confirmed, attention is turned to the estimation of ρ. Once ρ has been estimated, an estimate $\hat{G}$ of G can be calculated and used to produce β^{EGLS}. However, as in the case of heteroskedastic disturbances, it is computationally far easier to transform the variables and apply OLS to obtain β^{EGLS} than to estimate G and employ this estimate in the β^{EGLS} formula. The estimating equation must be transformed so as to create a new estimating equation, in the transformed variables, whose disturbance vector is spherical (i.e., the original disturbance, when transformed, is spherical). Applications of OLS to the transformed variables then creates β^{EGLS}. The appropriate transformation in the context of first-order autocorrelation is to replace each observation by that observation minus the estimated value of ρ times the previous period's observation (i.e., replace x_t with $x_t - \hat{\rho} x_{t-1}$). To avoid losing one observation by this procedure, the first observation x_1 should be transformed to $\sqrt{(1 - \hat{\rho}^2)}x_1$. The rationale for this is discussed in the technical notes to this section.

There are several different techniques employed to produce β^{EGLS}, all of them following the method outlined above, essentially differing only in the way in which they estimate ρ. (Some methods do not bother to do the special transformation of the first observation, but should be revised to do so.) The most popular techniques used to produce β^{EGLS} are described briefly below; all appear frequently in packaged computer regression programs.

(1) *Cochrane–Orcutt iterative least squares*

Regressing the OLS residuals on themselves lagged one period provides an estimate of ρ. Using this estimate, the dependent and independent variables can be transformed as described earlier and an OLS regression on these transformed variables gives β^{EGLS}. Using this β^{EGLS}, new estimates of the original disturbances can be made, by substituting β^{EGLS} into the original (untransformed) relationship, which should be 'better' than the OLS estimates (since β^{EGLS} is supposed to be 'better' than β^{OLS} in this context). Regressing these new residuals on themselves lagged one period provides a new (and presumably 'better') estimate of ρ. This procedure can be repeated until successive estimates of ρ are arbitrarily close.

(2) *Durbin's two-stage method*

The dependent variable is regressed on itself lagged, all the independent variables and all the independent variables lagged. This estimating relationship results from mathematical manipulations designed to transform the original estimating form into one with a spherical disturbance. This is illustrated in the technical notes to this section. The estimated coefficient of the lagged dependent variable in this new relation provides an estimate of ρ. This estimate is then used to transform the variables, as described earlier, and an OLS regression on these transformed variables generates β^{EGLS}.

(3) *Hildreth–Lu search procedure*

For any particular value of ρ, the dependent and independent variables can be transformed as described earlier and an OLS regression on transformed variables will generate a β^{EGLS}. The sum of squared residuals from this regression on transformed variables will be different for different values of ρ. The Hildreth–Lu procedure searches for the particular value of ρ that minimizes the sum of these squared residuals and adopts its corresponding β^{EGLS} as the estimator of β.

(4) *Maximum likelihood*

If the spherical disturbance u (from $\varepsilon_t = \rho\varepsilon_{t-1} + u_t$) can be assumed to have a specific distribution (a normal distribution, for example), the maximum likelihood technique can be applied to estimate ρ and β simultaneously. When u is distributed normally, it turns out that all four of the methods discussed here are asymptotically equivalent.

General Notes

7.2 Consequences of Violation

- The OLS estimator, by definition, maximizes R^2. The GLS estimator can be used to produce estimates of the dependent variables that can then be used to calculate an R^2 that must be less than the R^2 from OLS. In the context of the GLR model, however, since the GLS procedure minimizes a *generalized* sum of squared residuals, it is more appropriate to redefine the R^2 statistic so that it represents the proportion of the 'generalized variation' of the dependent variable explained by the independent variables. Fortunately, in many instances (but not all) the GLS technique of regressing on transformed variables (discussed in sections 7.3 and 7.4) automatically produces this new R^2. See Buse (1973) for a discussion of this.

- β^{GLS} is definitely superior (on the best linear unbiasedness criterion) to β^{OLS} in the GLR model, but β^{EGLS} might not be. Monte Carlo results reported in Griliches and Rao (1969), for example, indicate that for sample size 20, when the estimated first-order autocorrelation coefficient of the residuals is less than one-third in absolute value, β^{OLS} is more efficient than β^{EGLS}. In general, the nonsphericalness of the error terms must be quite severe to make β^{EGLS} superior to β^{OLS}.

- The true variance of β^{EGLS} is underestimated if the formula for the variance of β^{GLS} is used with $\hat{G}$ in place of G. This has implications for hypothesis testing using β^{EGLS}.

7.3   Heteroskedasticity

- Although it is usually the case that econometricians think in terms of error variances being positively related to independent variables, this is not necessarily the case. Error-learning models suggest that as time passes (and independent variables grow in size) errors will become smaller. Similarly, over time, data-collecting techniques improve so that errors from this source should decline in importance. In addition, it has been suggested that assuming an error-term variance that is declining over time could be useful since the correction procedure would explicitly give a heavier weight to recent data, which may more accurately reflect the world as it is today.

- Not all sources of heteroskedasticity can or should be captured via a relationship with an independent variable. For example, using grouped data leads to heteroskedasticity if the groups are not all the same size. In this case the error variances are proportional to the group sizes, so appropriate weighting factors can easily be deduced.

- Theory can sometimes suggest that an estimating relationship will be characterized by heteroskedasticity. The case of grouping data, noted earlier, is one example. As a second example, consider the case of a random coefficient. Suppose that $Y_t = \alpha + \beta_t X_t + \varepsilon_t$ where the random slope coefficient is given by $\beta_t = \beta + u_t$ with u_t an error with mean zero and variance σ_u^2. The estimating relationship becomes

$$Y_t = \alpha + \beta X_t + (\varepsilon_t + X_t u_t)$$

where the composite error term has variance $\sigma_t^2 + X_t^2 \sigma_u^2$. As a third example, suppose the error term is multiplicative rather than additive. Suppose $Y_t = (\alpha + \beta X_t)\varepsilon_t$ where $\varepsilon_t = 1 + u_t$ and u_t has mean zero and variance σ_u^2. The estimating form

$$Y_t = \alpha + \beta X_t + (\alpha + \beta X_t)u_t$$

is such that the composite error term has variance $(\alpha + \beta X_t)^2 \sigma_u^2$.

- The tests for heteroskedasticity described in the body of this chapter are general in that they do not use a specific functional form for the relationship between the error variance and the variables thought to determine that variance. To construct β^{EGLS}, a specific functional form is required (although it should be noted that Monte Carlo studies suggest that precise knowledge of this functional form is not crucial). One popular way to be more specific is through the Glejser (1969) test. In this test the absolute values of the OLS residuals are regressed, using several functional forms, on the variable(s) to which the variance of the disturbance term is thought to be related. Whether or not heteroskedasticity exists depends on whether or not the coefficient(s) of these regressions tests significantly different from zero. A variant of this approach, the modified Glejser test, is to use the squared values of the OLS residuals, rather than their absolute values, as the dependent variable. Another popular functional form was suggested by Park (1966); see the technical notes. If the relevant functional form is known (due to testing using the Glejser method, for example, or because theory has suggested a specific form), the maximum likelihood approach is possible. Here the parameters in the equation being estimated (i.e., β) and the parameter(s) in the relationship determining the error variances are estimated simultaneously. For elucidation, see Rutemiller and Bowers (1968). If the prerequisites for using the MLE approach are known to be valid (namely, knowledge of the distributional form of the error and the functional form of the relationship between the error variance and variable(s) determining that variance), this approach is the best choice.

- Several less common tests for heteroskedasticity exist, some of which are noted in the first edition of this book, p. 86. In addition, fancier versions of the tests cited here exist which try to account, for example, for the fact that the OLS residuals are themselves heteroskedastic on the null hypothesis that the true errors are homoskedastic. Chapter 11 of Judge *et al.* (1985) is an extensive survey of heteroskedasticity.

- Heteroskedasticity has been examined in conjunction with other violations of the CLR model. For example, Lahiri and Egy (1981) address the problem of nonlinear functional form and heteroskedasticity. Examples of its conjunction with autocorrelated errors are cited in the next section.

- Transforming an equation to correct for heteroskedasticity usually creates an estimating equation without an intercept term. Care must be taken in interpreting the R^2 from the resulting regression. Most researchers include an intercept anyway; this does little harm and avoids potential problems. For example, including an intercept prevents one kind of bias from arising when a relevant regressor has been omitted, as discussed in chapter 6.

- Before correcting for heteroskedasticity, each variable should be examined for possible transformations (e.g., changing aggregate to per capita or changing money to real) that might be appropriate in the context of the relationship in question. This may uncover the source of the heteroskedasticity. More generally, the heteroskedasticity may be due to an omitted explanatory variable or an incorrect functional form; Thursby (1982) suggests a means of discriminating between heteroskedasticity and mis–specification.

7.4   Autocorrelated Disturbances

- Recall from chapter 5 that autocorrelated residuals can arise from functional form or dynamic mis-specification. These possibilities should be investigated before concluding that EGLS is called for.

- The case of positively autocorrelated errors usually leads to an upward bias in the R^2 statistic. A high R^2 in conjunction with a low D–W statistic suggests that the model is mis-specified in some way. Regressing on first differences may reveal this. See Granger and Newbold (1974).

- Most of the tests used to detect autocorrelation only test for first-order autocorrelation. This should not blind one to other possibilities. It is quite possible, for example, that in models using quarterly data the errors are correlated with themselves lagged four periods. On this see Wallis (1972). Although it might seem reasonable to suppose that treating the residuals as first-order autocorrelated, when they are in fact second-order autocorrelated, would be better than just applying OLS, this is not necessarily the case: see Engle (1974). Beach and MacKinnon (1978b) examine the MLE for second-order autocorrelation. Vinod (1973) generalizes the D–W statistic for testing for higher-order autocorrelation. The Box–Pierce statistic (discussed in the technical notes of chapter 15) can be used here, along with the general methods of Box–Jenkins analysis, discussed in chapter 15.

- Godfrey (1978) and Breusch (1978) developed an LM test for autocorrelated errors when the alternative hypothesis is either qth-order autoregressive, $AR(q)$, *or* qth-order moving average, $MA(q)$. In spite of having such a general alternative hypothesis, it appears to have good power. One of its advantages is that it is appropriate even when a lagged value of the dependent variable serves as a regressor. (Durbin's h test is the most popular test in this context – see chapter 8.) As with most LM tests, it can be calculated as the sample size times the R^2 from an OLS regression. For a textbook exposition, see Johnston (1984) pp. 319–21.

- If serially correlated errors are determined to exist, on the basis of, say, a DW test, the first-order moving average, or MA(1), error process is as *a priori* plausible as the first-order autoregressive, or AR(1), process, but is seldom employed in applied work. (An AR(1) error process takes the form $\varepsilon_t = \rho\varepsilon_{t-1} + u_t$, whereas an MA(1) error process takes the form $\varepsilon_t = u_t + \theta u_{t-1}$ where the u_t are independently and identically distributed errors and ρ and θ are parameters.) This is because techniques for estimating in the context of MA(1) errors are computationally burdensome relative to those available for the context of AR(1) errors. MacDonald and MacKinnon (1985) present a computationally attractive estimation technique for the context of an MA(1) error process and argue that the common practice of ignoring the possibility of MA(1) errors cannot be justified. See Nicholls et al. (1975) for arguments favoring the use of MA errors.

- The inconclusive region of the DW test has been eliminated by Henshaw (1966), who derived an approximate distribution for the d statistic. The computational cost of this method has proved prohibitive, however. Theil and Nagar (1961) and Hannan and Terrell (1968) show that the upper distribution of the d statistic is a good approximation to its actual distribution if, as is likely in economic time-series, the regressors are changing slowly. Further work on this problem is summarized by Maddala (1977) pp. 285–6.

- Several alternative tests for autocorrelation exist (some of which were noted in the first edition of this book, pp. 87–8), but the DW test is the only test employed frequently by practitioners. An exception is Durbin's h statistic (discussed in chapter 8), used whenever a lagged value of the dependent variable serves as a regressor. For Monte Carlo evidence on tests for autocorrelated errors see L'Esperance and Taylor (1975).

- Many Monte Carlo studies have addressed the question of autocorrelated errors. A few general conclusions seem evident from these studies.
  (a) The possible gain from using EGLS rather than OLS can be considerable whereas the possible loss is small.
  (b) The special transformation for the first observation is important.
  (c) Standard errors for the EGLS estimator are usually underestimated.
  (d) The relative performance of estimating techniques is sensitive to the nature of the data matrix X.

(e) Improvement in current techniques is most likely to be achieved through better estimates of the autocorrelation coefficient ρ.

More specific conclusions are difficult to pin down. Beach and MacKinnon (1978a) present a convincing case for the MLE, noting that it retains the first observation and incorporates automatically the restriction that ρ be less than one in absolute value. Park and Mitchell (1980) present Monte Carlo evidence favouring the Cochrane–Orcutt method (called the Prais–Winsten method when it incorporates the special transformation for the first observation) with ρ estimated as

$$\hat{\rho} = \sum_{t=2}^{T} \hat{u}_t \hat{u}_{t-1} \Bigg/ \sum_{t=2}^{T-1} \hat{u}_t^2.$$

They note that this $\hat{\rho}$ minimizes the sum of squared errors for the transformed regression, the shorter summation in the denominator reduces the downward bias of the usual estimator of ρ. Oxley and Roberts (1982) note that the Cochrane–Orcutt method can find a local minimum and thus they recommend the Hildreth–Lu method.

- Chapter 8 of Judge *et al.* (1985) is an extensive survey of autocorrelated errors. See also Maddala (1977) p. 277–84.

- Autocorrelated errors is one violation of the CLR that has been examined in conjunction with other violations. Epps and Epps (1977) investigate autocorrelation and heteroskedasticity together. Savin and White (1978) and Tse (1984) address autocorrelated errors and nonlinear functional forms. Bera and Jarque (1982) examine the conjunction of autocorrelated errors, heteroskedasticity, nonlinearity and non-normality. Further examples are found in chapters 8 and 9.

- Estimating the variance–covariance matrix of the EGLS estimator is not as straightforward as it seems; see for example Miyazaki and Griffiths (1984).

Technical Notes

7.1 Introduction

- The matrix G is usually normalized by rewriting it as $\sigma^2 G_N$ where σ^2 is chosen so as to make the trace of G_N (the sum of the diagonal elements of G_N) equal T. This makes it comparable to the CLR case in which the variance–covariance matrix of ε is $\sigma^2 I$, where I has trace T.

7.2 Consequences of Violation

- The formula for β^{GLS} is given by $(X'G^{-1}X)^{-1}X'G^{-1}Y$ and the formula for its variance is given by $(X'G^{-1}X)^{-1}$ or $\sigma^2(X'G_N^{-1}X)^{-1}$. This variance–covariance matrix is 'smaller' than the variance–covariance matrix of β^{OLS}, given by the formula $\sigma^2(X'X)^{-1}(X'G_N X)(X'X)^{-1}$. Employing the usual formula $s^2(X'X)^{-1}$ to estimate this variance–covariance matrix of β^{OLS} gives a biased estimator, because the expected value of s^2 in the GLR model is no longer equal to σ^2, and because $(X'X)^{-1}$ does not equal $(X'X)^{-1}(X'G_N X)(X'X)^{-1}$. Goldberger (1964) pp. 239–42 traces through two special cases to show that in the case of only one independent variable (in addition to the constant term) the usual estimator is biased downward (a) if high variances correspond to high values of the independent variable, or (b) if the independent variable is positively serially correlated in the case of positive first-order autocorrelated errors (described in section 7.4)

The 'weighted' or 'generalized' sum of squared errors minimized by the GLS technique is given by $\varepsilon'G^{-1}\varepsilon$. The GLS estimator of σ^2 is given by $\hat{\varepsilon}'G^{-1}\hat{\varepsilon}/(T-K)$ where $\hat{\varepsilon}$ is the GLS estimate of ε. The maximum likelihood estimate of σ^2, for joint-normally distributed errors, is given by $\hat{\varepsilon}'G^{-1}\hat{\varepsilon}/T$.

7.3 Heteroskedasticity

- Breusch and Pagan (1979) show that their test statistic can be computed as one-half the regression (i.e., explained) sum of squares from a linear regression of $\hat{u}_t^2/\hat{\sigma}^2$ on a constant and the variables thought to affect the error variance. Here $\hat{u}_t$ is the OLS residual, $\hat{\sigma}^2$ is the average of the $\hat{u}_t^2$, and the statistic is distributed asymptotically as a chi-square with degrees of freedom equal to the number of variables thought to affect the error variance.

- Koenker (1981) notes that this Breusch–Pagan test is sensitive in small samples to its assumption that the errors are distributed normally (because it uses the result that the variance of $\hat{u}_t^2$ is $2\sigma^4$; this is where the ½ in this statistic comes from). He suggests replacing $2\hat{\sigma}^4$ by $\Sigma(\hat{u}_t^2 - \hat{\sigma}^2)^2/N$, where N is the sample size. The Breusch–Pagan statistic then becomes N times the (uncentred) R^2 in the regression of $\hat{u}_t^2 - \hat{\sigma}^2$ on the variables thought to affect the error variance. In this form it is seen that the White test (see below) is a special case of this 'studentized' Breusch–Pagan test, as noted by Waldman (1983).

- White (1980) shows that his test statistic can be computed as the sample size N times the R^2 from a regression of $\hat{u}_t^2$, the squares of the OLS residuals on a constant, the regressors from the equation being estimated, their squares and their cross-products. It is distributed asymptotically as a chi-square with degrees of freedom equal to the number of regressors (not counting the constant) in the regression used to obtain the statistic.

  This test detects heteroskedasticity only if it affects the consistency of the usual estimator of the variance–covariance matrix of the OLS estimator. It is possible to have heteroskedasticity which does not affect this consistency but none the less causes OLS to be less efficient than GLS (or EGLS). This could happen if the heteroskedasticity were related to a variable orthogonal to the regressors, their squares and their cross-products.

  Whenever White's test detects heteroskedasticity, he suggests using a heteroskedasticity-consistent estimator of the variance–covariance matrix of the OLS estimator. The essence of this suggestion is that G in the formula $(X'X)^{-1}X'GX(X'X)^{-1}$ given earlier is estimated by a diagonal matrix with the squared OLS residuals $\hat{u}_t^2$ along the diagonal. For computational considerations see Messer and White (1984).

- Szroeter (1978) introduced a class of tests applicable whenever the observations can be ordered on the basis of the true error variances. This class of tests uses the statistic

$$\bar{h} = \Sigma h_t \hat{u}_t^2 / \Sigma \hat{u}_t^2$$

where the h_t are constants having the same order as the error variances. Choice of the h_t, the observations over which the sums are taken and the means of calculating the $\hat{u}_t^2$ define a member of the class. Note that $\bar{h}$ is a weighted average of the h_t with the weights given by the $\hat{u}_t^2$. Under homoskedasticity $\bar{h}$ should be approximately equal to the simple average of the h_t: this is exploited to form the test. Judge *et al.* (1985) pp. 450–3 have a good exposition.

- When the error variance is proportional to a variable, so that, for example, $\sigma_t^2 = KX_t$, it is not necessary to estimate K to calculate β^{EGLS}. In fact, if the heteroskedasticity does actually take that form, the appropriate transformation is to divide all observations by $\sqrt{X_t}$, yielding a transformed relationship whose error is homoskedastic with variance K. The actual value of K is not needed; in this case β^{EGLS} is β^{GLS}. One way in which this correction can be upset is if there is 'mixed' heteroskedasticity so that $\sigma_t^2 = \gamma + KX_t$, where γ is some nonzero constant. Now the appropriate transformation is to divide by $\sqrt{(\gamma + KX_t)}$, so that it becomes necessary to estimate γ and K. But our estimates of γ and K are notoriously poor. This is because the 'observation' for σ_t^2 is the squared OLS residual $\hat{\varepsilon}_t^2$ so that this observation on σ_t^2 is in effect an estimate of σ_t^2 from a sample size of one. If we have such poor estimates of γ and K, might we be better off ignoring the fact that γ is nonzero and continuing to use the transformation of division by $\sqrt{X_t}$? Kennedy (1985a) suggests that, as a rule of thumb, division by $\sqrt{X_t}$ should be employed unless γ exceeds 15% of the average variance of the error terms.

- A wide variety of functional forms for the relationship between the error variance and the relevant independent variable are used in the Glejser and maximum likelihood contexts. One popular general form was suggested by Park (1966). Assume that $\sigma^2 = kx^\alpha$ where σ^2 is the error variance, k is a constant and x is relevant independent variable. This is estimated by adding a multiplicative disturbance term e^v, a log-normally distributed disturbance. Specific values of the parameter α correspond to specific relationships between the error variance and the independent variable. In particular, the case of $\alpha = 0$ corresponds to homoskedasticity.

- Under heteroskedasticity, the variances of all errors are in general different, each traditionally being estimated by the square of its corresponding OLS residual. MINQUEs, minimum norm quadratic unbiased estimates, attempt to improve on these variance estimates. See Vinod and Ullah (1981) pp. 113–14 for discussion and references.

7.4 Autocorrelated Disturbances

- In the simple model with only one independent variable and a first-order autocorrelated error term with autocorrelation coefficient ρ, the relative efficiency of β^{GLS} versus β^{OLS} (i.e., the ratio of the variances of β^{GLS} to that of β^{OLS}) is roughly $(1 - \rho^2)/(1 + \rho^2)$.

- The transformation of the dependent and independent variables used in obtaining the GLS estimates is derived as follows. Suppose the equation to be estimated is

$$y_t = \beta_1 + \beta_2 x_t + \varepsilon_t \quad \text{where} \quad \varepsilon_t = \rho\varepsilon_{t-1} + u_t .$$

Lagging and multiplying through by ρ, we get

$$\rho y_{t-1} = \rho\beta_1 + \rho\beta_2 x_{t-1} + \rho\varepsilon_{t-1} .$$

Subtracting this second equation from the first, we get

$$y_t - \rho y_{t-1} = \beta_1(1 - \rho) + \beta_2(x_t - \rho x_{t-1}) + (\varepsilon_t - \rho\varepsilon_{t-1})$$

or

$$y^*_t = \beta^*_1 + \beta_2 x^*_t + u_t .$$

This same technique can be used to derive the transformation required if the errors have a more complicated autocorrelation structure. For example, if the errors have a second-order autocorrelated structure so that $\varepsilon_t = \rho_1\varepsilon_{t-1} + \rho_2\varepsilon_{t-2} + u_t$, then x_t must be transformed to $x_t - \rho_1 x_{t-1} - \rho_2 x_{t-2}$.

- The special transformation for the first observation is deduced by noting that only if this transformation of the first observation is made will the general formula for β^{GLS} (in the context of first-order autocorrelation) correspond to the OLS regression in the transformed data. See Kadiyala (1968).

- The rationale behind Durbin's two-stage method is easily explained. Suppose that the equation being estimated is

$$y_t = \beta_1 + \beta_2 x_t + \varepsilon_t \quad \text{where} \quad \varepsilon_t = \rho\varepsilon_{t-1} + u_t .$$

Lagging and multiplying through by ρ we get

$$\rho y_{t-1} = \beta_1\rho + \beta_2\rho x_{t-1} + \rho\varepsilon_{t-1} .$$

which upon rearrangement becomes

$$y_t = \beta_1(1 - \rho) + \rho y_{t-1} + \beta_2 x_t - \beta_2\rho x_{t-1} + u_t .$$

This is a linear estimating function with a spherical disturbance u. Although the estimate of the coefficient of y_{t-1} is a biased estimate of ρ (see section 8.3), it is consistent. It might be thought that this estimate could be improved by incorporating the knowledge that the coefficient of x_{t-1} is minus the product of the coefficient of y_{t-1} and the coefficient of x_t. Monte Carlo studies have shown that this is not worth while.

- Most tests for autocorrelated errors employ the OLS residuals. Unfortunately, under the null hypothesis that the disturbances are spherical, the OLS residuals are *not* spherical, and thus tests of sphericalness using these OLS residuals are suspect. Recursive residuals, introduced in chapter 5, could be used in place of the OLS residuals. BLUS residuals are designed for this purpose, being constructed so as to be spherical under the null hypothesis that the errors are spherical. The name 'BLUS' comes from best linear unbiased scalar; the BLUS residuals have minimum variance among all linear unbiased estimators with spherical or 'scalar' variance–covariance matrix. See Theil (1971) pp. 205–35. Monte Carlo studies suggest that econometricians are better off sticking with the OLS residuals.

- Greenwald (1983) analyses the circumstances under which, in the GLR model, the traditional (CLR) estimator of the variance–covariance matrix is biased. In particular, if the correlation pattern across observations of the independent variable(s) is similar to the deviation pattern of the error covariance matrix from sphericalness, then the traditional formula understates true standard errors. This circumstance may arise frequently, since it is likely that the components of the 'random error' are likely to be economic data series similar to the independent variable(s). If there is no relationship between these correlation patterns, the traditional formula is asymptotically unbiased. Note the relationship between this result and that of White (discussed earlier) regarding heteroskedasticity.

8. Violating Assumption Four: Measurement Errors and Autoregression

8.1 Introduction

The fourth assumption of the CLR model specifies that the observations on the independent variables can be considered fixed in repeated samples. In many economic contexts the independent variables are themselves random (or stochastic) variables and thus could not have the same values in repeated samples. For example, suppose, as is common in econometric work, that a lagged value of the dependent variable appears as one of the independent variables. Because it is in part determined by the previous period's disturbance, it is stochastic and cannot be considered as fixed in repeated samples. (Recall that in repeated sampling new disturbance terms are drawn to create each repeated sample.)

This assumption of fixed regressors is made mainly for mathematical convenience; if the regressors can be considered to be fixed in repeated samples, the desirable properties of the OLS estimator can be derived quite straightforwardly. The essence of this assumption is that, if the regressors are nonstochastic, they are distributed independently of the disturbances. If this assumption is weakened to allow the explanatory variables to be stochastic but to be distributed independently of the error term, all the desirable properties of the OLS estimator are maintained; their algebraic derivation is more complicated, however, and their interpretation in some instances must be changed (for example, in this circumstance β^{OLS} is not, strictly speaking, a linear estimator). Even the maximum likelihood property of β^{OLS} is maintained if the disturbances are distributed normally and the distribution of the regressors does not involve either the parameter β or the variance of the disturbances, σ^2.

This fourth assumption can be further weakened at the expense of the small-sample properties of β^{OLS}. If the regressors are contemporaneously uncorrelated with the disturbance vector, the OLS estimator is biased but retains its desirable asymptotic properties. Contemporaneous uncorrelation in this context means that the nth observations on the regressors must be uncorrelated with the nth disturbance term, although they may be correlated with the disturbance terms associated with other regressor observations. In general, no alternative estimators are available with

111

superior small-sample properties, so the OLS estimator is retained on the basis of its desirable asymptotic properties.

If the regressors are contemporaneously correlated with the error term, the OLS estimator is even asymptotically biased. This is because the OLS procedure, in assigning 'credit' to regressors for explaining variation in the dependent variable, assigns, in error, some of the disturbance-generated variation of the dependent variable to the regressor with which that disturbance is contemporaneously correlated. Consider as an example the case in which the correlation between the regressor and the disturbance is positive. When the disturbance is higher the dependent variable is higher, and owing to the correlation between the disturbance and the regressor, the regressor is likely to be higher, implying that too much credit for making the dependent variable higher is likely to be assigned to the regressor. This is illustrated in Fig. 8.1. If the error term and the independent variable are positively correlated, negative values of the disturbance will tend to correspond to low values of the independent variable and positive values of the disturbance will tend to correspond to high values of the independent variable, creating data patterns similar to that shown in the diagram. The OLS estimating line clearly overestimates the slope of the true relationship. This result of overestimation with positive correlation between the disturbance and regressor does not necessarily hold when there is more than one explanatory variable, however. Note that the estimating line provides a much better fit to the sample data than does the true relationship; this causes the variance of the error term to be underestimated.

When there exists contemporaneous correlation between the disturbance and a regressor, alternative estimators with desirable small-sample properties cannot in general be found; as a consequence, the search for

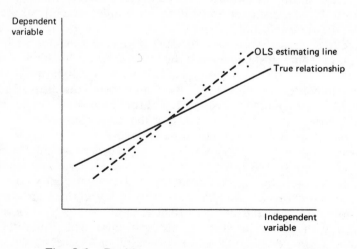

Fig. 8.1   Positive contemporaneous correlation

alternative estimators is conducted on the basis of their asymptotic properties. This should become clear in the discussions below of errors in variables and autoregression. Simultaneous equation estimation, an important example of this econometric problem, is discussed separately in chapter 9.

8.2 Errors in Variables

Many economists feel that the greatest drawback to econometrics is the fact that the data with which econometricians must work are so poor. A well-known quotation expressing this feeling is due to Josiah Stamp:

> The Government are very keen on amassing statistics – they collect them, add them, raise them to the nth power, take the cube root and prepare wonderful diagrams. But what you must never forget is that every one of those figures comes in the first instance from the village watchman, who just puts down what he damn pleases. [1929, pp. 258–9]

The errors-in-variables problem is concerned with the implication of using incorrectly measured variables, whether these measurement errors arise from the whims of the village watchman or from the use by econometricians of a proxy variable in place of an observable variable suggested by economic theory.

Errors in measuring the dependent variables are incorporated in the disturbance term; their existence causes no problems. When there are errors in measuring an independent variable, however, the fourth assumption of the CLR model is violated, since these measurement errors make this independent variable stochastic; the seriousness of this depends on whether or not this regressor is distributed independently of the disturbance. The original estimating equation, with correctly measured regressors, has a disturbance term independent of the regressors. Replacing one of these regressors by its incorrectly measured counterpart creates a new disturbance term, which, as shown in the technical notes to this section, involves the measurement error embodied in the new regressor. Because this measurement error appears in both the new regressor (the incorrectly measured independent variable) and the new disturbance term, this new estimating equation has a disturbance that is contemporaneously correlated with a regressor; thus the OLS estimator is biased even asymptotically.

There are two basic approaches to estimation in the presence of errors in variables.

(1) *Weighted regression*

The OLS procedure minimizes the sum of squared errors where these errors are measured in the vertical direction (the distance A in Fig. 8.2).

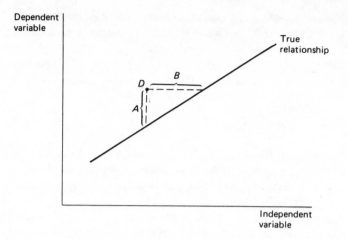

Fig. 8.2   Illustrating weighted regression

But if we have errors in measuring the independent variable, there exist errors in the horizontal direction as well (i.e., the data point D in Fig. 8.2 could be off the true line either because of a traditional error A or because of an error of size B in measuring the independent variable – or, as is most likely, because of a combination of both these types of errors). The least squares procedure should be modified to incorporate these horizontal errors; the problem in doing this is how to weight these two types of errors. This weighting is usually determined on the basis of the ratio of the variances of the two errors. Several special cases arise:

(a) If the variance of the vertical error is extremely large relative to the variance of the horizontal error, OLS is appropriate.
(b) If the variance of the horizontal error is extremely large relative to the variance of the vertical error, inverse least squares (in which x is regressed on y and the inverse of the coefficient estimate for y is used as the estimate of β) is appropriate.
(c) If the ratio of the variance of the vertical error to the variance of the horizontal error is equal to the ratio of the variances of the dependent and independent variables, we have the case of 'diagonal' regression, in which a consistent estimate turns out to be the geometric mean of the OLS and inverse least squares estimators.
(d) If the ratio of these error variances is unity, we have the case of 'orthogonal' regression, in which the sum of squared errors measured along a line perpendicular to the estimating line is minimized.

The great drawback of this procedure is that the ratio of the error variances is not usually known and cannot usually be estimated. This problem also characterizes the usually reliable maximum likelihood method. If the errors are all normally distributed (and independent of one another), the maximum likelihood estimates cannot be calculated without extra information (such as knowledge of the ratio of the error variances or knowledge of the variance of the measurement error).

(2) *Instrumental variables*

This method is useful for any situation in which a regressor is contemporaneously correlated with the disturbance. In this method a new independent variable (called an instrumental variable) must be found for each independent variable that is contemporaneously correlated with the disturbance. This new independent variable must be correlated with the original variable *and* be contemporaneously uncorrelated with the disturbance. The instrumental variables estimator is then found using a formula involving both the original variables and the new (instrumental) variables; it can be shown to be consistent.

The major problem with the instrument variables technique is that it is difficult to find a 'good' instrumental variable, i.e., an instrumental variable that is highly correlated with the independent variable with which it is associated, but uncorrelated with the disturbance. Usually the choice of an instrumental variable is highly arbitrary – there is no way of knowing whether the most efficient of the available instrumental variables has been chosen. Worse still, there is really no way of checking if the instrumental variable is in fact independent of the disturbance. (Economic theory may be of help here.) Another objection to this estimator is that it leads to much higher variances than OLS. The weaker the correlation between the instrumental variables and their associated independent variables, the larger is the variance–covariance matrix of the instrumental variable estimator. Because the typical case is one in which the instrumental variables are not highly correlated with the independent variable with which they are associated, this technique is often accused of obtaining consistency at the cost of a high variance; the OLS estimator could be preferred on the MSE criterion.

Several special cases of the instrumental variables approach should be noted.

(a) The most popular instrumental variable is the lagged value of the independent variable in question; it is usually correlated with the original independent variable, and, although it is correlated with the disturbance vector, because it is lagged it is not contemporaneously correlated with the disturbance (assuming the disturbance is not autocorrelated).

(b) The two-group method, in which the observations are split into two equal-sized groups on the basis of the size of the regressor and then the slope coefficient is estimated by the line joining the arithmetic means of the two groups, can be interpreted as an instrumental variables estimator with the instrumental variable taking the value − 1 if the regressor value is below its median value and +1 if above its median value.

(c) The three-group method, a variation of the two-group method in which the middle third of the observations is ignored, corresponds to using an instrumental variable with values −1, 0 and +1.

(d) In the Durbin method the independent variable is ranked by size and an instrumental variable is defined as the rank order (i.e., with values 1, 2, 3, ... *T*).

8.3 Autoregression

It is not uncommon in economics for a variable to be influenced by its own value in previous periods. For example, the habit-persistence theory of consumption suggests that consumption depends on the previous period's consumption, among other things. Whenever a lagged value of the dependent variable appears as a regressor in an estimating relationship, we have the case of *autoregression*. Because a lagged value of the dependent variable is stochastic (i.e., it was in part determined by a disturbance), using it as an independent variable (regressor) violates assumption 4 of the CLR model. The critical question is whether or not the lagged dependent variable is independent of the disturbance vector, or, failing that, contemporaneously independent of the disturbance.

The lagged dependent variable cannot be independent of the entire disturbance vector because the dependent variable is in part determined by the disturbance term. In particular, in the *t*th period the lagged dependent variable (i.e., the dependent variable value from the $(t − 1)$th period) is correlated with the $(t − 1)$th period's disturbance because this disturbance was one of the determinants of the dependent variable in that period. Furthermore, if this lagged dependent variable was in turn determined in part by the dependent variable value of the $(t − 2)$th period, then it will be correlated with the disturbance of the $(t − 2)$th period since that disturbance in part determined that period's dependent variable value. This reasoning can be extended to show that the lagged dependent variable is correlated with all of the past disturbances. However, it is *not* correlated with the current or future disturbances; thus, although the lagged dependent variable is not independent of the disturbance vector, it is contemporaneously independent of the disturbance. This means that, although β^{OLS} is a biased estimator of β, it is consistent and is on these grounds usually adopted as the most appropriate estimator.

It often happens that the autoregressive estimation problem arises not directly from specification of a habit-persistence theory, but indirectly through mathematical manipulations designed to transform an equation with estimation problems into a new estimating equation that is free of those problems. The following examples are typical of this.

(1) *Durbin two-stage method*   The first stage of the Durbin two-stage method for dealing with autocorrelated errors (discussed in section 7.4 and its associated technical notes) transforms the original estimating equation into one with a lagged dependent variable as a regressor. The coefficient estimate of this lagged dependent variable produces an estimate of ρ, the error autocorrelation coefficient, which is used in the second stage. Although this estimate is biased, it is consistent.

(2) *Koyck distributed lag*   Sometimes a dependent variable is determined by many or all past values of an independent variable, in addition to the current value of that independent variable. Estimating this *distributed lag* proves difficult, either because there are too many regressors relative to the number of observations (a degrees-of-freedom problem) or because the lagged values of the dependent variable are collinear with one another (the multicollinearity problem – see chapter 10). To circumvent these estimating problems the distributed lag coefficients are usually assumed to follow some specific pattern. A popular specification is the Koyck distributed lag in which these coefficients decline geometrically. This relationship can be mathematically manipulated (see the technical notes) to produce an estimating relationship that contains as independent variables only the current value of the original independent variable and the lagged value of the dependent variable. Thus a large estimating equation has been transformed into a much smaller autoregressive equation.

(3) *The partial-adjustment model*   Sometimes economic theory specifies that the desired rather than the actual value of the dependent variable is determined by the independent variable(s). This relationship cannot be estimated directly because the desired level of the dependent variable is unknown. This dilemma is usually resolved by specifying that the actual value of the dependent variable adjusts or is adjusted to the desired level according to some simple rule. In the *partial adjustment* or *rigidity* model the actual adjusts by some constant fraction of the difference between the actual and desired values. This is justified by citing increasing costs associated with rapid change, or noting technological, institutional or psychological inertia. As shown in the technical notes, mathematical manipulation of these two relationships (one determining the desired level and the second determining the adjustment of the actual level) creates an estimating equation that is autoregressive.

(4) *Adaptive expectations model*   Sometimes economic theory specifies that the dependent variable is determined by the anticipated or 'expected' value of the independent variable rather than by the current value of the independent variable. This relationship cannot be estimated directly because the anticipated values of the independent variables are unknown. This dilemma is usually resolved by specifying that the anticipated value of

the independent variable is formed by some simple rule. In the *adaptive expectations* model the anticipated value of the independent variable is formed by taking the last period's anticipated value and adding to it a constant fraction of the difference between last period's anticipated and actual values. This is justified by appealing to uncertainty and claiming that current information is discounted. As shown in the technical notes, mathematical manipulation of these two relationships (one determining the dependent variable and the second determining how anticipations are formed) creates an estimating equation that is autoregressive.

In each of these examples the lagged value of the dependent variable became a regressor in an estimating relationship through mathematical manipulation. When an estimating equation is created in this way, it is important to ensure that the disturbance term is included in the mathematical manipulations so that the character of the disturbance term in this final estimating equation is known. Too often researchers ignore the original disturbance and simply tack a spherical disturbance on to the relationship derived for estimating purposes. This leads to the adoption of the OLS estimator, which may be inappropriate.

In the second and fourth examples given above it happens that the mathematical manipulations create a disturbance term for the ultimate estimating relationship that is autocorrelated. This creates an estimating problem in which two assumptions of the CLR model are violated simultaneously – autocorrelated errors and a lagged dependent variable as a regressor. Unfortunately, it is not the case that the problem of simultaneous violation of two assumptions of the CLR model can be treated as two separate problems. The interaction of these two violations produces new problems. In this case the OLS estimator, although unbiased in the presence of autocorrelated errors alone, and consistent in the presence of a lagged dependent variable as a regressor alone, is asymptotically biased in the presence of both together. This asymptotic bias results because the lagged dependent variable is contemporaneously correlated with the autocorrelated disturbance; the tth period's disturbance is determined in part by the $(t - 1)$th period's disturbance and it in turn was one of the determinants of the lagged (i.e., $(t - 1)$th period's) dependent variable.

Early attempts to overcome this asymptotic bias used an instrumental variable for the lagged value of the dependent variable. The choice most often made was a lagged value of another regressor appearing in the estimating equation. Although this method produced a consistent estimator, it was not efficient because it made no effort to correct for the correlated error. Current estimators proposed to deal with this problem fall into two categories.

(1) *Maximum likelihood*

Simultaneous estimation of the parameters in the estimating equation and the parameter(s) characterizing the disturbance term via a maximum likelihood technique provides an asymptotically efficient estimate. Although it is computationally costly because search procedures must usually be employed, its use is advocated strongly by econometricians familiar with computer techniques for finding maximum likelihood estimates.

(2) *Generalized least squares*

For the case in which the disturbance is first-order autocorrelated, several variations of the generalized least squares methods (discussed in section 7.4) are sometimes used. They are essentially two- or three-step methods designed to circumvent the costly maximum likelihood search procedures. The most highly recommended of these is the Wallis method, in which the lagged value of an independent variable is used as an instrumental variable for the lagged dependent variable, the residuals from this estimation are used to estimate the first-order autocorrelation coefficient ρ, and then this estimate of ρ is used to create a generalized least squares estimator β^{EGLS}.

General Notes

8.1 Introduction

- The test procedure of Hausman (1978), discussed in chapter 5, can be used to test for violations of assumption 4. An instrumental variable (IV) estimator should be asymptotically unbiased regardless of the violation of assumption 4, whereas the OLS estimator will be unbiased if assumption 4 is met and otherwise asymptotically biased. A test of the difference between IV and OLS estimates is thus employed as a test of whether or not assumption 4 is violated.

8.2 Errors in Variables

- Morgenstern (1963) wrote an entire book examining the accuracy of economic data. Some spectacular examples of data fudging by government agencies can be found in Streissler (1970) pp. 27–9. (Example: a large overstatement of housing starts in Austria was compensated for by deliberately understating several subsequent housing start figures.) Streissler claims that often the econometrician more or less completely misunderstands what the statistics he works with really mean. A joke popular with graduate students illustrates this. After running many regressions a professor had discovered that the nation's output of soybeans followed a semi-logarithmic production function. He had just finished writing up his paper when on a visit to the office of the bureaucrat in charge of soybean statistics he noticed a sign which read, 'When in Doubt Use the Semi-Log'. A more serious example of this is provided by Shourie (1972). He notes that value added by the construction industry in Sri Lanka is usually estimated by the national accounts statistician as a constant multiple of imports of construction materials, so that a regression postulating that imports of construction materials were linearly related to value added in the construction industry would fit quite well.

- Although the coefficient estimates are biased (even asymptotically) in the errors-in-variables case, OLS is still appropriate for predicting the expected value of y given the measured value of x.

- In some instances it could be argued that economic agents respond to the measured rather than the true variables, implying that the original estimating equation should be specified in terms of the measured rather than the true values of the regressors. This eliminates the errors-in-variables problem.

- In the case of a single explanatory variable, errors in measuring this variable lead to negative correlation between the error term and the incorrectly measured regressor, causing β^{OLS} to be biased downward. When there is more than one independent variable, the direction of bias is more difficult to determine. See Levi (1973).

- Inverse least squares, in which the dependent variable becomes a regressor and the incorrectly measured independent variable becomes the regressand, provides an unbiased estimate of the inverse of β when there is no error in the vertical direction. The inverse of this estimate is a biased but consistent estimate of β. (Recall the technical notes to section 5.3.)

- When both vertical and horizontal errors exist, in large samples the OLS and inverse least squares estimates contain the value of β between them. Levi (1977) discusses bounded estimates. When the interval between these two estimates of β is small, it can be concluded that measurement errors are not a serious problem.

- On diagonal least squares see Leser (1974) pp. 23–4, and on orthogonal least squares see Malinvaud (1966) pp. 7–11. A major drawback of orthogonal least squares is that it is sensitive to the measurement units. For example, if the independent variable were measured in centimetres instead of metres, the estimated coefficient would not turn out to be 100 times the original estimated coefficient. On the maximum likelihood method see Maddala (1977) pp. 294–6.

- Feldstein (1974) suggests forming a weighted average of OLS and instrumental variable estimators to help reduce (at the expense of some bias) the inevitably large variance associated with instrumental variable estimation. Feldstein shows his estimator to be desirable on the mean square error criterion.

- For discussion of and references for the two- and three-group methods and the Durbin method, see Johnston (1984) pp. 430–2. All three methods produce consistent estimates under fairly general conditions; the two-group method is the least efficient of these, while the Durbin method is the most efficient. The intercept estimator for all these methods is found by passing a line with the estimated slope through the mean of all the observations.

- Often an explanatory variable is unobservable, but a proxy for it can be constructed. The proxy by definition contains measurement errors, and thus a biased estimate results. Forgoing the proxy and simply omitting the unobservable regressor also creates bias. McCallum (1972) and Wickens (1972) show that, on the criterion of asymptotic bias, using even a poor proxy is better than omitting the unobservable regressor. Using the MSE criterion, Aigner (1974) shows that using the proxy is preferred in most, but not all, circumstances.

- The maximum likelihood technique breaks down in the errors-in-variables context, basically because each observation carries with it an extra unknown (the true value of the unobservable variable), referred to as an incidental parameter. Johnston (1984) pp. 432–5 discusses how extra information in the form of knowledge of a variance or of a ratio of variances can be used to salvage the maximum likelihood approach.

- The use of incidental equations is often suggested as a means of improving estimation in the context of measurement errors. An incidental equation is an equation relating the unobservable variable to one or more observable variables plus an error term. The predicted values from an OLS regression of this equation can then be used as an instrumental variable for the unobservable variable. This technique is just a variant of the instrumental variable technique; it is in essence the two-stage least squares procedure discussed in chapter 9.

- The Ballentine of Fig. 8.3 can be used to illustrate the rationale behind the instrumental variable (IV) estimator. Suppose that Y is determined by X and an error term ε (ignore the dashed circle Z for the moment), but that X and ε are not independent. The lack of independence between X and ε means that the yellow area (representing the influence of the error term) must now overlap with the X circle. This is represented by the red area. Variation in Y in the red area is due to the influence of *both* the error term and the explanatory variable X. If Y were regressed on X, the information in the red-plus-blue-plus-purple area would be used to estimate β_x. This estimate is biased because the red area does not reflect variation in Y arising solely from variation in X. Some way must be found to get rid of the red area.

    The circle Z represents an instrumental variable for X. It is drawn to reflect the two properties it must possess:
    (1) It must be independent of the error term, so it is drawn such that it does not intersect the yellow or red areas.
    (2) It must be as highly correlated as possible with X, so it is drawn with a large overlap with the X circle.

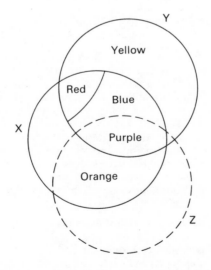

Fig. 8.3   Using an instrumental variable Z

Suppose X is regressed on Z. The predicted X from this regression, $\hat{X}$, is represented by the purple-plus-orange area. Now regress Y on $\hat{X}$ to produce an estimate of β_x; this in fact defines the IV estimator. The overlap of the Y circle with the purple-plus-orange area is the purple area, so information in the purple area is used to form this estimate; since the purple area corresponds to variation in Y arising entirely from variation in X, the resulting estimate of β_x is unbiased (strictly speaking, asymptotically unbiased).

Notice that, in constructing this estimate, although the bias arising from the red area is eliminated, the information set used to estimate β_x has shrunk from the red-plus-blue-plus-purple area to just the purple area. This implies that the variance of the IV estimator will be considerably higher than the variance of the OLS estimator, a reason why many researchers prefer to stick with OLS in spite of its asymptotic bias. It should now be apparent why the instrumental variable should be as highly correlated with X as possible: this makes the purple area as large as possible (at the expense of the blue area), reducing the variance of the IV estimator.

8.3   Autoregression

- For the extremely simple case in which $y_t = \beta y_{t-1} + \varepsilon_t$ with ε a spherical disturbance, the bias of the OLS estimator is approximately $-2\beta/T$, which disappears as T becomes large. The presence of extra regressors in the model also decreases this bias. Several suggestions for correcting for this bias (such as using the estimator $[(T/(T-2)]\beta^{OLS})$ have been suggested, but the correction factors increase the variance of the estimator and run the danger of increasing the mean square error. A Monte Carlo study by Copas (1966) suggests that β^{OLS} is better than the suggested alternatives. When the model has an intercept so that $y_t = \alpha + \beta y_{t-1} + \varepsilon_t$, then the bias in β^{OLS} is given by $-(1 + 3\beta)/T$. A suggested corrected estimator is $(T\beta^{OLS} + 1)/(T - 3)$, which Orcutt and Winokur (1969), on the basis of a Monte Carlo study, claim is superior.

- It may well be the case that the real world is characterized by some combination of the partial adjustment and adaptive expectation models. Waud (1968) discusses the estimation problems associated with mis-specification related to this possibility.

- The D–W statistic is biased towards 2 when a lagged dependent variable is a regressor. This means that in this context the DW test is biased towards not finding autocorrelated errors. In this circumstance Durbin (1970) has suggested on asymptotic grounds the h statistic, described in the technical notes to this section. Because this test is valid only asymptotically, several Monte Carlo studies have been undertaken to examine its small-sample properties, particularly as it compares to the traditional DW test. Unfortunately, these studies are inconclusive; for discussion and references see Judge *et al.* (1985) pp. 326–7. McNown and Hunter (1980) have suggested an alternative test, which is easy to calculate, has desirable asymptotic properties and, on the basis of their Monte Carlo study, appears to perform well in small samples. See the technical notes.

- In the autoregressive model with first-order autocorrelated errors the asymptotic bias in β^{OLS} is positive if $\rho > 0$ and negative if $\rho < 0$. This bias becomes smaller if more regressors are involved. In the simple model in which $y_t = \beta y_{t-1} + \varepsilon_t$ and $\varepsilon_t = \rho\varepsilon_{t-1} + u_t$, the OLS bias in estimating β is exactly the negative of the OLS bias in estimating ρ. See Malinvaud (1966) pp. 459–65.

- Kmenta (1971) pp. 481–7 discusses maximum likelihood estimation in the context of autocorrelated errors in the autoregressive model. If the errors are spherical, the maximum likelihood estimator is equivalent to the OLS estimator.

- Fomby *et al.* (1984) chapter 11 has a good textbook discussion of the conjunction of lagged dependent variables and autocorrelated errors.

- The Wallis method is not as efficient as the maximum likelihood method, basically because estimation of the coefficient of the lagged dependent variable is not independent of the estimation of the first-order autocorrelation coefficient (ρ) of the errors. Maddala (1971) therefore recommends iterating the Wallis method.

- Hatanaka (1974) has suggested a different two-step method which is asymptotically efficient, i.e., as efficient as maximum likelihood. Fomby *et al.* (1984) pp. 251–3 have a clear description.

- The correlated error term created in the Koyck distributed lag and the adaptive expectations examples is a moving-average error, not a first-order autocorrelated error. Its estimation cannot therefore be undertaken via the Wallis method. See the technical notes to this section for further discussion.

Technical Notes

8.2 Errors in Variables

- Suppose that the true relationship is

$$y = \beta_1 + \beta_2 x_2 + \varepsilon$$

but that x_2 is measured with error as z_2 where

$$z_2 = x_2 + u.$$

This implies that x_2 can be written as $z_2 - u$, and the first equation then becomes

$$y = \beta_1 + \beta_2(z_2 - u) + \varepsilon$$

$$y = \beta_1 + \beta_2 z_2 + (\varepsilon - \beta_2 u).$$

The new disturbance contains u, the error in measuring x_2, as does z_2. Notice that the correlation between z_2 and this new disturbance is negative, implying that β^{OLS} calculated by regressing y on z_2 will be biased downward.

- Let Z be a matrix of observations on instrumental variables corresponding to the matrix X of observations on the original variables. Any variable in X that is not contemporaneously correlated with the disturbance uses its own values as its instrumental variable in the matrix Z. The formula for the instrumental variable estimator β^{IV} is $(Z'X)^{-1}Z'Y$. An easy way of remembering this formula is to picture the OLS estimator as being derived by pre-multiplying the equation $Y = X\beta + \varepsilon$ by X' to get $X'Y = X'X\beta + X'\varepsilon$, dropping the last term, and solving for β to get $(X'X)^{-1}X'Y$; pre-multiplying by Z' instead of X' creates β^{IV}.

  This formula, $(Z'X)^{-1}Z'Y$, is equivalent to $(\hat{X}'\hat{X})^{-1}\hat{X}'Y$, the formula suggested by our earlier discussion using the Ballentine of Fig. 8.3.

8.3 Autoregression

- The Koyck distributed lag model may be written as

$$y_t = \beta x_t + \beta \lambda x_{t-1} + \beta \lambda^2 x_{t-2} + \beta \lambda^3 x_{t-3} + \ldots + \varepsilon_t$$

where $0 < \lambda < 1$ so that the influence of lagged values of the independent variable x declines geometrically. Lagging this equation one period and multiplying through by λ, we get

$$\lambda y_{t-1} = \beta \lambda x_{t-1} + \beta \lambda^2 x_{t-2} + \beta \lambda^3 x_{t-3} + \ldots + \lambda \varepsilon_{t-1}.$$

Subtracting the second equation from the first, we get

$$y_t = \lambda y_{t-1} + \beta x_t + (\varepsilon_t - \lambda \varepsilon_{t-1}) \qquad \cdots$$

an estimating equation of the autoregressive form, in which the number of regressors has shrunk to only two. Notice that the error term is autocorrelated, but not according to the first-order autocorrelation scheme discussed in chapter 7. This error is generated by a moving-average process; adjacent errors are correlated, but errors two or more periods distant are uncorrelated.

Estimation in this model is simplified a little because in this particular model (and in the adaptive expectations model) the coefficient of the lagged dependent variable is the same as the coefficient in the moving-average error term. See Johnston (1984) pp. 368–71 and Kmenta (1971) pp. 481–2, where an iterative search procedure, equivalent to maximum likelihood under the assumption of normal errors, is described for this case. In this special case the estimating problem can be reinterpreted as an errors-in-variables problem and estimated via the weighted regression method (recall section 8.2). See Kmenta (1971) pp. 483–4. This method is consistent, but is not as efficient as the asymptotically efficient maximum likelihood method.

- In the partial adjustment model the desired level of the dependent variable y^*, is determined by x, so that

$$y^*_t = \beta_0 + \beta_1 x_t + \varepsilon_t$$

and the actual adjusts by some fraction of the difference between the desired and the actual so that

$$y_t - y_{t-1} = \alpha(y^*_t - y_{t-1}) + u_t.$$

Substituting y^*_t from the first equation into the second equation we get, after manipulation,

$$y_t = \alpha\beta_0 + (1 - \alpha)y_{t-1} + \alpha\beta_1 x_t + (\alpha\varepsilon_t + u_t),$$

an estimating equation of the autoregressive form. In this case the error term is spherical.

- In the adaptive expectations model the dependent variable is determined by the anticipated value of the independent variable, x^*, so that

$$y_t = \beta_0 + \beta_1 x^*_t + \varepsilon_t.$$

The anticipated value is formed by updating last period's anticipated value by a fraction of its prediction error. Thus

$$x^*_t = x^*_{t-1} + \alpha(x_t - x^*_{t-1}) + u_t.$$

From the first equation $x^*_t = (y_t - \beta_0 - \varepsilon_t)/\beta_1$ and $x^*_{t-1} = (y_{t-1} - \beta_0 - \varepsilon_{t-1})/\beta_1$. Substituting these expressions into the second equation and simplifying, we get

$$y_t = \alpha\beta_0 + (1 - \alpha)y_{t-1} + \alpha\beta_1 x_t + [\varepsilon_t - (1 - \alpha)\varepsilon_{t-1} + \beta_1 u_t],$$

an estimating equation of the autoregressive form. In this case the error is of the moving-average type, similar to that found in the Koyck example.

- The Wallis (1967) method estimates ρ using the formula

$$\hat{\rho} = \frac{T}{T - 1}\left(\sum_{t=2}^{T} \hat{\varepsilon}_t \hat{\varepsilon}_{t-1} \middle/ \sum_{t=1}^{T} \hat{\varepsilon}_t^2\right) + \frac{k}{T}$$

where k is the number of unknown parameters in the original regression and $\hat{\epsilon}$ is the residual from the first-step regression. This adjusts for the small-sample bias of the usual estimator of ρ.

- Suppose $Y_t = \beta Y_{t-1} + \alpha X_t + \epsilon_t$ and $\epsilon_t = \rho \epsilon_{t-1} + u_t$ where u_t is a spherical disturbance. Durbin's h statistic is given by

$$h = \hat{\rho} \sqrt{\left(\frac{T}{1 - Tv}\right)}$$

where $\hat{\rho}$ is an estimate of ρ calculated from the OLS residuals, T is the sample size, and v is the estimated variance of the coefficient estimate of the lagged value of the dependent variable (in this case, the estimated variance of β^{OLS}). h is distributed asymptotically normally with mean zero and variance one. When $Tv > 1$ this statistic cannot be calculated; in this circumstance Durbin suggests an asymptotically equivalent test, namely, regress the OLS residual $\hat{\epsilon}_t$ on $\hat{\epsilon}_{t-1}$ and all the explanatory variables (in this case, just Y_{t-1} and X_t) and test against zero, in the usual way, the coefficient of $\hat{\epsilon}_{t-1}$.

- The test of McNown and Hunter is suggested through algebraic manipulation of the model above. If the relationship is lagged one period, multiplied through by ρ and then subtracted from the original relationship, the result can be rearranged to produce

$$Y_t = (\beta + \rho)Y_{t-1} + \alpha X_t - \rho\beta Y_{t-2} - \rho\alpha X_{t-1} + u_t.$$

An OLS regression on this equation can be used to test against zero the coefficient of X_{t-1}. If $\alpha \neq 0$, this coefficient will be zero if $\rho = 0$.

9. Violating Assumption Four: Simultaneous Equations

9.1 Introduction

In a system of simultaneous equations, all the endogenous variables are random variables – a change in any disturbance term changes *all* the endogenous variables since they are determined simultaneously. (An exception is a recursive system, discussed in the general notes.) Since the typical equation in a set of simultaneous equations has at least one endogenous variable as an independent variable, it does not fit the CLR mould: this endogenous variable cannot be considered as fixed in repeated samples. Assumption 4 of the CLR model is violated.

The character of the OLS estimator in this context depends on whether or not the endogenous variables used as regressors are distributed independently of the disturbance term in that equation. As noted above, though, when this disturbance term changes, the endogenous variable it determines directly changes, which in turn changes *all* of the other endogenous variables since they are determined simultaneously; this means that the endogenous variables used as regressors are contemporaneously correlated with the disturbance term in this equation (as well as with the disturbance term in all other equations). As a consequence, the OLS estimator is biased, even asymptotically, so that an alternative estimator is usually thought necessary.

A popular example used to illustrate this is a simple Keynesian system consisting of a consumption function

$$C = a + bY + \varepsilon$$

and an equilibrium condition

$$Y = C + I$$

where C (consumption) and Y (income) are endogenous variables and I (investment) is an exogenous variable. Consider the problem of estimating the consumption function, regressing consumption on income. Suppose the disturbance in the consumption function jumps up. This directly increases consumption, which through the equilibrium condition increases income. But income is the independent variable in the consumption function. Thus, the disturbance in the consumption function and the regressor are positively correlated. An increase in the disturbance term (directly implying an increase in consumption) is accompanied by an increase in income (also implying an increase in consumption). When estimating the influence of income on consumption, however, the OLS technique attributes *both* of these increases in consumption (instead of just the latter) to the accompanying increase in income. This implies that the OLS estimate of the marginal propensity to consume is biased upward, even asymptotically.

A natural response to this estimating problem is to suggest that the simultaneous system be solved and put into its reduced form. This means that every endogenous variable is expressed as a linear function of all the exogenous variables (and lagged endogenous variables, which are considered exogenous in this context). For the simple Keynesian example, the structural equations given above can be solved to give the reduced form equations

$$Y = \frac{a}{1-b} + \frac{1}{1-b} I + \frac{1}{1-b} \varepsilon$$

$$C = \frac{a}{1-b} + \frac{b}{1-b} I + \frac{1}{1-b} \varepsilon$$

which can be rewritten in more general form as

$$Y = \pi_1 + \pi_2 I + v_1$$

$$C = \pi_3 + \pi_4 I + v_2$$

where the π are parameters that are (nonlinear) functions of the structural form parameters and the v are the reduced-form disturbances, functions of the structural form disturbances.

Because no endogenous variables appear as independent variables in these reduced-form equations, if each reduced-form equation is estimated by OLS, the estimates of the reduced-form parameters, the π, are consistent (and if no lagged endogenous variables appear among the exogenous variables, these estimates are unbiased). Economic theory tells us that these reduced-form parameters are the long-run multipliers associated with the model. If a researcher is only interested in predicting the endogenous variables, or only wishes to estimate the size of these multipliers, he can simply use these estimates. If, however, he is interested in estimating the parameter values of the original equations (the structural parameters), these estimates of the reduced-form parameters are of help only if they can be used to derive estimates of the structural parameters (i.e., one suggested way of obtaining estimates of the structural parameters is to calculate them using estimates of the reduced-form parameters). Unfortunately, this is not always possible; this problem is one way of viewing the identification problem.

9.2   Identification

If you know that your estimate of a structural parameter is in fact an estimate of that parameter and not an estimate of something else, then that parameter is said to be identified: Identification is knowing that something is what you say it is.

The identification problem is a mathematical (as opposed to statistical) problem associated with simultaneous equation systems. It is concerned with the question of the possibility or impossibility of obtaining meaningful estimates of the structural parameters. There are two basic ways of describing this problem.

(1) *Can the reduced-form parameters be used to deduce unique values of the structural parameters?*   In general, different sets of structural parameter values can give rise to the same set of reduced-form parameters, so that knowledge of the reduced-form parameters does not allow the correct set of structural parameter values to be identified. (Hence the name 'identification' problem.) The set of equations representing the simultaneous equation system can be multiplied through by a transformation matrix to form a new set of equations with the same variables but different (i.e., transformed) parameters and a transformed disturbance. Mathematical manipulation shows that the reduced form of this new set of simultaneous equations (i.e., with a new set of structural parameters) is *identical* to the reduced form of the old set. This means that, if the reduced-form parameters were known, it would be impossible to determine which of the two sets of structural parameters is the 'true' set. Since in general a large number of possible transformations exists, it is usually impossible to identify the correct set of structural parameters given values of the reduced-form parameters.

(2) *Can one equation be distinguished from a linear combination of all equations in the simultaneous system?*   If it is possible to form a linear combination of the system's equations that looks just like one of the equations in the system (in the sense that they both include and exclude the same variables), a researcher estimating that equation would not know if the parameters he or she estimates should be identified with the parameters of the equation he or she wishes to estimate, or with the parameters of the linear combination. Since in general it is possible to find such linear combinations, it is usually impossible to identify the correct set of structural parameters.

The identification problem can be resolved if economic theory and extraneous information can be used to place restrictions on the set of simultaneous equations. These restrictions can take a variety of forms (such as use of extraneous estimates of parameters, knowledge of exact relationships among parameters, knowledge of the relative variances of disturbances, knowledge of zero correlation between disturbances in different equations, etc.), but the restrictions usually employed, called *zero restrictions*, take the form of specifying that certain structural parameters are zero, i.e., that certain endogenous variables and certain exogenous variables do not appear in certain equations. Placing a restriction on the structural parameters makes it more difficult to find a transformation of the structural equations that corresponds to the same reduced form, since that transformation must maintain the restriction. Similarly, the existence of the restriction makes it more difficult to find a linear combination of the equations that is indistinguishable from an original equation. If the econometrician is fortunate, there will be enough of these restrictions to eliminate *all* of the possible transformations and (what is equivalent) make it impossible to find one of those linear combinations. In this case the structural parameters are identified and can therefore be estimated.

A favourite example used to illustrate the identification problem, originally analysed by Working (1927), is the case of a supply and a demand curve for some good, each written in the normal fashion – quantity as a function of price. This, along with an equilibrium condition, represents a simultaneous system; observations on quantity and price reflect the intersection of these two curves in each observation period. The positions of the supply and demand curves in each period are determined by shifting the true supply and demand curves by the amount of their respective disturbances for that period. The observation points, then, are likely to be a cluster of points around the true equilibrium position, representing the intersections of the supply and demand curves as they jump around randomly in response to each period's disturbance terms. This is illustrated in Figs 9.1(a) and 9.1(b). The scatter of data in Fig. 9.1(b) suggests that it is impossible to estimate either the supply or the demand curve.

The supply and demand curves have the same included and excluded variables, so that regressing quantity on price generates estimates that could be estimates of the supply parameters, the demand parameters or, as is most likely, some combination of these sets of parameters.

Now suppose that an exogenous variable, say the level of income, is introduced as an independent variable in the demand function, and that it is postulated that this variable does *not* appear in the supply function (i.e., the coefficient of this exogenous variable in the supply function is zero). It is now the case that the demand function shifts in response to changes in this exogenous variable (to form D_1, D_2, D_3, etc. in Fig. 9.2a) as well as to changes in the disturbance term. This creates a scatter of observations as illustrated in Figs 9.2(a) and 9.2(b). This scatter of observations suggests that the supply curve can be estimated from the data (i.e., it is identified), but the demand curve cannot (i.e., it is unidentified). This is reflected in

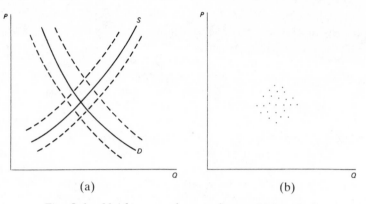

Fig. 9.1   Neither supply nor demand identified

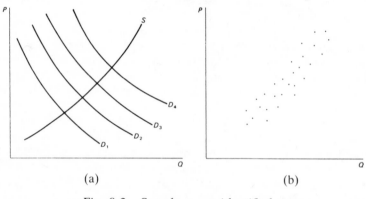

Fig. 9.2   Supply curve identified

the fact that any linear combination of the supply and demand curves gives an equation that looks like the demand curve, but no combination can be found that looks like the supply curve. Note, however, that it is not necessarily the case that a scatter of observations like this corresponds to an identified case; it is possible, for example, that the supply curve could itself have shifted with changes in the exogenous variable income, as illustrated in Fig. 9.3. This emphasizes the role of the restriction that the exogenous variable must not affect the supply curve; in general, identification results only through an appropriate set of restrictions.

In a simple example such as the foregoing, it is easy to check for identification; in more complicated systems, however, it is not so easy. In general, how does an econometrician know whether or not his system of simultaneous equations contains enough restrictions to circumvent the identification problem? This task is made a little simpler by the fact that

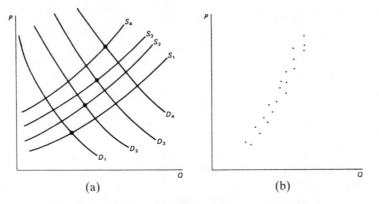

(a)   (b)

Fig. 9.3   Neither supply nor demand identified

each equation in a system of simultaneous equations can be checked separately to see if its structural parameters are identified. Mathematical investigation has shown that in the case of zero restrictions on structural parameters each equation can be checked for identification by using a rule called the *rank condition*. It turns out, however, that this rule is quite awkward to employ (see the technical notes to this section for further discussion of this rule), and as a result a simpler rule, called the *order condition*, is used in its stead. This rule only requires counting included and excluded variables in each equation (see the general notes to this section). Unfortunately, this order condition is only a necessary condition, not a sufficient one, so that, technically speaking, the rank condition must also be checked. Many econometricians do not bother doing this, however, gambling that the rank condition will be satisfied (as it usually is) if the order condition is satisfied. This procedure is not recommended.

If all equations in a system are identified, the system or model is said to be identified. If only some equations are identified, only the structural parameters associated with those equations can be estimated; structural parameters associated with unidentified equations cannot be estimated; i.e., there does not exist a meaningful way of estimating these parameters. The only way in which the structural parameters of these unidentified equations can be identified (and thus be capable of being estimated) is through imposition of further restrictions, or use of more extraneous information. Such restrictions, of course, must be imposed only if their validity can be defended.

If an equation is identified, it may be either 'just identified' or 'over-identified'. An equation is *just identified* if the number of identifying restrictions placed on the model is the minimum needed to identify the equation; an equation is *over-identified* if there are some extra restrictions beyond the minimum necessary to identify the equation. The case of over-identification seems to be the most prevalent. The relevance of this distinction relates to the choice of estimator. In some cases, applying a complicated estimation technique to a just-identified equation is no different from applying a simpler (and thus less costly) estimation technique. One technique (the indirect least squares estimator) can be applied only to just-identified equations. Discussion of the various estimators used in the simultaneous equations context should clarify this.

9.3   Single-equation Methods

The estimators described in this section are called 'single-equation' methods because they are used to estimate a system of simultaneous equations by estimating each equation (provided it is identified) separately. The 'systems' methods discussed in section 9.4 estimate all the (identified) equations in a system simultaneously; they are sometimes called 'full information' methods because they incorporate knowledge of all the restrictions in the system when estimating each parameter. Single-equation methods are sometimes called 'limited information' methods because they only utilize knowledge of the restrictions in the particular equation being estimated. Five single-equation methods are discussed in this section:

(1) Ordinary least squares (OLS)
(2) Indirect least squares (ILS)
(3) Instrumental variables (IV)
(4) Two-stage least squares (2SLS)
(5) Limited information, maximum likelihood (LI/ML)

Of all these methods, 2SLS is by far the most popular. The brief discussions of the other methods provide a useful perspective from which to view 2SLS and simultaneous equation estimation in general.

(1)   *Ordinary least squares (OLS)*

It is possible to use the OLS estimator and simply accept its asymptotic bias. This can be defended in several ways.

(a) Although the OLS estimator is biased, in small samples so also are all alternative estimators. Furthermore, the OLS estimator has minimum variance among these alternative estimators. Thus it is quite possible that in small samples the OLS estimator has minimum mean square error. Monte Carlo studies have shown, however, that this is true only in very small samples.
(b) According to Monte Carlo studies, the properties of the OLS estimator are less sensitive than the alternative estimators to the presence of estimation problems such as multicollinearity, errors in variables or

mis-specifications, particularly in small samples.
(c) Predictions from simultaneous equation models estimated by OLS often compare quite favourably with predictions from the same models estimated by alternative means.
(d) OLS can be useful as a preliminary or exploratory estimator.
(e) If a simultaneous equation system is recursive (described in the general notes to section 9.1), OLS is no longer asymptotically biased and is unbiased if there are no lagged endogenous variables and no correlation between disturbances in different equations. This is discussed in the general notes to section 9.1.

(2) *Indirect least squares (ILS)*

Suppose we wish to estimate a structural equation containing, say, three endogenous variables. The first step of the ILS technique is to estimate the reduced-form equations for these three endogenous variables. If the structural equation in question is just identified, there will be only one way of calculating the desired estimates of the structural equation parameters from the reduced-form parameter estimates. The structural parameters are expressed in terms of the reduced-form parameters, and the OLS estimates of the reduced-form parameters are plugged in these expressions to produce estimates of the structural parameters. Because these expressions are nonlinear, however, unbiased estimates of the reduced-form parameters produce only consistent estimates of the structural parameters, not unbiased estimates (recall the discussion of this in the technical notes to section 5.3). If an equation is over-identified, the extra identifying restrictions provide additional ways of calculating the structural parameters from the reduced-form parameters, all of which are *supposed* to lead to the same values of the structural parameters. But because the estimates of the reduced-form parameters do not embody these extra restrictions, these different ways of calculating the structural parameters create different estimates of these parameters. (This is because unrestricted estimates rather than actual values of the parameters are being used for these calculations, as illustrated in the technical notes to this section.) Because there is no way of determining which of these different estimates is the most appropriate, ILS is not used for over-identified equations. The other simultaneous equation-estimating techniques have been designed to estimate structural parameters in the over-identified case; many of these can be shown to be equivalent to ILS in the context of a just-identified equation, and to be weighted averages of the different estimates produced by ILS in the context of over-identified equations.

(3) *Instrumental variables (IV)*

As seen earlier in section 8.3, the instrumental variable technique is a general estimation procedure applicable to situations in which the independent variable is not independent of the disturbance. If an appropriate instrumental variable can be found for each endogenous variable that appears as a regressor in a simultaneous equation, the instrumental variable technique provides consistent estimates. The big problem with this approach, of course, is finding appropriate instrumental variables; exogenous variables in the system of simultaneous equations are considered the best candidates since they are correlated with the endogenous variables (through the interaction of the simultaneous system) and are uncorrelated with the disturbances (by the assumption of exogeneity).

(4) *Two-stage least squares (2SLS)*

This technique is a special case of the instrumental variable technique in which the 'best' instrumental variables are used. As noted above, the exogenous variables are all good candidates for instrumental variables; which is the best is difficult to determine. A natural suggestion is to combine all the exogenous variables to create a combined variable to act as a 'best' instrumental variable. A good instrumental variable is one that is highly correlated with the regressor for which it is acting as an instrument. This suggests regressing each endogenous variable being used as a regressor on all the exogenous variables in the system and using the estimated values of these endogenous variables from this regression as the required instrumental variables. (Each estimated value is the 'best' instrumental variable in the sense that, of all combinations of the exogenous variables, it has highest correlation with the endogenous variable.) This defines the 2SLS procedure:

Stage 1: regress each endogenous variable acting as a regressor in the equation being estimated on *all* the exogenous variables in the system of simultaneous equations (i.e., estimate the reduced form), and calculate the estimated values of these endogenous variables.

Stage 2: use these estimated values as instrumental variables for these endogenous variables *or* simply use these estimated values and the included exogenous variables as regressors in an OLS regression. (It happens that these two versions of the second stage give identical results.)

Because the 2SLS estimator is a legitimate instrumental variable estimator, we know that it is consistent. Monte Carlo studies have shown it to have small-sample properties superior on most criteria to all other estimators. They have also shown it to be quite robust (i.e., its desirable properties are insensitive to the presence of other estimating problems such as multicollinearity and specification errors). These results, combined with its low computational cost, have made the 2SLS estimator the most popular of all simultaneous equations estimators. Since it is equivalent to ILS in the just-identified case, 2SLS is usually applied uniformly to all identified equations in the system.

(5) *Limited information, maximum likelihood (LI/ML)*

In this technique, estimates of the reduced-form parameters are created by maximizing the likelihood function of the reduced-form disturbances *subject* to the zero restrictions on the structural parameters in the equation being estimated. (Only that part of the reduced form corresponding to the endogenous variables appearing in the structural equation in question need be estimated.) These estimates of the reduced-form parameters are then used, as in ILS, to create estimates of the structural parameters; because the zero restrictions have been built into the reduced-form estimates, the multiple ILS estimates of the over-identified case all turn out to be the same. In the just-identified case LI/ML is identical to ILS and 2SLS if the errors are distributed normally. An alternative (equivalent) way of viewing this procedure is as an application of instrumental variables: the reduced-form parameter estimates from this technique can be used to calculate estimated values of the endogenous variables included in the equation being estimated, and these can in turn be used as instrumental variables as in the 2SLS procedure. The LI/ML estimator is therefore consistent.

The usual assumption made is that the structural disturbances are distributed multivariate normally, implying that the reduced-form disturbances are also distributed multivariate normally. Under this condition the LI/ML is identical to the limited information, least generalized variance (LI/LGV) and the limited information, least variance ratio (LI/LVR) estimators, discussed in the technical notes to this section. Furthermore, these estimators, and the 2SLS estimator which just happens to share the same asymptotic variance–covariance matrix, are at least as efficient asymptotically as any other estimator using the same amount of information. (This follows from maximum likelihood properties.)

9.4   Systems Methods

Systems estimating procedures estimate *all* the identified structural equations together as a set, instead of estimating the structural parameters of each equation separately. These systems methods are also called 'full information' methods because they utilize knowledge of *all* the zero restrictions in the entire system when estimating the structural parameters. Their major advantage is that, because they incorporate all of the available information into their estimates, they have a smaller asymptotic variance–covariance matrix than single-equation estimators. By the same token, however, if the system is mis-specified (if an alleged zero restriction is incorrect, for example) the estimates of *all* the structural parameters are affected, rather than, in the case of single-equation estimation techniques, only the estimates of the structural parameters of one equation. This, and their high computational costs, are the major drawbacks of the systems methods. The two major systems methods are discussed briefly below.

(1) *Three-stage least squares (3SLS)*

This method is the systems counterpart of 2SLS. Its structure is based on an alternative interpretation of 2SLS: if a single equation is multiplied through (transformed) by the matrix of observations on *all* the exogenous variables in the system, applying the GLS to this new (transformed) relationship creates the 2SLS estimates. Now if all the equations to be estimated are transformed in this way, stacked one on top of the other, and then this stack is rewritten as a single, very large, equation, applying GLS to this giant equation should produce the 2SLS estimates of each of the component equations. Because the nonspherical disturbance of this giant equation can incorporate nonzero correlations between disturbances in different equations, however, these estimates can differ from the 2SLS estimates and can in fact be more efficient. This defines the 3SLS procedure.

The variance–covariance matrix of this giant equation's disturbance can be shown to involve the matrix of observations on all the exogenous variables in the system and the contemporaneous variance–covariance matrix of the structural equation's disturbances. (This matrix contains the variances of each equation's disturbances along the diagonal and the covariance between equation's disturbances in the off-diagonal positions.) The former matrix is known but the latter must be estimated (from estimates of the structural equations' disturbances). The 3SLS procedure can be summarized as follows:

Stage 1: calculate the 2SLS estimates of the identified equations.

Stage 2: use the 2SLS estimates to estimate the structural equations' errors, and then use these to estimate the contemporaneous variance–covariance matrix of the structural equations' errors.

Stage 3: apply GLS to the large equation representing all the identified equations of the system.

The 3SLS estimator is consistent and in general is asymptotically more efficient than the 2SLS estimator. If the disturbances in the different structural equations are uncorrelated, so that the contemporaneous variance–covariance matrix of the disturbances of the structural equations is diagonal, 3SLS reduces to 2SLS.

(2) *Full information, maximum likelihood (FI/ML)*

This systems method corresponds to the single-equation technique LI/ML. In this technique estimates of *all* the reduced-form parameters (rather than just those corresponding to the endogenous variables included in a particular equation) are created by maximizing the likelihood function of the reduced-form disturbances, subject to the zero restrictions on *all* the structural parameters in the system. The usual assumption made is that the structural disturbances, and thus the reduced-form disturbances, are distributed multivariate normally. Under this condition the FI/ML estimator and the 3SLS estimator, which shares the same asymptotic variance–covariance matrix, are at least as efficient asymptotically as any other estimator that uses the same amount of information. (This follows from maximum likelihood properties.)

General Notes

9.1 Introduction

- The Hausman test, described in chapter 5 and again in chapter 8, can be used to test for endogeneity of regressors.

- Not all sets of equations are simultaneous. Several equations might be connected not because they interact, but because their error terms are related. For example, if these equations are demand functions, a shock affecting demand for one good may spill over and affect demand for other goods. In this case, estimating these equations as a set, using a single (large) regression, should improve efficiency. This technique, due to Zellner (1962) is called SURE (seemingly unrelated regression estimation); a description is given in the technical notes.

- Lagged values of endogenous variables are treated as exogenous variables, because for determination of the current period's values of the endogenous variables they are given constants. For this reason the exogenous and lagged endogenous variables are often called *predetermined* variables. Their use as regressors creates reduced-form estimates that are biased but asymptotically unbiased (assuming the errors are not autocorrelated), as noted in section 8.3. This is not of concern in the context of structural simultaneous equation estimation, because all estimators used in this context are biased anyway; they are chosen on the basis of their asymptotic properties.

- Not all simultaneous equations systems suffer from the simultaneous equation estimation bias described in this chapter. A *recursive system* is one in which there is unidirectional dependency among the endogenous variables. The equations can be ordered such that the first endogenous variable is determined only by exogenous variables, the second determined only by the first endogenous variable and exogenous variables, the third by only the first two endogenous variables and exogenous variables, and so forth. There must be no feedback from an endogenous variable to one lower in the causal chain. In a recursive system, a change in the disturbance in the fourth equation, for example, affects directly the fourth endogenous variable, which in turn affects the higher-ordered endogenous variables in the system, but does *not* affect the lower-ordered endogenous variables. Because only lower-ordered variables appear as regressors in the fourth equation, there is no contemporaneous correlation between the disturbance and the regressors in the fourth equation. If there is no correlation between disturbances in different equations, OLS estimation is consistent, and if no lagged endogenous variables appear among the exogenous variables in the equation, it is unbiased.

- For an interesting discussion of problems associated with applying current econometric techniques to the estimation of simultaneous equation systems, see Kmenta (1972).

9.2   Identification

- Goldberger (1964) pp. 312–13 shows how transforming structural parameters creates a new set of structural parameters with the same reduced-form parameters.

- Before the identification problem was recognized by economists, demand studies for agricultural products were undertaken using OLS. They gave good results, though, because the demand curve was relatively stable whereas the supply curve was quite erratic. This provides an example of how extraneous information could be used to identify an equation. If there is no exogenous variable in either the supply or the demand equation but the disturbance term in the supply equation is known to have a very high variance relative to the disturbance term in the demand equation, the data observations should trace out a demand curve in the same sense that a supply curve was traced out in Fig. 9.2. Thus, prior knowledge of the relative variances of the disturbances can aid in identification.

- The popularity of zero restrictions as a means of identifying equations probably stems from the fact that this method is easier to apply and has been given formal mathematical treatment. Other means do exist, however. Johnston (1984) pp. 463–6 and Maddala (1977) pp. 226–8 discuss the use of restrictions on the contemporaneous variance–covariance matrix of the simultaneous system. (This matrix contains the variance of the disturbance in each equation along the diagonal, and the contemporaneous covariances between equations' disturbances in the off-diagonal positions.) Christ (1966) pp. 334–43 discusses the use of restrictions on the range of an error term, knowledge of the ratio of two error term variances, and knowledge of the covariance between two equations' error terms. Maddala (1977) pp. 228–31 discusses non-homogeneous restrictions, nonlinearities and cross-equation restrictions.

- The order condition is written in many different (equivalent) ways in textbooks, all involving counting included and excluded variables of different types. The best of these ways is to check if there are enough exogenous (predetermined) variables excluded from the equation in question to provide an instrumental variable for each of the endogenous variables appearing as regressors in that equation. (The number of excluded exogenous variables must be greater than or equal to the number of included endogenous variables less 1.) Maddala (1977) p. 234 gives some reasons why this way of checking the order condition is preferred to others.

- An equation is 'just identified' if there are exactly enough exogenous variables excluded from the equation to act as instrumental variables for the endogenous variables appearing as regressors in that equation. It is over-identified if there are more than enough excluded exogenous variables.

- Over-identification can be thought of as a case in which the specification of the structural equation imposes restrictions on the reduced form.

- Identifying restrictions cannot be tested (because their validity must be assumed for meaningful estimation), but, as explained in the technical notes, over-identifying restrictions *can* be tested. Such tests, when undertaken, usually reject the over-identifying restrictions, casting doubt on the identifying restrictions since the over-identifying restrictions cannot be separated from the identifying restrictions. A sceptic might use this fact to explain why economists seldom undertake such tests.

9.3 Single-equation Methods

- Little is known about the small-sample properties of simultaneous equation estimators. Several Monte Carlo studies exist, however; for a survey see Challen and Hagger (1983) pp. 117–21 or Johnston (1972) pp. 408–20. Unfortunately, the results from these studies are not clear-cut, mainly because the results are peculiar to the model specifications used in the Monte Carlo experiments. Furthermore, it turns out that many methods are not robust, in the sense that their performance on the usual estimating criteria is sensitive to things such as sample size, specification errors, the presence of multicollinearity, etc. This makes it difficult to draw general conclusions concerning the relative desirability of the many simultaneous equation estimators. These Monte Carlo studies have consistently ranked 2SLS quite highly, however, so that many econometricians recommend 2SLS for general use.

- Researchers use estimates of the asymptotic variances of simultaneous equation estimators to undertake hypothesis tests; although these estimates are usually underestimates of the true variances, alternative methods have not proved superior. See Maddala (1974).

- The estimators discussed in this chapter assume that the errors are not autocorrelated. In the presence of autocorrelated errors these estimators are inconsistent if lagged values of the endogenous variables appear as exogenous variables (recall section 8.3). Goldfeld and Quandt (1972) chapter 7 discuss the problem, recommending the maximum likelihood techniques. Much recent research has been directed at this problem, most of it based on Fair (1970). Fair claims that for strongly autocorrelated errors it is more important to correct for that problem than for the simultaneous equation bias. Godfrey (1976) discusses testing for autocorrelated errors in simultaneous equations with lagged endogenous variables.

- Carter (1973) discusses the use of OLS as a preliminary or exploratory estimator in simultaneous equation systems.

- Khazzoom (1976) has developed a technique (using a 'generalized inverse') that allows indirect least squares to be applied to over-identified equations.

- In large econometric models it may be impossible to apply 2SLS because the total number of exogenous variables in the system exceeds the number of observations, making calculation of the reduced form (the first stage of 2SLS) impossible. This problem is usually solved by using, in the first stage of 2SLS, a small number of principal components in place of the exogenous variables excluded from the equation in question. See McCarthy (1971). A principal component is a linear combination of variables that captures as much of the variation in those variables as it is possible to capture via a linear combination of those variables (see section 10.4).

- When 2SLS is applied to an over-identified equation, a particular endogenous variable is chosen, from the set of endogenous variables included in that equation, to be the left-hand-side variable in that equation, and is given the coefficient 1. If the econometrician is uncertain of this specification, and a different endogenous variable is picked to play this role, the 2SLS procedure creates different estimates of the *same* parameters (i.e., after renormalizing to put a coefficient of 1 on the original variable chosen to be the left-hand-side variable). The LI/ML method does not suffer from this normalization problem; it creates a unique estimate that lies between the extremes of the different possible 2SLS estimates. The fact that 2SLS is sensitive to the normalization choice should not necessarily be viewed as a disadvantage, however. It could be claimed that this sensitivity allows economic theory (which usually suggests a specific normalization) to inject some extra information into the estimating procedure. See Fisher (1976) for further discussion.

- Challen and Hagger (1983) chapter 6 contains an excellent discussion of practical reasons (such as nonlinearities, undersized samples, autocorrelated errors and computational cost) why most simultaneous equations systems are estimated by OLS, or some variant thereof, rather than by one of the more sophisticated estimating techniques introduced in this chapter.

9.4   Systems Methods

- The superiority of 3SLS is slight if the contemporaneous variance–covariance matrix of the structural equations' disturbances is only slightly different from a diagonal matrix or the sample size is small so that it cannot be well estimated. Mikhail (1975) suggests, on the basis of a Monte Carlo study, that 3SLS is better than 2SLS if the contemporaneous covariance between the error terms of two equations exceeds one-third.

- 3SLS, like 2SLS, is not invariant to the choice of normalization.

- The 3SLS method can be iterated by using the original 3SLS estimates to create new estimates of the structural disturbances and repeating the rest of the 3SLS calculations. This 'iterated 3SLS' estimator has the same asymptotic properties as the original 3SLS estimates. Monte Carlo studies have not shown it to be markedly superior to 3SLS.

- If there is extraneous information concerning the contemporaneous variance–covariance matrix of the structural equations' errors, or if there are lagged endogenous variables, FI/ML is asymptotically more efficient than 3SLS.

- Rothenberg and Leenders (1964) have suggested an estimating technique called linearized maximum likelihood (LML) which is a short-cut version of FI/ML. Although it reduces the considerable computational cost of FI/ML, it is still more burdensome than 3SLS. Recent developments in computers and their software packages have made maximum likelihood methods more viable. In particular, Parke (1982) has reduced dramatically the computational costs of FIML and 3SLS estimation for large, nonlinear simultaneous equation models.

- The estimating techniques discussed in this chapter are designed to estimate the structural parameters. It may be, however, that the econometrician is only interested in the reduced-form parameters, in which case he could avoid estimating the structural parameters and simply estimate the reduced-form parameters by applying OLS to each of the reduced-form equations (i.e., regress each endogenous variable on all the exogenous variables in the system). If some structural equations are over-identified, however, more efficient estimates of the reduced-form parameters can be obtained by taking structural parameter estimates (that incorporate the over-identifying restrictions) and using them to estimate directly the reduced-form parameters. Although these 'derived' reduced-form estimates are biased (whereas the OLS reduced-form estimates are not), they are consistent, and, because they incorporate the over-identifying information, are asymptotically more efficient than the OLS reduced-form estimates. Monte Carlo studies have shown the derived reduced-form estimates to have desirable small-sample properties. Of course, if the over-identifying restrictions are untrue, the OLS reduced-form estimates will be superior; a suggested means of testing over-identifying restrictions is through comparison of predictions using OLS reduced-form estimates and derived reduced-form estimates. Liu (1960) claims that all simultaneous equations systems are under-identified and that, therefore, structural estimation is impossible, and prediction must be undertaken with the reduced form.

Technical Notes

9.1 Introduction

- SURE consists of writing a set of individual equations as one giant equation. Suppose there are N equations $Y_i = X_i \beta_i + \varepsilon_i$ where the subscript i refers to the ith equation. (Here each Y_i, β_i and ε_i are vectors; X_i is a data matrix.) These equations are written as

$$
\begin{bmatrix} Y_1 \\ Y_2 \\ \vdots \\ Y_n \end{bmatrix} = \begin{bmatrix} X_1 & & \\ & X_2 & O \\ & & \ddots \\ O & & X_n \end{bmatrix} \begin{bmatrix} \beta_1 \\ \beta_2 \\ \vdots \\ \beta_n \end{bmatrix} + \begin{bmatrix} \varepsilon_1 \\ \varepsilon_2 \\ \vdots \\ \varepsilon_n \end{bmatrix}
$$

or $Y^* = X^* \beta^* + \varepsilon^*$.

Now if we allow contemporaneous correlation between the error terms across equations, so that, for example, the tth error term in the ith equation is correlated with the tth error term in the jth equation, the variance–covariance matrix of ε will not be diagonal. Estimating these error correlations and the diagonal elements (by using the residuals from each equation estimated separately) should allow estimation of the variance–covariance matrix of ε^* and generation of EGLS estimates of β^*. Aigner (1971) pp. 197–204 has a good textbook exposition.

9.2 Identification

- The order condition for identification through the use of zero restrictions can be generalized in terms of homogenous linear restrictions: an equation is identified if there are $G - 1$ independent homogeneous linear restrictions on the parameters of that equation, where G is the number of equations in the system. (A linear homogeneous restriction equates to zero a linear combination of parameter values; for example, it may be specified that consumption is a function of disposable income so that the coefficient on income is equal in value but opposite in sign to the coefficient on taxes – their sum would be zero.) A similar generalization exists for the rank condition. See Fisher (1966) chapter 2.

- The 'impossible to find a linear combination' view of identification can be used to check informally the rank condition for instances in which the order condition holds. A visual inspection of the pattern of included, and excluded variables in a system of equations can often verify that:
  (a) it is not possible to form a linear combination of the equations in the system that looks like the equation being tested for identification;
  (b) it is obviously possible to do so; or
  (c) it is only possible to do so if the values of the parameters in the system bear a particular (and unlikely) relationship to one another.
  Examples of these three cases are given below. If an econometrician is not confident that his visual inspection for the possibility of a linear combination was adequate, he can test the rank condition formally: the matrix of parameters (from all equations) associated with all the variables excluded from the equation in question must have rank equal to one less than the number of equations in the system.

- *Examples of case (a)* Suppose we have the following two-equation model, where the y are endogenous variables, the x are exogenous variables and the θ are parameters. (For simplicity the constant terms and the normalization choice are ignored.)

$$\theta_1 y_1 + \theta_2 y_2 + \theta_3 x_1 = 0$$
$$\theta_4 y_1 + \theta_5 y_2 \qquad = 0$$

The second equation is identified by the order condition and there is clearly no way in which these equations can be combined to produce a new equation looking like the second equation; the rank condition must be satisfied. This is the example illustrated by Fig. 9.2.

- *Examples of case (b)* Suppose a third equation is added to the previous example, introducing a new endogenous variable y_3 and a new exogenous variable x_2. The first equation now satisfies the order condition (because of the extra exogenous variable in the system). But the sum of the first and second equations yields an equation containing the same variables as the first equation, so the rank condition cannot be satisfied for this equation. In general, this problem arises whenever all the variables contained in one equation form a subset of variables in another equation; this is fairly easy to check visually.
  Not all examples of case (b) are so easy to check, however. Consider the following four-equation example:

$$\theta_1 y_1 \qquad\qquad + \theta_2 y_3 \qquad\qquad + \theta_3 x_1 \qquad\qquad\qquad = 0$$
$$\qquad \theta_4 y_2 + \theta_5 y_3 + \theta_6 y_4 + \theta_7 x_1 \qquad\qquad = 0$$
$$\theta_8 y_1 + \theta_9 y_2 \qquad\qquad\qquad + \theta_{10} x_2 + \theta_{11} x_3 = 0$$
$$\theta_{12} y_1 + \theta_{13} y_2 \qquad + \theta_{14} y_4 + \theta_{15} x_1 \qquad\qquad = 0$$

The second equation satisfies the order condition, but if θ_1/θ_{12} times the fourth equation is subtracted from the first equation, a new equation is created that has the same included and excluded variables as the second equation, so the rank condition is not satisfied for this equation.

- *Examples of case (c)* Suppose we have the following three-equation model:

$$\theta_1 y_1 + \theta_2 y_2 \qquad\qquad + \theta_3 x_1 \qquad\qquad = 0$$
$$\theta_4 y_1 \qquad + \theta_5 y_3 \qquad + \theta_6 x_2 = 0$$
$$\theta_7 y_1 + \theta_8 y_2 + \theta_9 y_3 + \theta_{10} x_1 + \theta_{11} x_2 = 0$$

The first equation is identified by the order condition. If it happens that $\theta_5 = k\theta_9$ and $\theta_6 = k\theta_{11}$, then the second equation minus k times the third equation (i.e., a particular linear combination of the second and third equations) will create an equation with the same included and excluded variables as the first equation; the rank condition is not met. In practice, the third case is usually ignored, since the probability is virtually zero that the true values of the parameters are related in this way.

9.3 Single-equation Methods

● Consider estimating by indirect least squares the just-identified supply equation corresponding to the example illustrated in Fig. 9.2. Ignoring constant terms for simplicity, suppose the demand equation can be written as $q = \beta p + \gamma y$ where q is quantity, p is price and y is income (exogenously determined). Write the supply function as $q = \delta p$. Solving these equations for the reduced form, we get

$$p = \frac{\gamma}{\delta - \beta} y = \pi_1 y$$

$$q = \frac{\gamma \delta}{\delta - \beta} y = \pi_2 y \ .$$

OLS estimation of these reduced-form equations yields unbiased estimates $\hat{\pi}_1$ and $\hat{\pi}_2$ of π_1 and π_2. Since $\pi_2/\pi_1 = \delta$, $\hat{\pi}_2/\hat{\pi}_1$ is the ILS estimate of δ; this estimate is not unbiased, since $\hat{\pi}_2/\hat{\pi}_1$ is a nonlinear function of $\hat{\pi}_1$ and $\hat{\pi}_2$, but it is consistent.

Now suppose that an additional exogenous variable, advertising, affects demand but not supply (e.g., an additional, over-identifying restriction, that the coefficient of advertising is zero in the supply equation, is imposed). The demand equation is now written as

$$q = \beta p + \gamma y + \theta a$$

where a is advertising. The reduced-form equations become

$$p = \frac{\gamma}{\delta - \beta} + \frac{\theta}{\delta - \beta} a = \pi_1 y + \pi_3 a$$

$$q = \frac{\gamma \delta}{\delta - \beta} y + \frac{\theta \delta}{\delta - \beta} a = \pi_2 y + \pi_4 a.$$

OLS estimation of these reduced-form equations yields unbiased estimates $\pi_1{}^*$, $\pi_2{}^*$, $\pi_3{}^*$ and $\pi_4{}^*$ of π_1, π_2, π_3 and π_4. Since $\pi_2/\pi_1 = \delta$ and $\pi_4/\pi_3 = \delta$, there are two different ILS estimates of δ, namely $\pi_2{}^*/\pi_1{}^*$ and $\pi_4{}^*/\pi_3{}^*$. Only if the estimation of π incorporates the zero restrictions will these two estimates of δ be the same.

In Fig. 9.2 we saw that identification was possible because shifts in the demand curve due to income changes traced out the supply curve. With the extra exogenous variable advertising, we now find that the supply curve is also traced out by shifts in the demand curve arising from changes in advertising expenditures. The indirect least squares procedure thus has two ways of estimating the supply curve: from variations in supply due to variations in income, or from variations in supply due to variations in advertising, illustrating the over-identification phenomenon.

● When the disturbances are distrubuted normally, the LI/ML method is identical to the *limited information, least variance ratio (LI/LVR)* method. In this technique the structural equation to be estimated is rewritten so that all the endogenous variables appearing in that equation are on the left-hand side and all the included exogenous variables and the disturbance are on the right-hand side. Suppose a particular set of values is chosen for the parameters of the included endogenous variables and a composite endogenous variable is calculated. This composite endogenous variable is a linear function of the included exogenous variables plus a disturbance term. Regressing this composite endogenous variable on the exogenous variables included in the equation should produce a sum of squared residuals only slightly larger than the sum of squared residuals obtained from regressing it on *all* the exogenous variables in the system, since the exogenous variables not included in the equation should have little explanatory power. The LI/LVR chooses the set of values of the (structural) parameters of the included endogenous variables so as to minimize the ratio of the former sum of squared residuals to the latter sum of squared residuals. This ratio is called the variance ratio; hence the name 'least variance ratio'. Econometricians have derived mathematically a means of doing this without having to search over all possible sets of parameter values of the included endogenous variables (see Wonnacott and Wonnacott, 1970, pp. 376–9). Once the parameter estimates of the included endogenous variables have been found, the composite endogenous variable is simply regressed on the included exogenous variables to find estimates of the (structural) parameters of the included exogenous variables. This technique can be shown to be identical to the limited information, least generalized variance method (discussed below) as well as to the LI/ML method. Computationally, however, the LI/LVR method is easier than the others, so it is the one employed in practice. Its computational cost is higher than that of 2SLS, however.

- It is interesting that 2SLS can be shown to minimize the difference between the numerator and the denominator of the least variance ratio.

- The least variance ratio should only slightly exceed 1 if the excluded exogenous variables do in fact all have zero coefficients. If some of the excluded variables should have been included, this ratio will exceed 1 by a significant amount. A test of over-identifying restrictions is based on this idea. An alternative test is based on the difference between the numerator and the denominator of this ratio. See Murphy (1973) pp. 476–80.

- When the disturbances are distributed normally the LI/ML method is also identical to the *limited information, least generalized variance (LI/LGV)* method. This technique, like LI/ML, is based on the idea that ILS could be applied to an over-identified equation if the reduced-form parameter estimates had built into them the zero restrictions on the structural parameters in that equation. To build these zero restrictions into the reduced-form parameter estimates, the reduced-form parameters must be estimated as a *set* of equations (including only those reduced-form equations corresponding to the endogenous variables appearing in the structural equation being estimated) instead of individually. When estimating a single equation the sum of squared residuals is usually minimized; when estimating an entire set of equations simultaneously, however, it is not obvious what should be minimized. The estimated *contemporaneous variance–covariance matrix* of the disturbances of the set of equations is used to resolve this problem. This matrix has the sum of squared residuals from each equation in the diagonal positions, and the sum of cross-products of disturbances from different equations in the off-diagonal positions, with each element divided by the sample size. The determinant of the contemporaneous variance–covariance matrix is called the generalized variance. The LI/LGV technique minimizes this generalized variance *subject to* the zero restrictions on the structural parameters in the equation being estimated. The estimates of the reduced-form parameters so obtained may be used to estimate the structural parameters; this can now be done in spite of the over-identification because the over-identifying restrictions are built into the estimates of the reduced-form parameters.

- It might seem more natural to minimize the trace (the sum of the diagonal elements) of the estimated contemporaneous variance–covariance matrix of the reduced-form disturbances rather than its determinant, since that corresponds more closely to the concept of minimizing the sum of squared residuals (i.e., minimizing the trace would minimize the sum of the sum of squared residuals in each equation). This approach has drawbacks, however, as noted in Wonnacott and Wonnacott (1970) pp. 365–71.

- Minimizing the generalized variance would be equivalent to minimizing the sum of squared residuals associated with each individual reduced-form equation (i.e., running GLS on each equation separately) were it not for the restrictions.

- Many simultaneous equation estimating techniques can be interpreted as using instrumental variables for the endogenous variables appearing as regressors. The OLS technique can be thought of as using the endogenous variables themselves as instrumental variables; the 2SLS technique uses as instrumental variables the calculated values of the endogenous variables from the reduced-form estimation. The *k-class estimator* uses an instrumental variable calculated as a weighted average of the instrumental variables used by the OLS and the 2SLS techniques. The weighting factor is k; when $k = 1$ the k-class estimator is identical to 2SLS, and when $k = 0$ it is identical to OLS. When k is equal to the variance ratio from the LI/LVR estimator, the k-class estimator is identical to the LI/ML, LI/LVR and LI/LGV estimators. When the limit of k as the sample size goes to infinity is 1 (as is the variance ratio), the k-class estimator is consistent and has the same asymptotic variance–covariance matrix as the 2SLS, LI/ML, LI/LVR and LI/LGV estimators.

- The *fix-point* and *iterative instrumental variables* methods (see Dutta, 1975, pp. 317–26) are iterative procedures in which initial estimates of the structural parameters are used to create estimates of the endogenous variables, which in turn are used to generate, via an OLS or IV procedure, new estimates of the structural parameters. This process is repeated until convergence is attained. Extensions of these iterative techniques are discussed by Giles (1973) pp. 74–9. Such iterative techniques are of value in estimating very large systems of simultaneous equations.

9.4 Systems Methods

- The systems methods discussed in this chapter assume that disturbances in each individual structural equation are spherical, that disturbances in different time periods in different equations are independent, and that this contemporaneous variance–covariance matrix is the same in each time period. (For cross-sectional data, the reference to 'time period' must be replaced by 'individual' or 'firm' or whatever is relevant.)

- When the errors are distributed normally, the FI/ML method is equivalent to the *full-information, least generalized variance* (FI/LGV) method, the systems counterpart of LI/LGV. In this method, all the reduced-form equations (rather than just those corresponding to the included endogenous variables in a particular equation) are estimated by minimizing the determinant of the estimated contemporaneous variance–covariance matrix of the reduced-form disturbances, subject to the zero restrictions from *all* the structural equations.

- In *simultaneous least squares* (SLS), a method developed by Brown (1960), the weighted trace of the contemporaneous variance–covariance matrix of the reduced-form disturbances is minimized, subject to the zero restrictions on all the structural equations. The weights are the reciprocals of the estimated variances of the associated dependent variables.

- Dhrymes (1973) notes that derived reduced-form estimates may not be asymptotically more efficient than the OLS reduced-form estimates if a limited (rather than a full) information technique is used to estimate the structural parameters; although it does use over-identifying constraints, it does not make use of all the data.

10. Violating Assumption Five: Multicollinearity

10.1 Introduction

The fifth assumption of the CLR model specifies that there are no exact linear relationships between the independent variables and that there are at least as many observations as independent variables. If either half of this assumption is violated, it is mechanically impossible to compute the OLS estimates; i.e., the estimating procedure simply breaks down for mathematical reasons, just as if someone tried to divide by zero.

Both of these phenomena are rare. Most economists recognize that it is impossible to estimate n parameter values with less than n numbers and so ensure that their sample size is larger than the number of parameters they are estimating. In fact, they usually seek out the largest available sample size to ensure that the difference between the sample size and the number of parameters being estimated (this difference is the degrees of freedom) is as large as possible, since the variances of their estimates are usually smaller the larger is the number of degrees of freedom. An exact linear relationship between the independent variables usually occurs only in data that have been constructed by the researcher (an example is given in chapter 13); with care this can be avoided, or the regression problem can be reformulated when the computer rejects the regression run. To have an exact linear relationship in raw data is indeed a fluke.

It is quite possible, however, to have an *approximate* linear relationship among independent variables – in fact, such approximate relationships are very common among economic variables. It is often said in jest that, while one econometrician is regressing a dependent variable on several independent variables in the hopes of finding a strong relationship, another econometrician somewhere else in the world is probably regressing one of those independent variables on some of the other independent variables in the hopes of showing *that* to be a strong linear relationship. Although the estimation procedure does not break down when the independent variables are highly correlated (i.e., approximately linearly related), severe estimation problems arise. *Multicollinearity* is the name given to this phenomenon. Although technically the fifth assumption of the CLR model is violated only in the case of *exact* multicollinearity (an *exact* linear relationship among some of the regressors), the presence of multicollinearity (an *approximate* linear relationship among some of the regressors) leads

146

to estimating problems important enough to warrant our treating it as a violation of the CLR model.

Multicollinearity does not depend on any theoretical or actual linear relationship among any of the regressors; it depends on the existence of an approximate linear relationship in the data set at hand. Unlike most other estimating problems, this problem is caused by the particular sample available. Multicollinearity in the data could arise for several reasons. For example, the independent variables may all share a common time trend, one independent variable might be the lagged value of another that follows a trend, some independent variables may have varied together because the data were not collected from a wide enough base, or there could in fact exist some kind of approximate relationship among some of the regressors. If economists could collect data from controlled experiments, the multicollinearity problem could be eliminated by proper experimental design – the observations on the independent variables would be constructed so as to be orthogonal (the opposite of collinear). Economists are almost never in the position of conducting controlled experiments, however, and thus often must worry about the effects of multicollinearity in their data.

10.2 Consequences

The OLS estimator in the presence of multicollinearity remains unbiased and in fact is still the BLUE. The R^2 statistic is unaffected. In fact, since all the CLR assumptions are (*strictly*) speaking) still met, the OLS estimator retains all its desirable properties as noted in chapter 3. The major undesirable consequence of multicollinearity is that the variances of the OLS estimates of the parameters of the collinear variables are quite large. These high variances arise because in the presence of multicollinearity the OLS estimating procedure is not given enough independent variation in a variable to calculate with confidence the effect it has on the dependent variable. As a result, the consequences of this undesirable feature of the sample are indistinguishable from the consequences of inadequate variability of the regressors in a data set, an interpretation of multicollinearity which has unfortunately not been well understood by practitioners.

Consider the case in which a dependent variable is being regressed on two highly correlated independent variables. Variation in the two regressors can be classified into three types: variation unique to the first regressor, variation unique to the second regressor, and variation common to both. In measuring the effect of the first regressor on the dependent variable (i.e., in estimating its coefficient) only variation in the first regressor unique to that regressor can be used; variation in the first regressor that is shared by the second regressor cannot be used because there would be no way of knowing whether the dependent variable variation was due to variation in the first or in the second variable. The

OLS procedure uses *only* variation unique to the first regrssor in calculating the OLS estimate of the coefficient of the first regressor; it uses only variation unique to the second regressor in calculating the coefficient estimate of the second regressor. For the purpose of calculating coefficient estimates, the common variation is ignored. (It is used, however, for prediction purposes and in calculating R^2.) When the regressors are highly correlated, most of their variation is common to both variables, leaving little variation unique to each variable. This means that the OLS procedure has little information to use in making its coefficient estimates, just as though it had a very small sample size, or a sample in which the independent variable did not vary much. Any estimate based on little information cannot be held with much confidence – it will have a high variance. The higher the correlation between the independent variables (the more severe the multicollinearity), the less information used by the OLS estimator to calculate the parameter estimates and thus the greater the variances.

As another way of looking at this, consider the information that was cast aside. It consists of variation in the dependent variable explained by common variation in the two regressors. If this common explanation were known to be due to one regressor rather than the other, the estimate of the two regressors' coefficients might have to be considerably changed. But the allocation of this common explanation between the two regressors is unknown. It is this uncertainty as to which variable deserves the credit for the jointly explained variation in the dependent variable that creates the uncertainty as to the true values of the coefficients being estimated and thus causes the higher variances of their estimates.

Having high variances means that the parameter estimates are not precise (they do not provide the researcher with reliable estimates of the parameters) and hypothesis testing is not powerful (diverse hypotheses about the parameter values cannot be rejected). As an example of this, consider the case illustrated in Fig. 10.1. The confidence ellipse (recall section 4.3) for the two parameter estimates is long, narrow and tilted, reflecting the collinearity in the regressors. If the influence on the dependent variable of the common variation is in fact due to the first regressor, β_1 will be large and β_2 small, implying a true parameter value set in the lower right of the ellipse. If it is due to the second regressor, β_2 will be large and β_1 small, implying a true parameter value set in the upper left of the confidence ellipse. There is a high (negative) covariance between the two estimators. In Fig. 10.1 the ellipse covers part of the vertical axis and part of the horizontal axis, implying that the individual hypothesis $\beta_1 = 0$ cannot be rejected and the individual hypothesis $\beta_2 = 0$ cannot be rejected. But the ellipse does not cover the origin, so that the joint hypothesis that both β_1 and β_2 are zero is rejected. Although the researcher knows that at least one of these variables is relevant, the correct specification is difficult to determine without sound guidance from economic theory. Thus a

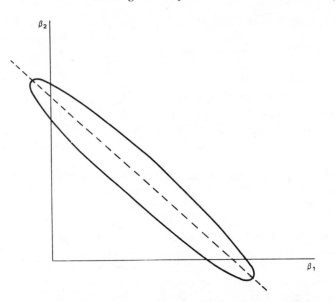

Fig. 10.1   High negative covariance arising from collinearity

second consequence of multicollinearity is that it can easily lead to specification errors (which in this context is quite serious since the parameter estimates are very sensitive to the model specification).

10.3   Detecting Multicollinearity

Much controversy has surrounded the question of detecting the existence of multicollinearity. One reason for this is that many of the detection methods suggested are inadequate and have justifiably been criticized. But there exists a far more important reason. The only remedy for undesirably high variances is somehow to incorporate additional information in the estimating procedure. This remedy is the same regardless of whether these undesirably high variances were caused by multicollinearity or inadequate variation of the regressors in the data set. If it doesn't make any difference whether high variances of coefficient estimates are due to collinearity or to inadequate variability in the data, why bother trying to detect multicollinearity? This is an awkward question. The usual response is that, through efforts to detect the existence of multicollinearity, a researcher may be led to consider explicitly extra information that will be more likely (than other kinds of extra information) to reduce the variances in question. On the other hand, he/she for this same reason may be led more quickly to incorporate false information. This perspective is important to keep in mind whenever employing methods for detecting multicollinearity.

It is common for researchers to claim that multicollinearity is at work whenever their hypothesized signs are not found in the regression results, when variables that they know *a priori* to be important have insignificant *t* values, or when various regression results are changed substantively whenever an explanatory variable is deleted. Unfortunately, none of these conditions is either necessary or sufficient for the existence of collinearity, and furthermore none provides any useful suggestions as to what kind of extra information might be required to solve the estimation problem they represent.

Another popular means of detecting multicollinearity is through the use of the correlation matrix. Computer printouts of most regression packages include a matrix of simple correlation coefficients between all pairs of the independent variables. The off-diagonal elements contain the simple correlation coefficients for the given data set; the diagonal elements are all unity since each variable is perfectly correlated with itself. A high value (about 0.8 or 0.9 in absolute value) of one of these correlation coefficients indicates high correlation between the two independent variables to which it refers. This method does detect collinearity between two specific variables and thus can suggest what kind of extra information (e.g., that one of these variables' coefficients is zero) might be most useful in solving the problem; but it does not allow detection of a case in which three or more variables are collinear with no two taken alone exhibiting high correlation.

A less common, but more satisfactory, way of detecting multicollinearity is through the use of the *condition indices* of the data matrix. These numbers are given by the eigenvalues of the matrix $X'X$, where X is the data matrix, divided into the largest eigenvalue. A high index reflects the presence of collinearity.

10.4   What to Do

There are two basic options for researchers faced with multicollinearity.

(1) *Do nothing*

The existence of multicollinearity in a data set does not necessarily mean that the coefficient estimates in which the researcher is interested have unacceptably high variances. The classic example of this is estimation of the Cobb–Douglas production function: the inputs capital and labour are highly collinear, but none the less good estimates are obtained. This has led to the rule of thumb, 'Don't worry about multicollinearity if the R^2 from the regression exceeds the R^2 of any independent variable regressed on the other independent variables.' Another rule of thumb sometimes used is 'Don't worry about multicollinearity if the *t* statistics are all greater than 2.'

A second reason for following a course of inaction can be illustrated by Fig. 10.1. It should be clear from this diagram that, although the variances of the estimates of β_1 and β_2 are high, the variance of an estimate of the linear combination of β_1 and β_2 given by the dashed line is low. Consequently, if the researcher's interest centres on this linear combination, the multicollinearity need not be of concern. This might happen, for example, if the estimated equation is to be used for prediction purposes and the multicollinearity pattern is expected to prevail in the situations to be predicted.

(2) *Incorporate additional information*

This remedy can be discussed under several headings.

(a) *Obtain more data*   Because the multicollinearity problem is essentially a data problem, additional data that do not contain the multicollinearity feature could solve the problem. Even getting additional data with the same multicollinearity character would help, since a larger sample size would provide some additional information, helping to reduce variances.

(b) *Formalize relationships among regressors*   If it is believed that the multicollinearity arises not from an unfortunate data set but from an actual approximate linear relationship among some of the regressors, this relationship could be formalized and the estimation could then proceed in the context of a simultaneous equation estimation problem.

(c) *Specify a relationship among some parameters*   Economic theory may suggest that two parameters should be equal, that the sum of several elasticities should be unity, or, in general, that there exists a specific relationship among some of the parameters in the estimating equation. Incorporation of this information, via methods discussed in chapter 11, will reduce the variances of the estimates. As an example, consider specifying that the coefficients of a lag structure take the form of a Koyck distributed lag (i.e., they decline geometrically), as discussed in section 8.3.

(d) *Drop a variable*   A popular means of avoiding the multicollinearity problem is by simply omitting one of the collinear variables. If the true coefficient of that variable in the equation being estimated is zero, this is a correct move. If the true coefficient of that variable is *not* zero, however, a specification error is created. As noted in section 5.2, omitting a relevant variable causes estimates of the parameters of the remaining variables to be biased (unless some of these remaining variables are uncorrelated with the omitted variable, in which case their parameter estimates remain unbiased). The real question here is whether, by dropping a variable, the econometrician can reduce the variance of the remaining estimates by enough to compensate for this bias introduced. This suggests the use of the MSE criterion in undertaking a decision to drop a variable. This approach should not be adopted cavalierly, since, as noted by Drèze (1983, p. 296), 'setting a coefficient equal to zero because it is estimated with poor precision amounts to elevating ignorance to arrogance.'

(e) *Incorporate estimates from other studies*   If an extraneous estimate of the coefficient of one of the variables involved in the multicollinearity is available, it can be used, via the mixed estimation technique described in chapter 11, to alleviate the high variance problem occasioned by the multicollinearity. If this is done, however, care must be taken to ensure that the extraneous estimate is relevant. For example, estimates from cross-sectional studies are often used to alleviate time-series multicol-linearity, but cross-section estimates relate to the long-run version of many parameters, rather than the short-run version relevant for time-series studies.

(f) *Form a principal component*   The variables that are collinear could be grouped together to form a composite index capable of representing this group of variables by itself. Such a composite variable should be created only if the variables included in the composite have some useful combined economic interpretation, otherwise the empirical results will have little meaning. For example, in undertaking a study of the effect of marketing activity on consumer demand, a researcher might find that variables representing different dimensions of marketing activity are highly col-linear; some combination of these variables could readily be interpreted as a 'marketing variable' and its use in the model would not confuse the meaning of the empirical results. The most popular way of constructing such a composite index is to use the first principal component of the variables in question.

(g) *Shrink the OLS estimates*   By shrinking the OLS estimates towards the zero vector, a researcher may be able to reduce the risk (the sum of the MSEs of each individual parameter estimate) of the estimates. Implicitly, this is equivalent to incorporating the *ad hoc* stochastic prior information that the true β is close to the zero vector. The two most popular means of doing this are the ridge estimator and the Stein estimator.

General Notes

10.2   Consequences

- Leamer (1983b) pp. 300–3 stresses the fact that collinearity as a cause of weak evidence (high variances) is indistinguishable from inadequate data variability as a cause of weak evidence.

- The Ballentine portrays the multicollinearity phenomenon succinctly. Consider Fig. 3.2, in the general notes to chapter 3. Multicollinearity is reflected by a large overlap between the X and Z circles. This could create a large red area at the expense of the blue or green areas. These blue and green areas reflect the information used to estimate β_x and β_z; since less information is used, the variances of these parameter estimates are larger.

- In addition to creating high variances of coefficient estimates, multicollinearity has the related undesirable property that calculations based on the data matrix are unstable in that slight variations in the data matrix, such as addition or deletion of an observation, lead to large changes in parameter estimates. An example of this is provided in Beaton *et al.* (1976), who perturb a set of collinear data by adding random numbers between -0.5 and $+0.5$ (i.e., they have added a rounding error beyond the last published digit). These small perturbations change drastically most parameter estimates. Incorporating additional information into the estimation procedure tends to stabilize estimates in this respect, as well as reducing variances.

10.3 Detecting Multicollinearity

- The use of condition indices for the detection of multicollinearity is advocated in persuasive fashion by Belsley *et al.* (1980) chapter 3. As a rule of thumb, a condition index greater than 30 indicates strong collinearity.

- The inverse of the correlation matrix is also used in detecting multicollinearity. The diagonal elements of this matrix are called variance inflation factors, VIF_i. They are given by $(1 - R_i^2)^{-1}$ where R_i^2 is the R^2 from regressing the ith independent variable on all the other independent variables. A high VIF indicates an R_i^2 near unity and hence suggests collinearity. As a rule of thumb, for standardized data a $VIF_i > 10$ indicates harmful collinearity.

- Multicollinearity detection methods suggested by Farrar and Glauber (1967) have become undeservedly popular. For a summary of the critiques of these methods, see Belsley *et al.* (1980) pp. 93–5.

- Belsley (1984b) notes that centring data (expressing them as deviations from their means) can produce meaningless and misleading collinearity diagnostics.

10.4 What to Do

- The do-nothing approach is supported by Conlisk (1971), who shows that multicollinearity can be advantageous in several special circumstances. He gives examples of estimation of a linear combination of the parameters, estimation of the intercept, estimation in the presence of certain kinds of *a priori* information, estimation when there are unequal costs associated with different observations, and estimation in the context of autocorrelated residuals.

- It must be stressed that the incorporation-of-additional-information approach will 'solve' the multicollinearity problem (in the sense of generating a lower MSE) only if the extra information is 'close' to being correct. This is discussed at length in chapter 11.

- Silvey (1969) discusses the nature of additional data that would be most useful in resolving the multicollinearity problem.

- The discussion in the body of this chapter of solving multicollinearity by dropping a variable is a special case of the more general problem of testing any linear restriction to see whether or not adding that restriction will reduce MSE. See Toro-Vizcarrondo and Wallace (1968). It is a kind of pretest estimator, discussed in chapter 11.

- Feldstein (1973) suggests using a weighted average of the estimates obtained with and without dropping a variable, where the weights, chosen to minimize MSE, involve the value of the t statistic used to test whether or not that variable's coefficient is significantly different from zero. This principle is similar to that underlying the Stein estimator, discussed in chapter 11.

- The problem of high variances could be solved by adding (rather than dropping) a variable. Adding a variable that was incorrectly excluded could markedly reduce the estimate of the error variance, which implies lower estimated variances of all coefficient estimates.

- Kuh and Meyer (1957) discuss problems associated with the use of extraneous estimates to avoid multicollinearity. See also Adams (1965) and Baltagi and Griffin (1984).

- The first principal component of a set of variables is a weighted average of the variables in which the weights are chosen to make the composite variable reflect the maximum possible proportion of the total variation in the set. Additional principal components can be calculated (i.e., the second principal component is orthogonal to the first and uses weights designed to incorporate within it the maximum possible proportion of the remaining variation in the original variables), but the first principal component usually captures enough of the variation in the set to be an adequate representative of that set on its own.

- The principal components technique as described in the body of this chapter is not the usual way in which it is advocated. If there are J explanatory variables, then J principal components can be constructed, each orthogonal to the others. If the regression is run on some of these J principal components, rather than on the original J variables, the results of this regression can be transformed to provide estimates $\hat{\beta}$ of the coefficients β of the original variables. If all J principal components are used, the resulting $\hat{\beta}$ is identical to the $\hat{\beta}$ obtained by regressing on the original, collinear data: nothing is gained. The rationale of the principal components method is not to include all of the principal components in the preliminary stage; by dropping some of the principal components, this method produces different estimates of β, with smaller variances. The reduction in variances occurs because implicitly this technique incorporates the extra information that particular linear combinations of the original regressors (namely the dropped principal components) are zero. Alternatively, this could be viewed as specifying (assuming) that the approximate linear relationship(s) among the regressors that cause(s) the multicollinearity is (are) exact. For discussion see Judge *et al.* (1985) pp. 909–12. For an instructive example of an application of this technique, see Sanint (1982).

- The ridge estimator is given by the formula

$$(X'X + kI)^{-1} X'Y = (X'X + kI)^{-1} X'X \beta^{OLS}$$

where k is a non-negative number and in a more general formulation can be a diagonal matrix. For $k = 0$ the ridge estimator is identical to the OLS estimator. As k becomes more and more positive, β^{OLS} is shrunk more and more towards the zero vector. The rationale behind the ridge estimator is that there exists a number k such that the MSE of the ridge estimator is less than the MSE of β^{OLS}.

Unfortunately, this k value is not known: it depends on the unknown parameters of the model in question, namely that k is less than $2\sigma^2\ \beta'\beta$. A wide variety of different methods of selecting k have been suggested, all using the sample data. This produces a stochastic k, implying that the existence of an MSE-reducing, non-stochastic k is no longer relevant. In particular, it is in the presence of multicollinearity that it is difficult to use the data to obtain an accurate estimate of k, implying that the ridge estimator is not likely to offer much improvement on β^{OLS} in the presence of multicollinearity. Fomby *et al.* (1984) pp. 300–2 have a concise exposition of this.

- There exists a plethora of Monte Carlo studies examining the relative merits of different ways of choosing k to operationalize the ridge estimator. For a critical review of many of these studies, see Draper and Van Nostrand (1979), who conclude (p. 464) that 'The extended inference that ridge regression is "always" better than least squares is, typically, completely unjustified.' This conclusion is not shared by all, however – see for example Lin and Kmenta (1982). Ridge regression is in fact a topic of considerable debate. Vinod and Ullah (1981) chapter 7 are proponents, Draper and Van Nostrand (1979) are opponents, and Judge *et al.* (1980) pp. 471–87 fall in between. Smith and Campbell (1980) and ensuing discussion illustrates some facets of this debate.

- The ridge estimator can be viewed as the OLS estimator incorporating the stochastic constraint that β is the zero vector. The extent of the shrinking towards the zero vector (the magnitude of k) depends on the 'variance' of this additional information that β is 'close' to the zero vector. In a Bayesian interpretation (see chapter 12) the extent of the shrinking depends on the confidence with which it is believed that β is the zero vector. Why should a researcher be prepared to incorporate this particular extra information? Vinod and Ullah (1981) p. 187 offer the justification that 'In the absence of specific prior knowledge it is often scientifically conservative to shrink toward the zero vector.' On the other hand, Judge *et al.* (1980) p. 494 comment that 'These estimators work by shrinking coefficients ... toward zero. This is clearly a desperation measure.'

- A concise exposition of the use of the Stein estimator in the context of multicollinearity can be found in Hill *et al.* (1981) and Mittelhammer and Young (1981). This estimator, discussed in chapter 11, is in essence a weighted average of the OLS estimates with and without extra information, where the weights are determined by the value of the F statistic used for testing the validity of the extra information. Although in some types of problems this guarantees an improvement in risk (MSE), in the regression context the Stein estimator dominates the OLS estimator only if $tr(X'X)^{-1} > 2d_L$ where d_L is the largest characteristic root of $(X'X)^{-1}$. Unfortunately, the presence of multicollinearity is likely to cause this condition not to hold. For discussion see Hill and Ziemer (1984, 1982) and for examples with economic data see Aigner and Judge (1977).

- Like the ridge estimator, the Stein estimator can be given a Bayesian interpretation; if the stochastic prior for β is chosen to be the zero vector, the ridge and Stein estimators differ only in that implicitly they use different variance–covariance matrices for this prior vector. Unlike the ridge estimator, however, the Stein estimator is commonly used for problems not involving multicollinearity and so the choice of a nonzero prior vector is more readily considered. For example, a principal components estimate of β could be chosen as the extra information to serve as the prior vector.

- A drawback of addressing multicollinearity by using ridge, Stein or pretest estimators is that these estimators have unknown distributions so that hypothesis testing cannot be undertaken.

Technical Notes

- The variance of a parameter estimate β_k^{OLS} is given by Stone (1945) as

$$\frac{1}{T - K} \frac{\sigma_y^2}{\sigma_k^2} \frac{1 - R^2}{1 - R_k^2}$$

where σ_y^2 is the variance of the dependent variable, σ_k^2 is the variance of the kth independent variable and R_k^2 is the R^2 from a regression of the kth independent variable on all the other independent variables. This formula shows that

(a) the variance of β_k^{OLS} decreases as the kth independent variable ranges more widely (σ_k^2 higher);

(b) the variance of β_k^{OLS} increases as the independent variables become more collinear (R_k^2 higher) and becomes infinite in the case of exact multicollinearity;

(c) the variance of β_k^{OLS} decreases as R^2 rises, so that the effect of a high R_k^2 can be offset by a high R^2.

11. Incorporating Extraneous Information

11.1 Introduction

Economic data are not easy to deal with. For example, they are frequently characterized by multicollinearity, and seldom is the correct specification known. Because of problems like these, econometric estimates often lack efficiency. If extraneous (*a priori*) information, available from economic theory or previous studies, can be incorporated into the estimation procedure, efficiency can be improved. This is the case even if the extraneous information employed is incorrect (as it often is): more information cannot help but reduce variance. But incorrect extraneous information creates bias, so trading off variance and bias (usually through the MSE criterion) becomes a question of central importance in this context.

The purpose of this chapter is to describe a variety of ways in which extraneous information can play a role in improving parameter estimates. The discussion of this chapter is entirely in the classical mould. Bayesians claim that the most logical and consistent way of incorporating extraneous information is through the use of Bayes' theorem; the Bayesian approach is discussed at length in chapter 12.

11.2 Exact Restrictions

The extraneous information might take the form of an exact restriction involving some of the parameters to be estimated. For example, economic theory might suggest that the sum of a number of propensities is equal to 1, or that the value of one parameter is twice the value of another. If this restriction is linear it can be used to eliminate mathematically one parameter, and a new estimating equation can be constructed with fewer parameters and fewer independent variables. (These new independent variables are linear combinations of the original independent variables.) The parameter estimates of the new estimating equation can be used to create estimates of the original parameters.

This method is analytically equivalent to restricted least squares, a technique in which the sum of squared error terms is minimized subject to the extraneous information restriction. The resulting estimator can be shown to be the BLUE in the CLR model extended to include the extraneous information. If the extraneous information restriction is non-linear (for example, that the product of two parameters is equal to a third parameter), computer-assisted numerical techniques similar to those used for nonlinear least squares must be used to minimize the sum of squared residuals subject to the nonlinear constraint.

11.3 Stochastic Restrictions

Another form of extraneous information is a stochastic restriction, the most common example of which is an estimate of a parameter from a previous study. Such restrictions must be written with an error term, so that, for example, an extraneous unbiased estimate $\hat{\beta}_k$ of β_k must be written as

$$\hat{\beta}_k = \beta_k + v$$

where v is an error term (with variance equal to the variance of $\hat{\beta}_k$). This information is incorporated into the estimation procedure by interpreting the stochastic restriction as an extra sample observation. In the example of $\hat{\beta}_k$, the extra observation consists of a value of 1 for the kth independent variable, zero values for all the other independent variables, and a value of $\hat{\beta}_k$ for the dependent variable. The variance of the error term (v) associated with this extra 'observation' is the variance of $\hat{\beta}_k$ and is *not* equal to the variance of the error terms associated with the regular sample observations. Thus GLS, not OLS, should be applied to this 'augmented' sample to produce an efficient estimate. This technique is called the *mixed estimator* because it mixes stochastic sample and stochastic prior information.

11.4 Pre-test Estimators

Our discussion of extraneous information so far has assumed that the information employed is correct when in general it is often the case that this is not known with certainty. In actual applications, a common practice is to test information for its validity, before estimation; if the hypothesis that the information/restriction is true is accepted, the restricted OLS estimator is used, and if this hypothesis is rejected, the unrestricted OLS estimator is used. This methodology defines what is called a pre-test estimator: an estimator of an unknown parameter is chosen on the basis of the outcome of a pre-test.

To illustrate the nature of pre-test estimators and their implications, consider the following popular example. Suppose a researcher is uncertain whether or not the variable z should be included as a regressor and consequently decides to include/exclude z on the basis of a t test at, say, the 5% level. Two cases must be examined.

(a) *z is in fact irrelevant.* In this case the t test will correctly exclude z in repeated samples 95% of the time. But 5% of the time it will incorrectly be included, so that in 5% of the repeated samples the OLS estimator used will not have its desirable properties, implying that, *overall*, these desirable properties in repeated samples do not characterize the pre-test estimator. In this case, if z is not orthogonal to the other regressors, the variance of the pre-test estimator of the other slope coefficients will be higher than if z were omitted without testing. No bias is created.

(b) *z is in fact relevant.* In this case the t test will correctly include z a percentage of times equal to the power P of the test, a percentage that becomes greater and greater as the slope coefficient of z becomes more and more different from zero. But $(100 - P)\%$ of the time z will be incorrectly excluded, so that in $(100 - P)\%$ of repeated samples the OLS estimator used will not have its desirable properties. Once again, *overall*, this pre-test estimator will not have the desirable properties of the appropriate OLS estimator. In this case the pre-test estimator exhibits bias.

This failure of the pre-test estimator to achieve the properties of the OLS estimator using the correct specification is called *pre-test bias*. One of its major implications is that the traditional hypothesis-testing methodology, which depends on an estimator having certain properties in repeated samples, is now much more complicated; traditional formulae, such as the traditional formula for the standard error, cannot be used, and the correct measures are difficult to calculate.

The most dramatic implication of the pre-test bias phenomenon occurs when econometricians use sequential or 'stepwise' testing procedures (sometimes called 'data mining'), in which a large number of different hypotheses are tested to select a relatively small set of independent variables out of a much larger set of potential independent variables, greatly increasing the probability of adopting, by chance, an incorrect set of independent variables. This problem has been exacerbated by the advent of the computer. There is an unfortunate tendency among econometricians to do more computing than thinking when model-building; the pre-test bias phenomenon is sometimes described by the phrase, 'Compute first and think afterwards.'

Most econometricians ignore the pre-test bias problem; in fact, few even admit its existence. The main counter-argument to pre-test bias is that without pre-testing we must rely on an *assumption* concerning what variables are included in the set of independent variables. Is the probability that pre-testing yields an incorrect set of independent variables greater than or less than the probability that the econometrician has selected the 'correct' assumption? Pre-testing is simply a means of providing additional evidence to aid the econometrician in selecting the appropriate set of independent variables. So long as the econometrician views this as evidence to be evaluated sensibly in light of other considerations (such as economic theory), rather than as a mechanical procedure, pre-test bias should not be of great concern. A more cogent counter-argument is to note that an examination of the mean square error (MSE) properties of the pre-test estimator, relative to its competitors, needs to been undertaken to determine how serious this problem is. The next section examines this question.

11.5   Extraneous Information and MSE

If extraneous information is incorrect, an estimator incorporating this information, or a pre-test estimator that sometimes (in repeated samples) incorporates this information, will be biased. This complicates the decision to incorporate extraneous information because the reduction in variance from its incorporation might be more than offset by the bias introduced. As is usual when faced with such a trade-off, econometricians turn to the mean square error (MSE) criterion.

Risk functions, portrayed in Fig. 11.1, can be used to show the MSE associated with relevant estimators in the context of some set of restrictions. The vertical axis measures *risk*, the sum of the MSEs of the estimators of each element of the parameter vector. The horizontal axis measures the extent to which the restrictions are *not* met i.e., the degree of "falsity" of the extraneous information.

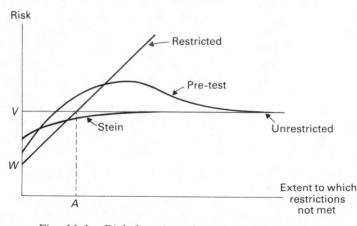

Fig. 11.1   Risk functions for selected estimators

Recall that MSE can be broken into the sum of the variance and the square of the bias. The unrestricted OLS estimator has zero bias and a constant variance regardless of the truth of the restrictions, so its risk function is drawn as a horizontal line at V, where V is the sum of the variances of the unrestricted OLS estimators of the elements of the parameter vector. The restricted OLS estimator has a smaller variance than the unrestricted OLS estimator, and, when the restriction is true, also has no bias. Thus, when the restriction is true (i.e., at the vertical axis in Fig. 11.1), the risk of the restricted OLS estimator is lower than V, say W. As the restriction becomes more and more false, the restricted estimator retains its small variance but suffers a greater and greater bias; reflecting this, the risk function for the restricted OLS estimator slopes upward.

Consider now the pre-test estimator. When the restrictions are true it has no bias, and, being a mixture of the restricted and unrestricted OLS estimators, it has a variance between the variances of these two estimators. Thus its risk function cuts the vertical axis between V and W. When the restrictions are far from true, the pre-test estimator should almost always correctly reject the restrictions so that the risk of the pre-test estimator should be virtually the same as the risk of the unrestricted OLS estimator. This is shown in Fig. 11.1 by the risk function of the pre-test estimator approaching asymptotically the risk function of the unrestricted OLS estimator.

The pre-test estimator performs reasonably well when the restrictions are either very close to being met or quite far from being met. In between, however, as illustrated in Fig. 11.1, it does not do so well. The reason for this is that in this intermediate position the pre-test does not invariably accept or invariably reject; the percentage of times in repeated samples that it accepts the restrictions is substantial, as is the percentage of times that it rejects those restrictions. The estimates produced when it (correctly) rejects are distributed around the true unknown parameter value, but the estimates produced when it (incorrectly) accepts are biased and thus are distributed around some other unknown parameter value. Consequently, *overall*, both bias and a larger variance are created.

The explanation of the preceding paragraph suggests that the undesirable risk properties of the pre-test estimator stem from its dichotomous nature, namely the fact that it jumps between the unrestricted OLS formula to the restricted OLS formula. An ingenious alternative to the pre-test estimator that avoids this problem, yet still retains the flavour of the pre-test concept, is to use as an estimator a weighted average of the restricted and unrestricted OLS estimators, with the weights a function of the magnitude of the F statistic used to test the restrictions. This is the essence of the *Stein estimator*. The success of this principle is reflected in Fig. 11.1 by the risk function of the Stein estimator. Note that it lies everywhere below the risk function of the unrestricted OLS estimator (i.e., it dominates the unrestricted OLS estimator), a result which astounded the statistics world when it was first derived.

General Notes

11.1 Introduction

- Not all forms of extraneous information are discussed here. For example, information concerning the variance–covariance matrix of the disturbance can clearly be incorporated directly into GLS estimation. The role of information in the form of identifying restrictions for simultaneous equations was discussed in chapter 9.

- As an example of how incorrect information can reduce variance, suppose the incorrect information that $\beta = 6.5$ is employed. Then $\hat{\beta}_R$, the estimate of β incorporating this information, is $\hat{\beta}_R = 6.5$, ignoring the data. The variance of this estimate is clearly zero, the smallest possible variance.

- It is an overstatement to claim that the introduction of extraneous information must reduce variance. It is possible to create examples in which this is not the case. Such examples rely on interaction of incorrect information with another incorrect feature of the analysis. For example, Taylor (1976) shows that extraneous information can worsen estimates if the econometrician assumes that the variance–covariance matrix of the disturbance is spherical when it in fact is not. Rothenberg (1973) p. 57 gives an example in which using the MSE criterion in conjunction with inequality constraints produces a worse estimate than if the constraints had been ignored.

- The problem of estimating *distributed lags* is one in which extraneous information plays a prominent role. For a variety of reasons (summarized nicely by Judge *et al.* (1980) pp. 623–9), economic relationships can be expected to be such that lagged values of the explanatory variable(s) appear as regressors. Although none of the CLR model assumptions is violated, so that OLS is an appropriate estimating procedure, invariably lagged values of an explanatory variable are highly collinear, causing the OLS estimates to have high variances. (If the lags are long, the resulting loss in degrees of freedom exacerbates this problem.) Any of the techniques suggested for addressing the multicollinearity problem (discussed in chapter 10) could be used here, but by far the most popular method employed in this context is the incorporation of extraneous information by specifying a *lag distribution*.

  A lag distribution function gives the magnitude of the coefficient of a lagged explanatory variable, expressed as a function of the lag. By specifying that this function takes a particular form, extra information is injected into the estimation procedure. A wide variety of specifications have been suggested for this purpose, some examples of which are the arithmetic, inverted V, Almon, Shiller, harmonic, geometric, Pascal, rational, gamma and exponential. For a concise summary, see Judge *et al.* (1980) p. 631.

  Lag distributions are characterized as finite or infinite, depending on the time required for the lag effect to vanish completely. The most popular finite lag distribution is the *Almon polynomial lag distribution*. In this technique the n coefficients of the lagged explanatory variables are assumed to lie on a polynomial (i.e., a function of the lag length) of order r. This allows for a flexible lag structure with a reduction in the number of parameters that require estimation if r is less than n. It can be viewed as imposing a specific set of linear constraints on OLS estimation. *Shiller's distributed lag* is a variant of this in which these restrictions are stochastic, incorporated via the mixed estimation technique; the coefficients of the lagged explanatory variable lie close to, rather than on, a polynomial. The main problem with the Almon lag is determining n and r. Pre-testing is usually employed for this purpose, resulting in estimators with unknown properties.

The most popular infinite lag distribution is the *Koyck geometric distributed lag*. Earlier discussion of this technique (chapter 8) showed that it could be estimated by an autoregressive model with an autocorrelated error. One disadvantage of this lag structure is that the coefficients of the lagged explanatory variable(s) continually decline – they cannot first rise and then decline, a pattern thought by many to be *a priori* attractive and one which should not be ruled out of consideration. One way of addressing this problem is to allow unrestricted coefficients on the first few lagged variables and then impose the geometric pattern. Two generalizations of the geometric lag, the *Pascal* and the *rational* lags, discussed briefly in the technical notes, can also be used to provide a more flexible structure in this regard.

Good textbook presentations of distributed lags and their associated estimation problems are Judge *et al.* (1985) chapters 9 and 10, and Maddala (1977) chapter 16.

11.2 Exact Restrictions

- An example can illustrate how a restricted least squares estimate is found when the restriction is linear. Suppose $y = \alpha + \beta x + \gamma z + \varepsilon$ and it is known that $3\beta + \gamma = 1$. Substituting $\gamma = 1 - 3\beta$ into this equation and rearranging produces the relationship $(y - z) = \alpha + \beta(x - 3z) + \varepsilon$. The restricted OLS estimates $\hat{\alpha}_R$ and $\hat{\beta}_R$ are found by regressing $(y - z)$ on a constant and $(x - 3z)$; then $\hat{\gamma}_R$ is computed as $1 - 3\hat{\beta}_R$. The sum of squared errors resulting from this regression is the restricted sum of squared errors.

- An exact linear restriction is tested using the traditional F test, as expounded in chapter 4, in which the difference between the restricted and unrestricted sum of squared errors plays a prominent role.

- Many computer regression packages cannot be run without an intercept term. Consequently, to incorporate the information that the intercept is zero, the computer must be tricked. Hawkins (1980) and Casella (1983) have useful suggestions.

- As an example of a nonlinear restriction, recall Durbin's two-stage method of dealing with autocorrelated errors. In the technical notes to section 7.2, the first stage estimating relationship is shown to be such that one slope coefficient is the negative of the product of two other slope coefficients.

- Economic theory sometimes suggests inequality restrictions, such as that a parameter be negative or that it lie between zero and one. By minimizing the sum of squared errors subject to the inequality constraint(s), these restrictions can be incorporated. Unfortunately, it is not possible to accomplish this via a regression technique; a quadratic programming formulation of this problem is required. For an exposition, see Judge *et al.* (1985) pp. 62–4. For large samples, when the variance of the parameter estimates can be expected to be quite small, (correct) inequality constraints are invariably met, and thus little is lost by ignoring them.

11.3   Stochastic Restrictions

- The mixed estimation method was developed in its most general form by Theil and Goldberger (1961). They expressed the set of stochastic linear restrictions in the form $r = R\beta + u$ where r is a known vector and R a known matrix. This generalized the technique of Durbin (1953), in which r is a vector of parameter estimates from a previous study and R is an identity matrix. As makes intuitive sense, the mixed estimator approaches the restricted OLS estimator as the variance of u approaches zero, and approaches the unrestricted OLS estimator as the variance of u becomes very large. Srivastava (1980) is an annotated bibliography of estimation using stochastic constraints.

- A popular way of incorporating a stochastic restriction is to assume that it is an exact restriction. Suppose for example that an extraneous estimate $\hat{\beta}_k$ of β_k is available. A popular way of utilizing this information is to subtract $\hat{\beta}_k$ times the kth independent variable from the dependent variable and then regress this new dependent variable on the remaining independent variables. The obvious deficiency of this method is that it does not use the sample data to improve on the estimate of β_k. It is therefore not as efficient as the mixed estimator. This is explained in the technical notes to this section.

- The stochastic restrictions of the mixed estimator could be developed and interpreted in subjective fashion as is done in the Bayesian approach (see chapter 12). This creates a means of introducing subjective prior information into classical statistics, although, as should be clear from a reading of chapter 12, this requires a schizophrenic view of probability.

- The compatability statistic developed by Theil (1963) is the means usually employed to test whether or not stochastic extraneous information is unbiased; i.e., it tests whether or not the stochastic restrictions are compatible with the data at hand. It is a straightforward application of the Wald statistic, very similar in form and interpretation to the Wald statistic discussed in the technical notes to section 5.40. There a Wald statistic was used to test for the equality of parameters in two data sets when the variance of the error term differed between the two data sets.

11.4   Pre-test Estimators

- The literature in the area of pre-test bias is difficult. Exceptions are Wallace and Ashar (1972) and Wallace (1977).

- A straightforward corollary of the pre-test bias phenomenon is the fact that researchers should not use the same sample evidence for both generating a hypothesis and testing it.

- The terminology 'data mining' is often used in the context of pre-test bias. In particular, researchers often run a large number of different regressions on a body of data looking for significant t statistics (at, say, the 5% level). Using this approach invalidates traditional hypothesis-testing procedures because such data mining is likely by chance to uncover significant t statistics; i.e., the final results chosen are much more likely to embody a type I error than the claimed 5%. Lovell (1983) offers a rule of thumb for deflating the exaggerated claims of significance generated by such data-mining procedures: when search has been conducted for the best k out of c candidate explanatory variables, a regression coefficient that appears to be significant at the level $\hat{\alpha}$ should be regarded as significant at only level $\alpha = (c/k)\,\hat{\alpha}$.

- The pre-testing phenomenon can arise in a variety of contexts. Some recent Monte Carlo studies are King and Giles (1984) and Griffiths and Beesley (1984), who examine pre-testing for autocorrelated errors, and Morey (1984), who examines pre-testing for specification error. Zaman (1984) conjectures that discontinuous functions of the data (such as pre-test estimators which jump from one estimator to another on the basis of a pre-test) are inadmissable, and that consequently shrinkage or weighted-average estimators like the Stein estimator are superior.

11.5   Extraneous Information and MSE

- Judge *et al.* (1985) pp. 72–90 and Fomby *et al.* (1984) chapter 7 have textbook discussions of pre-test and Stein estimators. Efron and Morris (1977) have an interesting elementary presentation of the Stein estimator. Judge and Bock (1978) pp. 309–11 has an excellent summary of the properties of pre-test and Stein rule estimators.

- Stein-type estimators do have disadvantages. They have unknown small-sample distributions and thus cannot be used to test hypotheses or construct confidence intervals. They assume that the errors are distributed normally. As noted in the general notes to chapter 10, in the regression context they dominate OLS only under certain circumstances, unlikely to be met by collinear data. And last, the loss function with respect to which they are superior is the sum of the MSEs of the estimators of the individual components of the parameter vector, and depends on there being at least three of these components. Nothing can be said about possible improvement of the MSE of the estimator of any individual component.

- The last point made above can be illustrated by an example from Efron and Morris (1977). Suppose we have data on the incidence of a disease in several regions of a small country. The unrestricted OLS estimate of the unknown true incidence for each region is given by the mean of the data for each region. But although the incidence of disease is likely to differ from region to region, the facts that these regions belong to the same country, and are or are close to being contiguous, suggest that these incidence parameters may all be very similar. A not unreasonable restriction to suggest in this context, then, is that all the incidences are identical. Using this restriction, a Stein estimate of the incidence for each region can be created, accomplished by 'shrinking' each unrestricted OLS estimate above towards the overall mean of the data. Now suppose the national government plans to set up medical facilities in each region to combat this disease, and wants to use the estimates of regional disease incidence to determine how much of its budget it should allocate to each region. In this case the sum of the individual MSEs is the relevant criterion and the Stein estimates should be used for this purpose. If, however, a regional government is making a decision of how much money to spend on its own medical facility, only one MSE is relevant, and the Stein estimator may not be the best one to use.

- The Stein estimator can be interpreted as 'shrinking' the unrestricted OLS estimator towards the restricted OLS estimator, where the extent of the shrinking depends on the magnitude of the F statistic used to test the restrictions. The formula used for the shrinking factor can sometimes shrink the unrestricted OLS estimator beyond the restricted OLS estimator. By truncating this shrinking factor so as to prevent this from happening, an estimator superior to the Stein estimator is created. It is called the Stein *positive rule* estimator. The name derives from the popular application to zero restrictions: the positive rule estimator prevents the sign of the Stein estimator from differing from that of the unrestricted OLS estimator.

Technical Notes

11.1 Introduction

- Suppose Y_t is determined by X_t and all its past values, with the coefficient on X_{t-i} written as β_i. The *Pascal distributed lag* specifies that

$$\beta_i = \alpha \binom{r + i - 1}{i} (1 - \lambda)^r \lambda^i$$

for $0 < \lambda < 1$ an unknown parameter and order r an integer. When $r = 1$ this clearly collapses to the geometric lag, but when $r > 1$ this generalization of the geometric lag produces a single-humped distribution function. Algebraic manipulation yields the relationship

$$Y_t = \alpha(1 - \lambda)^r (1 - \lambda L)^{-r} X_t + \varepsilon_t$$

where L is the lag operator ($L^i X_t = X_{t-i}$). When multiplied out, $(1 - \lambda L)^{-r}$ is an infinite lag. Multiplying through the relationship by $(1 - \lambda L)^r$ creates an autoregression equation of order r with an autocorrelated error; it is in this form that estimation is undertaken.

- The equation above for Y_t with the Pascal lag has a polynomial in L in the denominator of the right-hand side. A natural generalization is to specify a polynomial in L also in the numerator, so that

$$Y_t = \frac{P(L)}{Q(L)} X_t + \varepsilon_t$$

where $P(L)$ and $Q(L)$ are polynomials in L of order p and q. This defines the *rational distributed lag*. By suitable choice of p and q, virtually any lag function can be approximated very closely; for practical applications p and q need not be very large to accomplish this (q in particular need not exceed 3). Multiplying through by $Q(L)$ creates an estimating form

$$Y_t = \beta_0 X_t + \beta_1 X_{t-1} + \ldots + \beta_p X_{t-p} - \alpha_1 Y_{t-1} - \ldots - \alpha_q Y_{t-q} + \varepsilon_t^*$$

where ε_t^* is autocorrelated.

11.3 Stochastic Restrictions

- Calculation of the mixed estimator can be illustrated by an example. Suppose we are estimating $y = \alpha + \beta x + \gamma z + \varepsilon$ for which we have T observations. Assume the CLR model assumptions hold with the variance of ε given by σ^2. Suppose from a previous study we have an estimate $\hat{\gamma}$ of γ with variance $V(\hat{\gamma})$. Thus we could write $\hat{\gamma} = \gamma + u$ where the variance of u is $V(\hat{\gamma})$. The estimating equation for the mixed estimator is given by $y^* = x^*\theta + \varepsilon^*$, where

$$y^* = \begin{bmatrix} y_1 \\ y_2 \\ \vdots \\ y_T \\ \hat{\gamma} \end{bmatrix} ; x^* = \begin{bmatrix} 1 & x_1 & z_1 \\ 1 & x_2 & z_2 \\ \vdots & & \\ 1 & x_T & z_T \\ 0 & 0 & 1 \end{bmatrix} ; \varepsilon^* = \begin{bmatrix} \varepsilon_1 \\ \varepsilon_2 \\ \vdots \\ \varepsilon_T \\ u \end{bmatrix} ; \theta = \begin{bmatrix} \alpha \\ \beta \\ \gamma \end{bmatrix}$$

and the variance–covariance matrix of ε^* is given by

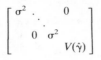

- Consider the following two methods of estimating β in the relationship $y = \alpha + \beta x + \gamma z + \varepsilon$.
  - (a) Ignore the estimate $\hat{\gamma}$ from a previous study and regress y on a constant, x, and z to obtain β^{OLS}.
  - (b) Replace γ by $\hat{\gamma}$, rearrange to get $(y - \hat{\gamma}z) = \alpha + \beta x + \varepsilon$, and regress $(y - \hat{\gamma}z)$ on a constant and x to obtain β^*. (This is a popular means of incorporating stochastic information.)

  Notice that method (a) utilizes only the information about γ in the data at hand to help in estimating β, ignoring the information about γ from the previous study. In contrast, method (b) above utilizes only the information about γ from the previous study, ignoring the information about γ in the data at hand. The mixed estimator is superior to these two alternatives because it incorporates both sources of information about γ into the estimate of β.

- In the example above, the variance of β^{OLS} is smaller than the variance of β^* if the variance of the OLS estimate of γ from method (a) is smaller than the variance of $\hat{\gamma}$ from the previous study. For a derivation see Goldberger (1964) pp. 258–9.

11.5   Extraneous Information and MSE

- The explanation of the risk function of the pre-test estimator in Fig. 11.1 was couched in terms of a type I error of 5%. It is easy to see that a type I error of 1% would create a different risk function, one lower on the left and higher on the right. This raises the question of what level of type I error is the optimum choice. Several criteria have been suggested in this regard. For example, the type I error could be chosen so as to minimize the maximum vertical distance in Fig. 11.1 between the risk function for the pre-test estimator and the minimum of the risk functions for the restricted and unrestricted OLS estimators. Wallace (1977) summarizes this literature.

- The usual measure of the extent to which the restrictions are not met – the horizontal axis of Fig. 11.1 – is the non-centrality parameter of the F statistic used to test the restrictions.

- In Fig. 11.1 the restricted OLS estimator is the best estimator if the case at hand lies to the left of point A, and the unrestricted OLS estimator is the best estimator if we are to the right of point A. This suggests that, rather than testing for the validity of the restrictions, we should test for whether or not the restrictions are close enough to being met that we are to the left of point A. This is the principle on which the tests of Toro-Vizcarrondo and Wallace (1968), Wallace and Toro-Vizcarrondo (1969) and Wallace (1972) are based. This pre-testing procedure is much more sophisticated than the usual pre-testing procedure.

12.   The Bayesian Approach

12.1   Introduction

There exist two very different approaches to statistics. The traditional 'classical' or 'frequentist' approach is what has been presented heretofore in this book; almost all econometrics textbooks exposit this approach, with little or no mention of its competitor, the Bayesian approach. One reason for this is the violent controversy among statisticians concerning the relative merits of the Bayesian and non-Bayesian methods, centring on the very different notions of probability they employ. This controversy not-withstanding, it seems that the main reason the Bayesian approach is used so seldom in econometrics is that there exist several practical difficulties with its application. In recent years, with the development of a variety of computer packages, these practical difficulties have for the most part been overcome; it therefore seems but a matter of time before Bayesian analyses become common in econometrics.

One purpose of this chapter is to explain the fundamentals of the Bayesian approach, with particular reference to the difference between Bayesian and non-Bayesian methods. A second purpose is to discuss the practical difficulties which, as alleged earlier, have prevented the adoption of the Bayesian approach. No effort is made to present the mechanics of Bayesian methods; textbook expositions are available for this purpose.

12.2   What is a Bayesian Analysis?

Suppose that, for illustrative purposes, we are interested in estimating the value of an unknown parameter, β. Using the classical approach, the data are fed into an estimating formula $\hat{\beta}$ to produce a specific point estimate $\hat{\beta}_0$ of β. If $\hat{\beta}_0$ is the maximum likelihood estimate, it maximizes the likelihood function, shown in Fig. 12.1. Associated with $\hat{\beta}$ is a sampling distribution, also illustrated in Fig. 12.1, indicating the relative frequency of estimates $\hat{\beta}$ would produce in hypothetical repeated samples. This sampling distribution is drawn using a dashed line to stress that it is unknown. If the assumptions of the classical normal linear regression model hold, as is usually assumed to be the case, the MLE $\hat{\beta}$ is the OLS estimator and its sampling distribution is normal in form, with mean equal to the true (unknown) value of β. Any particular estimate $\hat{\beta}_0$ of β is viewed as a random drawing from this sampling distribution, and the use of $\hat{\beta}_0$ as a

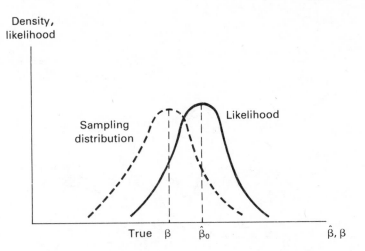

Fig. 12.1   The classical sampling distribution

point estimate of β is defended by appealing to the 'desirable' properties, such as unbiasedness, of the sampling distribution of $\hat{\beta}$. This summarizes the essentials of the classical, non-Bayesian approach.

The output from a Bayesian analysis is very different. Instead of producing a point estimate of β, a Bayesian analysis produces as its prime piece of output a density function for β, called the 'posterior' density function. This density function relates to β, not $\hat{\beta}$, so it most definitely is *not* a sampling distribution; it is interpreted as reflecting the odds the researcher would give when taking bets on the true value of β. For example, the researcher should be willing to bet three dollars, to win one dollar, that the true value of β is above the lower quartile of his or her posterior density for β. This 'subjective' notion of probability is a conceptually different concept of probability from the 'frequentist' or 'objective' concept employed in the classical approach; this difference is the main bone of contention between the Bayesians and non-Bayesians.

Following this subjective notion of probability, it is easy to imagine that *before* looking at the data the researcher could have a 'prior' density function for β, reflecting the odds that he or she would give, before looking at the data, if asked to take bets on the true value of β. This prior distribution, when combined with the data via Bayes theorem, produces the posterior distribution referred to above. This posterior density function is in essence a weighted average of the prior density and the likelihood (or 'conditional' density, conditional on the data), as illustrated in Fig. 12.2.

It may seem strange that the main output of the Bayesian analysis is a density function instead of a point estimate as in the classical analysis. The

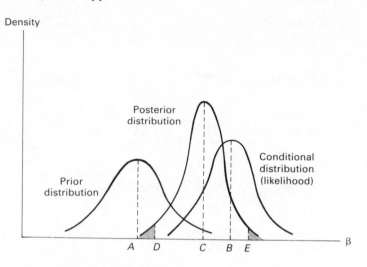

Density

Posterior
distribution

Conditional
distribution
(likelihood)

Prior
distribution

A   D   C   B E   β

Fig. 12.2   Obtaining the posterior distribution

reason for this is that the posterior can be used as input to decision problems, only one example of which is the problem of choosing a point estimate. An illustration of how the posterior can be used in this way should clarify this. To begin, a loss function must be specified, giving the loss incurred, using a specific point estimate β_0^*, for every possible true value of β. The expected loss associated with using β_0^* can be calculated by taking the expectation over all possible values of β, using for this calculation the posterior density of β. Note that this expectation is *not* taken over repeated samples.

This is illustrated in Fig. 12.3 for two choices of point estimate, β_0^* and β_1^*. The loss function is drawn for each as quadratic in the difference between the true value of β and the point estimate, so that each is minimized when β equals the point estimate. For each the expected loss is calculated by taking a weighted average of the losses associated with all possible values of β, using the height of the posterior density for the weights. This produces L_0 and L_1, respectively, as the expected losses associated with the point estimates β_0^* and β_1^*. Clearly β_1^* is preferred to β_0^* since L_1 is less than L_0. The Bayesian point estimate is that point estimate having the lowest expected loss. In the example of Fig. 12.3, where the loss function is quadratic and the posterior distribution symmetric, the mean β_m^* of the posterior distribution would be chosen as the point estimate of β.

To summarize, the Bayesian approach consists of three steps.

(1) A prior distribution is formalized, reflecting the researcher's beliefs about the parameter(s) in question before looking at the data.

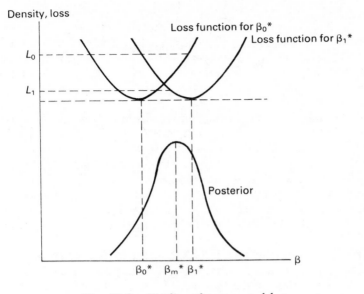

Fig. 12.3   Finding the expected loss

(2) This prior is combined with the data, via Bayes theorem, to produce the posterior distribution, the main output of a Bayesian analysis.
(3) This posterior is combined with a loss or utility function to allow a decision to be made on the basis of minimizing expected loss or maximizing expected utility. This third step is optional.

12.3   Advantages of the Bayesian Approach

The Bayesian approach claims several advantages over the classical approach, of which the following are some examples.

(a) The Bayesian approach is concerned with how information in data modifies a researcher's beliefs about parameter values and allows computation of probabilities associated with alternative hypotheses or models; this corresponds directly to the approach to these problems taken by most researchers.
(b) Extraneous information is routinely incorporated in a consistent fashion in the Bayesian method through the formulation of the prior; in the classical approach such information is more likely to be ignored, and when incorporated is usually done in *ad hoc* ways.
(c) The Bayesian approach can tailor the estimate to the purpose of the

study, through selection of the loss function; in general, its compatability with decision analysis is a decided advantage.

(d) There is no need to justify the estimating procedure in terms of the awkward concept of the performance of the estimator in hypothetical repeated samples; the Bayesian approach is justified solely on the basis of the prior and the sample data.

A more complete, and more persuasive, listing of the advantages of the Bayesian approach can be found in Zellner (1974). The essence of the debate between the frequentists and the Bayesians rests on the acceptability of the subjectivist notion of probability. Once one is willing to view probability in this way, the advantages of the Bayesian approach are compelling. But most practitioners, even though they have no strong aversion to the subjectivist notion of probability, do not choose to adopt the Bayesian approach. The reasons are practical in nature.

(1) Formalizing prior beliefs into a prior distribution is not an easy task.
(2) The mechanics of finding the posterior distribution are formidable.
(3) Convincing others of the validity of Bayesian results is difficult because they view those results as being 'contaminated' by personal (prior) beliefs.

In recent years these practical difficulties have been overcome by the development of appropriate computer software. These problems are discussed in the next section.

12.4   Overcoming Practitioners' Complaints

(1) *Choosing a prior*

In the words of Smith and Brainard (1976), a prior distribution tries to capture the 'information which gives rise to that almost inevitable disappointment one feels when confronted with a straightforward estimation of one's preferred structural model'. Non-Bayesians usually employ this information to lead them to add, drop or modify variables in an *ad hoc* search for a 'better' result. Bayesians incorporate this information into their prior, exploiting it *ex ante* in an explicit, up-front fashion; they maintain that, since human judgement is inevitably an ingredient in statistical procedures, it should be incorporated in a formal, consistent manner.

Although non-Bayesian researchers do use such information implicitly in undertaking *ad hoc* specification searches, they are extremely reluctant to formalize this information in the form of a prior distribution or to believe that others are capable of doing so. Leamer (1983b) p. 298 has expressed this sentiment cogently:

'It seems clear to me that the principal resistance to Bayesian methods is expressed in the incredulous grin which greets Bayesians when they make statements like: 'We need to begin with a multivariate prior distribution for the parameter vector β.'

To those unaccustomed to the Bayesian approach, formulating a prior can be a daunting task. This prompts some researchers to employ an 'ignorance' prior, which, as its name implies, reflects complete ignorance about the values of the parameters in question. In this circumstance the outcome of the Bayesian analysis is based on the data alone; it usually produces an answer identical, except for interpretation, to that of the classical approach. Cases in which a researcher can legitimately claim that he or she has absolutely no idea of the values of the parameters are rare, however; in most cases an 'informative' prior must be formulated. There are three basic ways in which this can be done.

(a) *Using previous studies*   A researcher can allow results from previous studies to define his or her prior. An earlier study, for example, may have produced an estimate of the parameter in question, along with an estimate of that estimate's variance. These numbers could be employed by the researcher as the mean and variance of his or her prior. (Notice that this changes dramatically the interpretation of these estimates.)

(b) *Placing hypothetical bets*   Since the prior distribution reflects the odds the researcher would give, before looking at the data, when taking hypothetical bets on the value of the unknown parameter β, a natural way of determining the prior is to ask the researcher (or an expert in the area, since researchers often allow their prior to be determined by advice from experts) various questions relating to hypothetical bets. For example, via a series of questions a value β_0 may be determined for which the researcher would be indifferent to betting that the true value of β (a) lies above β_0, or (b) lies below β_0. As another example, a similar series of questions could determine the smallest interval that he or she would be willing to bet, at even odds, contains the true value of β. Information obtained in this way can be used to calculate the prior distribution.

(c) *Using predictive distributions*   One problem with method (b) above is that for many researchers, and particularly for experts whose opinions may be used to formulate the researcher's prior, it is difficult to think in terms of model parameters and to quantify information in terms of a distribution for those parameters. They may be more comfortable thinking in terms of the value of the dependent variable associated with given values of the independent variables. Given a particular combination of values of the independent variables, the expert is asked for his or her assessment of the corresponding value of the dependent variable (i.e., a prior is formed on the dependent variable, not the parameters). This distribution, called a 'predictive' distribution, involves observable variables rather than un-observable parameters, and thus should relate more directly to the expert's knowledge and experience. By eliciting facts about an expert's predictive distributions at various settings of the independent variables, it is possible to infer the expert's associated (implicit) prior distribution concerning the parameters of the model.

For many researchers, even the use of these methods cannot allow them to feel comfortable with the prior developed. For these people the only way in which a Bayesian analysis can be undertaken is by structuring a range of prior distributions encompassing all prior distributions the resear-cher feels are reasonable. This approach is advocated under subsection (3) below as a necessary component of Bayesian analyses.

(2) *Finding the posterior*

The algebra of Bayesian analyses is more difficult than that of classical analyses, especially in multidimensional problems. For example, the classical analysis of a multiple regression with normally distributed errors in the Bayesian context requires a multivariate normal-gamma prior which, when combined with a multivariate normal likelihood function, produces a multivariate normal-gamma posterior from which the posterior marginal distribution (marginal with respect to the unknown variance of the error term) of the vector of slope coefficients can be derived as a multivariate t distribution. This both sounds and is mathematically demanding.

From the practitioner's viewpoint, however, this mathematics is not necessary. Bayesian textbooks spell out the nature of the priors and likelihoods relevant to a wide variety of estimation problems, and discuss the form taken by the resulting output. Armed with this knowledge, the practitioner can call on several computer packages to perform the calcula-tions required to produce the posterior distribution. A summary of available computer packages is given by Press (1980). In general, computa-tional difficulties can no longer be used as an excuse to shun the Bayesian approach.

(3) *Convincing others*

The problem Bayesians have of convincing others of the validity of their results is captured neatly by Blyth (1972) p. 20:

> However meaningful and helpful such numbers [Bayesian results] are to the author, they are meaningless and irrelevant to his reader. . . . what the reader wants to know from the author is 'Leaving your opinions out of this, what does your experimental evidence say?'

One way of addressing this problem is either to employ an ignorance prior or to employ a prior reflecting only results of earlier studies. But a better way of resolving this problem is to report a range of empirical results corresponding to a range of priors. This procedure has several advantages. First, it should alleviate any uncomfortable feeling the researcher may have with respect to his or her choice of prior. Second, a realistic range of priors should encompass the prior of an adversary, so that the range of results reported should include a result convincing to that adversary. Third, if the results are not too sensitive to the nature of the prior, a strong case can be made for the usefulness of these results. And fourth, if the results are sensitive to the prior, this should be made known so that the usefulness of such 'fragile' results can be evaluated in that light.

General Notes

12.1 Introduction

- Hey (1983) is a good reference for the Bayesian approach at the most elementary level. Novick and Jackson (1974) is invaluable at the intermediate level. Zellner (1971) is an excellent advanced reference, very comprehensive in its coverage of the Bayesian view of econometric problems. Judge *et al.* (1985) chapter 4 is a useful up-to-date reference. Zellner and Richard (1973) is an instructive application.

- Studying both Bayesian and non-Bayesian methods provides a much better understanding of statistics than that provided by studying only one approach. Weber (1973) examines the history of the Bayesian controversy.

12.2 What is a Bayesian Analysis?

- It cannot be stressed too strongly that the main difference between Bayesians and non-Bayesians is the concept of probability employed. For the Bayesian probability is regarded as representing a degree of reasonable belief; numerical probabilities are associated with degrees of confidence that the researcher has in propositions about empirical phenomena. For the non-Bayesian (or 'frequentist'), probability is regarded as representing the frequency with which an event would occur in repeated trials.

- The concept of a confidence interval can be used to illustrate the different concepts of probability employed by the Bayesians and non-Bayesians. In Fig. 12.2 the points D and E are placed such that 2.5% of the area under the posterior distribution appears in each tail; the interval DE can then be interpreted as being such that the probability that β falls in that interval is 95%. This is the way in which many clients of classical/frequentist statisticans want to and do interpret classical 95% confidence intervals, in spite of the fact that it is illegitimate to do so. The comparable classical confidence interval must be interpreted as either covering or not covering the true value of β, but being calculated in such a way that, if such intervals were calculated for a large number of repeated samples, then 95% of these intervals would cover the true value of β.

- In Fig. 12.2, the prior distribution is combined with the likelihood function (representing the data) to produce the posterior distribution, drawn as having the smallest variance because it incorporates information from the other two distributions. In many cases the mean C of the posterior distribution can be viewed as a weighted average of the mean A of the prior distribution and the mean B of the likelihood function, where the weights are the inverses of the variances (called the *precisions*) of the respective distributions. As the sample size becomes larger and larger, the likelihood function becomes narrower and narrower, and more and more closely centred over the true value of β. Since the variance of this conditional distribution becomes smaller and smaller (i.e., its precision becomes greater and greater), the role played by the prior becomes less and less. Asymptotically, the prior is completely swamped by the data, as it should be.

- When the decision problem is one of choosing a point estimate for β, the estimate chosen depends on the loss function employed. For example, if the loss function is quadratic, proportional to the square of the difference between the chosen point estimate and the true value of β, then the mean of the posterior distribution is chosen as the point estimate. If the loss is proportional to the absolute value of this difference, the median is chosen. A zero loss for a correct estimate and a constant loss for an incorrect estimate leads to the choice of the mode. The popularity of the squared error or quadratic loss function has led to the mean of the posterior distribution being referred to as the Bayesian point estimate. Note that, if the posterior distribution is symmetric with a unique global maximum, these three examples of loss functions lead to the same choice of estimate. For an example of an alternative loss function tailored to a specific problem, see Varian (1974).

- The ignorance prior is sometimes called a 'diffuse', 'uniform', 'equiproportional' or 'non-informative' prior. Its opposite is called an informative prior; an informative Bayesian analysis is one employing an informative prior. Using an ignorance prior allows a Bayesian to produce estimates identical to those of a classical analysis, with the all-important difference of interpretation (owing to the different concepts of probability).

- If the disturbances are assumed to be distributed normally, if the prior distribution is uniform (reflecting ignorance) and if the loss function is symmetric (such as in the three examples given earlier), the Bayesian estimator is identical to the OLS estimator. If the prior distribution is uniform and if the loss function is of the third form described above, the Bayesian estimator is identical to the maximum likelihood estimator (MLE). Under general conditions the Bayesian estimator and the MLE coincide in large samples (although their interpretation differs), since in large samples the prior is swamped by the actual data.

- Although the Bayesian approach rejects the concept of repeated samples, it is possible to ask how the Bayesian estimator would perform on criteria utilizing hypothetical repeated samples. Under certain conditions, as noted in the preceding paragraph, it is identical to the OLS estimator or the MLE and thus would have the same properties in repeated samples as these estimators. When the uniform prior is not used, a normal prior is often employed. In this case the Bayesian estimate is biased in repeated samples (but asymptotically unbiased) unless by luck the mean of the prior is the true parameter value. The variance of the Bayesian estimator is in general smaller, however, because it incorporates more information (i.e., the prior itself is extra information) than the classical techniques. This is evidenced by the sharper interval estimates usually associated with the Bayesian technique.

- The Bayesian would object strenuously to being evaluated on the basis of hypothetical repeated samples because he/she does not believe that justification of an estimator on the basis of its properties in repeated samples is relevant. He/she would maintain that because the estimate is calculated from the data at hand it must be justified on the basis of those data. The Bayesian recognizes, however, that reliance on an estimate calculated from a single sample could be dangerous, particularly if the sample size is small. In the Bayesian view sample data should be tempered by subjective knowledge of what the researcher feels are most likely to be the true value of the parameter. In this way the influence of atypical samples (not unusual if the sample size is small) is moderated. The classical statisticians, on the other hand, fear that calculations using typical samples will become contaminated with poor prior information.

12.3   Advantages of the Bayesian Approach

- Additional sample information is easily incorporated in a standard way via the Bayesian technique (the current posterior distribution is used as the prior in a new estimation using the additional data). Thus the Bayesian approach incorporates a formal and explicit learning model, corresponding directly with the learning process in research.

- Non-Bayesians argue that one's prior beliefs are not always easily expressed in the form of a prior distribution and thus it may be better to incorporate such imprecise information in a thoughtful (ad hoc) fashion than to insist that it be forced into a formal prior.

12.4   Overcoming Practitioners' Complaints

- A Bayesian analysis employing a prior based on results from a previous study would produce estimates similar to those of the method of mixed estimation outlined in chapter 11, except of course for interpretation.

- Not all previous studies match up perfectly with the study at hand. Results from previous studies may relate to slightly different variables under slightly different circumstances so that they cannot be used directly as suggested in the body of this chapter. A researcher may have to assimilate subjectively a wide array of related empirical studies to formulate a prior; this would have to be done using one of the other two methods for formulating priors discussed earlier.

- Formulation of a prior using information gained from questions relating to hypothetical bets is straightforward if the functional form of that prior is specified. This functional form is usually chosen so as to facilitate calculation of the posterior for the problem at hand. For example, if we are attempting to estimate the parameter of a binomial distribution, the derivation of the posterior is much easier if the prior takes the form of a beta distribution. In this example the beta prior is a 'natural conjugate prior' since it yields a posterior that also is a beta distribution. This choice of a natural conjugate form for the prior is innocuous: very few people have prior information so precise that it cannot be approximated adequately by a natural conjugate distribution. 'Conjugate' may or may not be related to the adjective 'conjugal': A conjugate distribution is a suitable mate for the model's distribution in that it produces offspring of its own kind.

- Given the distributional form of the prior, only answers to a small number of hypothetical betting questions are required to produce an actual prior.

Additional betting questions are none the less asked, with their answers providing a check on the 'coherence' of this prior; if answers to later questions are inconsistent with the fitted prior based on answers to earlier questions, this incoherence is used to prompt further thought on the nature of the prior beliefs in question. An iterative process ensues, leading eventually to the formulation of a coherent prior. Most undergraduate texts on Bayesian statistics have a section giving a detailed illustration of this process; for an example see Jones (1977) chapter 13. All this sounds like a lot of work. Thanks to Novick *et al.* (1983), however, there exists an interactive computer package (CADA) which relieves the analyst of almost all of the drudgery; the entire process is monitored by a computer-directed conversational dialogue, allowing priors to be formulated efficiently and painlessly. Examples of how CADA operates in this respect can be found in Novick and Jackson (1974) pp. 160–6, 217–23.

- Formulating priors by using predictive distributions is described and illustrated by Kadane *et al.* (1980), who also refer to a computer package implementing this approach. CADA also includes a variant of this approach. One advantage of the predictive distribution approach is that it does not impose a specific model on the researcher/expert and thus the elicited information could allow detection of a nonlinearity in the implicit model. Kadane *et al.* (1980) discusses the relative merits of the predictive distribution method and the method of eliciting hypothetical bets, which they call the structural method.

- There exists considerable evidence that people can be inaccurate in their personal assessments of probabilities; for references see Hogarth (1975), Leamer (1978) chapter 10, Lindley, Tversky and Brown (1979), Wallsten and Budescu (1983), and Fischhoff and Beyth-Marom (1983). The existence of this phenomenon underlines the importance of reporting estimates for a range of priors.

- The suggestion of reporting the fragility of empirical estimates (for both Bayesian and non-Bayesian methods) is advanced in convincing fashion by Leamer and Leonard (1983). They illustrate graphically for a two-dimensional case how the set of possible coefficient estimates is affected by the nature of the prior information. In one case they examine, the set of possible estimates is bounded by estimates generated by regressions formed by omitting different combinations of variables thought *a priori* to have coefficients close to zero in value. This example illustrates the kind of Bayesian prior information corresponding to "information" employed by a classical statistican in a typical ad hoc specification search. To aid practitioners in reporting the fragility of their estimates, Leamer and Leonard have developed a computer package SEARCH (Seeking Extreme and Average Regression Coefficient Hypotheses), capable of calculating the range of coefficient estimates associated with a range for the variance of the prior. Examples of this methodology can be found in Leamer and Leonard (1983), Leamer (1983a, 1984 and 1981). Ziemer (1984) speculates that fragility analysis will serve as a compromise between the *ad hoc* pre-test/search methods now in common use and the unfamiliar shrinkage/Bayesian methods advocated by theorists.

Technical Notes

- Bayes' Theorem is derived from the fact that the probability of obtaining the data and the parameters can be written either as:

$$\text{Prob(data and parameters)} = \text{Prob(data|parameters) Prob(parameters)}$$

or:

$$\text{Prob(data and parameters)} = \text{Prob(parameters|data) Prob(data)}$$

Equating these two expressions and rearranging, we get Bayes' Theorem:

$$\text{Prob(parameters|data)} = \frac{\text{Prob(data|parameters) Prob(parameters)}}{\text{Prob(data)}}.$$

The denominator can be calculated by integrating over all parameter values, so it becomes a normalization factor. The left-hand side of the expression is the *posterior* distribution, the Prob(parameters) *after* the sample. The right half of the right-hand side is the *prior* distribution, the Prob(parameters) *before* the sample. The left half of the right-hand side is the likelihood function. (Recall section 2.9 and its technical notes.) Thus, according to Bayes' Theorem the posterior distribution is given by the product of the prior distribution, the likelihood function and a normalization factor.

- Bayesians compare models by using the *posterior odds ratio*. Bayes' rule can be used as above to deduce the posterior probability of model i as

$$\text{Prob(model } i\text{|data)} = \frac{\text{Prob(model } i\text{) Prob(data|model } i\text{)}}{\text{Prob(data)}}$$

where prob(model i) is the prior probability of model i and Prob(data/model i) is the probability of having obtained the data given that they have been generated by model i. This latter term, called the *marginal* or *predictive* density, is a marginal probability, marginal with respect to the unknown parameter vector β. Thus Prob(data|model i) is calculated by taking a weighted average of Prob(data|model i, β) for all possible values of β, using as weights the heights of the prior density of β. Thus the marginal density is a weighted average of likelihoods.

Models are compared by forming the posterior odds ratio

$$\frac{\text{Prob(model } i\text{|data)}}{\text{Prob(model } j\text{|data)}} = \frac{\text{Prob(model } i\text{) Prob(data|model } i\text{)}}{\text{Prob(model } j\text{) Prob(data|model } j\text{)}}.$$

Model choice is undertaken with explicit consideration of losses associated with incorrect choices. For example, if there are only two models, i and j, and the cost of choosing model i when model j is correct is twice the cost of choosing model j when model i is correct, then model i will be chosen if the posterior odds ratio above exceeds two.

13. Dummy Variables

Explanatory variables are often qualitative in nature (e.g., wartime versus peacetime, male versus female, east versus west versus south), so that some proxy must be constructed to represent them in a regression. Dummy variables are used for this purpose. A dummy variable is an artificial variable constructed such that it takes the value unity whenever the qualitative phenomenon it represents occurs, and zero otherwise. Once created, these proxies, or 'dummies' as they are called, are used in the CLR model just like any other explanatory variable, yielding standard OLS results.

The exposition below is in terms of an example designed to illustrate the roles dummy variables can play, give insight to how their coefficients are estimated in a regression, and clarify the interpretation of these coefficient estimates.

13.1   A Step Function Example

Consider data on the incomes of doctors, professors and lawyers, exhibited in Fig. 13.1 (where the data have been ordered so as to group observations into the professions), and suppose it is postulated that an individual's

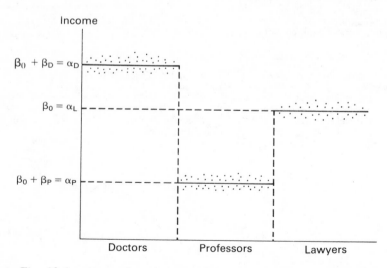

Fig. 13.1   A step function example of using dummy variables

income depends on his or her profession, a qualitative variable. We may write this model as

$$Y = \alpha_D D_D + \alpha_P D_P + \alpha_L D_L + \varepsilon \tag{1}$$

where D_D is a dummy variable taking the value one whenever the observation in question is a doctor, and zero otherwise; D_P and D_L are dummy variables defined in like fashion for professors and lawyers. Notice that the equation in essence states that an individual's income is given by the coefficient of his or her related dummy variable plus an error term. (For a professor, for example, D_D and D_L are zero and D_P is one, so (1) becomes $Y = \alpha_P + \varepsilon$.)

From the structure of equation (1) and the configuration of Fig. 13.1, the logical estimate of α_D is the average of all doctors' incomes, of α_P the average of all professors' incomes, and of α_L the average of all lawyers' incomes. It is reassuring, then, that if Y is regressed on these three dummy variables, these are exactly the estimates that result.

13.2   Using an Intercept

Equation (1) as structured does not contain an intercept. If it did, perfect multicollinearity would result (the intercept variable, a column of ones, would equal the sum of the three dummy variables) and the regression could not be run. None the less, more often than not, equations with dummy variables do contain an intercept. This is accomplished by omitting one of the dummies to avoid perfect multicollinearity.

Suppose D_L is dropped, for example, creating

$$Y = \beta_0 + \beta_D D_D + \beta_P D_P + \varepsilon. \tag{2}$$

In this case, for a lawyer D_D and D_P are zero, so a lawyer's expected income is given by the intercept β_0. Thus the logical estimate of the intercept is the average of all lawyers' incomes. A doctor's expected income is given by equation (2) as $\beta_0 + \beta_D$; thus the logical estimate of β_D is the difference between the doctors' average income and the lawyers' average income. Similarly, the logical estimate of β_P is the difference between the professors' average income and lawyers' average income. Once again, it is reassuring that, when regression (2) is undertaken (i.e., regressing Y on an intercept and the dummy variables D_D and D_P), exactly these results are obtained. The crucial difference is that with an intercept included the interpretation of the dummy variable coefficients changes dramatically.

With no intercept, the dummy variable coefficients reflect the expected income for the respective professions. With an intercept included, the omitted category (profession) becomes a base or benchmark to which the others are compared. The dummy variable coefficients for the remaining categories measure the extent to which they differ from this base. This base in the example above is the lawyer profession. Thus the coefficient β_D, for example, gives the *difference* between the expected income of a doctor and the expected income of a lawyer.

Most researchers find the equation with an intercept more convenient because it allows them to address more easily the questions in which they usually have the most interest, namely whether or not the categorization makes a difference and if so by how much. If the categorization does make a difference, by how much is measured directly by the dummy variable coefficient estimates. Testing whether or not the categorization is relevant can be done by running a t test of a dummy variable coefficient against zero (or, to be more general, an F test on the appropriate set of dummy variable coefficient estimates).

13.3   Adding Another Qualitative Variable

Suppose now the data in Fig. 13.1 are rearranged slightly to form Fig. 13.2, from which it appears that gender may have a role to play in determining income. This issue is usually broached in one of two ways. The most common way is to include in equations (1) and (2) a new dummy variable D_F for gender to create

$$Y = \alpha^*_D D_D + \alpha^*_P D_P + \alpha^*_L D_L + \alpha^*_F D_F + \varepsilon \tag{1*}$$

$$Y = \beta^*_0 + \beta^*_D D_D + \beta^*_P D_P + \beta^*_F D_F + \varepsilon \tag{2*}$$

where D_F takes the value 1 for a female and 0 for a male. Notice that no dummy variable D_M representing males is added; if such a dummy were added perfect multicollinearity would result, in equation (1*) because $D_D + D_P + D_L = D_F + D_M$ and in equation (2*) because $D_F + D_M$ is a column of 1s, identical to the implicit intercept variable. The interpretation of both α^*_F and β^*_F is as the extent to which being female changes income, regardless of profession. α^*_D, α^*_P and α^*_L are interpreted as expected income of a male in the relevant profession; a similar reinterpretation is required for the coefficients of equation (2*).

The second way of broaching this issue is to scrap the old dummy variables and create new dummy variables, one for each category illustrated in Fig. 13.2. This produces

$$Y = \alpha_{FD} D_{FD} + \alpha_{MD} D_{MD} + \alpha_{FP} D_{FP} + \alpha_{MP} D_{MP}$$
$$+ \alpha_{FL} D_{FL} + \alpha_{ML} D_{ML} + \varepsilon \tag{1'}$$

and

$$Y = \beta'_0 + \beta_{FD} D_{FD} + \beta_{MD} D_{MD} + \beta_{FP} D_{FP} + \beta_{MP} D_{MP}$$
$$+ \beta_{FL} D_{FL} + \varepsilon \;. \tag{2'}$$

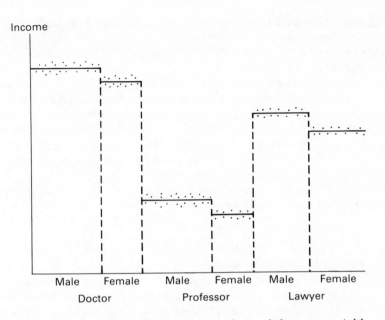

Fig. 13.2   Adding gender as an additional dummy variable

The interpretation of the coefficients is straightforward: α_{FD}, for example, is the expected income of a female doctor, and β_{FD} is the extent to which the expected income of a female doctor differs from that of a male lawyer.

The key difference between these two methods is that the former method forces the difference in income between male and female to be the same for all professions whereas the latter does not. The latter method allows for what are called interaction effects. In the former method a female doctor's expected income is the sum of two parts, one attributable to being a doctor and the other attributable to being a female; there is no role for any special effect that the combination or interaction of doctor and female might have.

13.4   Interacting with Quantitative Variables

All of the foregoing examples are somewhat unrealistic in that they are regressions in which all the regressors are dummy variables. In general, however, quantitative variables determine the dependent variable as well as qualitative variables. For example, income in an earlier example may also be determined by years of experience, E, so that we might have

$$Y = \gamma_0 + \gamma_D D_D + \gamma_P D_P + \gamma_E E + \varepsilon .$$

(3)

In this case the coefficient γ_D must be interpreted as reflecting the difference between doctors' and lawyers' expected incomes, taking account of years of experience (i.e., assuming equal years of experience).

Equation (3) is in essence a model in which income is expressed as a linear function of experience, with a different intercept for each profession. (On a graph of income against experience, this would be reflected by three parallel lines, one for each profession.) The most common use of dummy variables is to effect an intercept shift of this nature. But in many contexts it may be that the slope coefficient γ_E could differ for different professions, either in addition to or in place of a different intercept. (This could be viewed as a kind of interaction effect.)

This case is handled by adding special dummies to account for slope differences. Equation (3) becomes

$$Y = \gamma_0^* + \gamma_D^* D_D + \gamma_P^* D_P + \gamma_E^* E + \gamma_{ED}^*(D_D E) \\ + \gamma_{EP}^*(D_P E) + \varepsilon . \qquad (4)$$

Here $(D_D E)$ is a variable formed as the 'product' of D_D and E; it consists of the value of E for each observation on a doctor, and 0 elsewhere. The special 'product' dummy $(D_P E)$ is formed in similar fashion. The expression (4) for observations on a lawyer is $\gamma_0^* + \gamma_E^* E + \varepsilon$, so γ_0^* and γ_E^* are the intercept and slope coefficients relevant to lawyers. The expression (4) for observations on a doctor is $\gamma_0^* + \gamma_D^* + (\gamma_E^* + \gamma_{ED}^*) E + \varepsilon$, so the interpretation of γ_D^* is as the difference between the doctors' and the lawyers' intercepts and the interpretation of γ_{ED}^* is as the difference between the doctors' and the lawyers' slope coefficients. Thus this special 'product' dummy variable can allow for changes in slope coefficients from one data set to another and thereby capture a different kind of interaction effect.

Equation (4) is such that each profession has its own intercept and its own slope. (On a graph of income against experience, the three lines, one for each profession, need not be parallel.) Because of this there will be no difference between the estimates resulting from running this regression and the estimates resulting from running three separate regressions, each using just the data for a particular profession. Thus in this case using dummy variables is of no value. The dummy variable technique is of value whenever restrictions of some kind are imposed on the model in question. Equation (3) reflects such a restriction; the slope efficient γ_E is postulated to be the same for all professions. By running equation (3) as a single regression, this restriction is imposed and more efficient estimates of all parameters result. As another example, suppose that years of education were also an explanatory variable but that it is known to have the same slope coefficient in each profession. Then adding the extra explanatory variable years of education to equation (4) and performing a single regression produces more efficient estimates of all parameters than would be the case if three separate regressions were run. (It should be noted that running a single, constrained regression incorporates the additional assumption of a common error variance.)

General Notes

- The terminology 'dummy variable' has invited irreverent remarks. One of the best is due to Machlup (1974) p. 892: 'Let us remember the unfortunate econometrician who, in one of the major functions of his system, had to use a proxy for risk and a dummy for sex.'

- Gujarati (1978) chapter 13 has a good textbook discussion of dummy variables and the uses to which they can be put.

- Care must be taken in evaluating models containing dummy variables designed to capture structural shifts or seasonal factors, since these dummies could play a major role in generating a high R^2, hiding the fact that the independent variables have little explanatory power.

- When a regression linear in logarithms includes a dummy variable, for example $\ln Y = \alpha_0 + \alpha_1 \ln X + \alpha_2 D + \varepsilon$, the coefficient α_2 of the dummy variable D is interpreted as the percentage impact on Y of the qualitative variable it represents. For a semi-logarithmic functional form, however (e.g., $Y = \beta_0 + \beta_1 \ln X + \beta_2 D + \varepsilon$), the coefficient β_2 of the dummy variable only approximates this percentage impact and must be adjusted. See Halvorson and Palmquist (1980) and Kennedy (1981a).

- A popular use of dummy variables is for seasonal adjustment. Setting dummies up to represent the seasons and then including these variables along with the other regressors eliminates seasonal influences in so far as, in a linear model, these seasonal influences affect the intercept term (or, in a log-linear model, these seasonal influences can be captured as seasonal percentage impacts on the dependent variable). Should the slope coefficients be affected by seasonal factors, a more extensive de-seasonalizing procedure would be required, employing 'product' dummy variables. Johnston (1984, pp. 234–9) has a good discussion of using dummies to de-seasonalize. It must be noted that much more elaborate methods of de-seasonalizing data exist. For a survey see Pierce (1980). See also Raveh (1984). Robb (1980) and Gersovitz and MacKinnon (1978) suggest innovative approaches to seasonal factors. See also Judge *et al.* (1985) pp. 258–62 for discussion of the issues involved.

- Dummy variable coefficients are interpreted as showing the extent to which behaviour in one category deviates from some base (the 'omitted' category). Whenever there exists more than two categories, the presentation of these results can be awkward, especially when laymen are involved; a more relevant, easily understood base might make the presentation of these results more effective. For example, suppose household energy consumption is determined by income and the region in which the household lives. Rather than, say, using the South as a base and comparing household energy consumption in the North East, North Central and West to consumption in the South, it may be more effective, as a means of presenting these results to laymen, to calculate dummy variable coefficients in such a way as to compare consumption in each region with the national average. A simple adjustment permits this. See Suits (1984) and Kennedy (1985b).

- The dummy variable method of structuring the Chow (see section 5.4) test is straightforward. Suppose Y is a linear function of X and Z and the question at hand is whether the coefficients are the same in period 1 as in period 2. A dummy variable D is formed such that D takes the value zero for observations in period 1 and the value one for observations in period 2. 'Product' dummy variables DX and DZ are also formed (i.e., DX takes the value X in the period 2 and is 0 otherwise). Then the equation

$$Y = \beta_0 + \alpha_0 D + \beta_1 X + \alpha_1(DX) + \beta_2 Z + \alpha_2(DZ) + \varepsilon \qquad (1)$$

is formed.

Running regression (1) as is allows the intercept and slope coefficients to differ from period 1 to period 2. This produces SSE unrestricted. Running regression (1) forcing α_0, α_1 and α_2 to be 0 forces the intercept and slope coefficients to be identical in both periods. An F test, structured in the usual way, can be used to test whether or not the vector with elements α_0, α_1 and α_2 is equal to the zero vector. Notice that the former regression is equivalent to running two separate regressions, one for each period, and the latter is equivalent to running one regression on all data. Thus this method is identical to that given earlier, in section 5.4, for the Chow test.

- The advantage of the dummy variable variant of the Chow test is that it can easily be modified to test subsets of the coeficients. Suppose, for example, that it is known that, in equation (1) above, β_2 changed from period 1 to period 2 and that it is desired to test whether or not the other parameters (β_0 and β_1) changed. Running regression (1) as is gives the unrestricted SSE for the required F statistic, and running (1) without D and DX gives the restricted SSE. The required degrees of freedom are 2 for the numerator and $T-6$ for the denominator, where T is the total number of observations.

Notice that a slightly different form of this test must be used if, instead of knowing (or assuming) that β_2 had changed from period 1 to period 2, we knew (or assumed) that it had *not* changed. Then running regression (1) without DZ gives the unrestricted SSE and running regression (2) without D, DX and DZ gives the restricted SSE. The degrees of freedom are 2 for the numerator and $T-5$ for the denominator.

- Using dummies to capture a change in intercept or slope coefficient, as described above, allows the line being estimated to be discontinuous. (Try drawing a graph of the curve – at the point of change it 'jumps'.) Forcing continuity creates what is called a *piecewise linear model*; dummy variables can be used to force this continuity, as explained, for example, in Pindyck and Rubinfeld (1981) pp. 126–7. This model is a special case of a *spline function*, in which the linearity assumption is dropped. For an exposition see Suits *et al.* (1978). Poirier (1976) has an extended discussion of this technique and its applications in economics.

- Dummy variables can be used to facilitate the calculation of forecasts, forecast errors and related confidence intervals; see Salkever (1976).

- Dummy variables are sometimes used when pooling time-series and cross-sectional data. In this context it is often assumed that the intercept varies across the N cross-sectional units and/or across the T time periods. In the general case $(N-1) + (T-1)$ dummies can be used to incorporate this. (Computationally, it is not necessary to run a regression with all these extra variables: see Dielman (1983) pp. 114–15). These dummy variable coefficients represent ignorance – they are inserted merely for the purpose of measuring shifts in the regression line arising from unknown variables. Some researchers feel that this type of ignorance should be treated in a fashion similar to the general ignorance represented by the error term and have accordingly proposed the *variance components/error components* model for pooling.

In this model there is an overall intercept and an error term with three components: $u_i + v_t + \varepsilon_{it}$. The u_i are independently and identically distributed with zero mean and variance σ_u^2; they represent the extent to which the ith cross-sectional unit's intercept differs from the overall intercept. The v_t are independently and identically distributed with zero mean and variance σ_v^2; they represent the extent to which the tth time period's intercept differs from the overall intercept. The ε_{it}, with zero mean and variance σ_ε^2, represent the traditional error term unique to each observation. All three of these errors are assumed to be mutually independent. In this formulation the extent to which the dummy variable intercept coefficients differ across cross-sectional units is assumed to be randomly distributed, as is the extent to which they differ across time periods. Thus it can be classified as a random parameter model, discussed in chapter 5.

Estimation of the error components model is undertaken using an EGLS technique because the variance–covariance matrix of the composite error term is nonspherical. (The diagonal of this matrix is given by $\sigma_u^2 + \sigma_v^2 + \sigma_t^2$; off-diagonal elements corresponding to the same time period are σ_t^2, off-diagonal elements corresponding to the same cross-section unit are σ_u^2, and all other off-diagonal elements are zero.) For further discussion of this method and its many variants, including allowing the slope coefficients to vary as well as the intercepts, see Judge *et al.* (1985) chapter 13. Dielman (1983) is a useful survey; he also summarizes relevant computer software.

Mundlak (1978) has examined the relative merits of these two approaches to pooling. When using the dummy variable approach, inference is conditional on the particular intercept values inherent in the data at hand, and since no specific assumptions are made about the distribution of these intercepts, there is less danger of making a specification error. A disadvantage is the large number of degrees of freedom used up. If the distributional assumptions (e.g., that the intercepts for each cross-sectional unit can be viewed as random drawings from the same distribution) of the error components model are correct, then this technique should create a more efficient estimator. Mundlak argues that the error components approach will be seriously inappropriate only if the random intercepts are correlated (as they are likely to be) with the explanatory variables. A test for this is offered by Hausman (1978). Johnston (1984) pp. 405–7 stresses that the choice between these two pooling methods depends on the institutional realities of the problem at hand.

Technical Notes

- *Analysis of variance* is a statistical technique designed to determine whether or not a particular classification of the data is meaningful. The total variation in the dependent variable (the sum of squared differences between each observation and the overall mean) can be expressed as the sum of the variation between classes (the sum of the squared differences between the mean of each class and the overall mean, each times the number of observations in that class) and the variation within each class (the sum of the squared difference between each observation and its class mean). This decomposition is used to structure an F test to test the hypothesis that the between-class variation is large relative to the within-class variation, which implies that the classification is meaningful, i.e., that there is a significant variation in the dependent variable between classes.

If dummy variables are used to capture these classifications and a regression is run, the dummy variable coefficients turn out to be the class means, the between-class variation is the regression's 'explained' variation, the within-class variation is the regression's 'unexplained' variation, and the analysis of variance F test is equivalent to testing whether or not the dummy variable coefficients are significantly different from one another. The main advantage of the dummy variable regression approach is that it provides estimates of the magnitudes of class variation influences on the dependent variables (as well as testing whether the classification is meaningful).

Analysis of covariance is an extension of analysis of variance to handle cases in which there are some uncontrolled variables that could not be standardized between classes. These cases can be analysed by using dummy variables to capture the classifications and regressing the dependent variable on these dummies and the uncontrollable variables. The analysis of covariance F tests are equivalent to testing whether the coefficients of the dummies are significantly different from one another. These tests can be interpreted in terms of changes in the residual sums of squares caused by adding the dummy variables. Johnston (1972) pp. 192–207 has a good discussion.

In light of the above, it can be concluded that anyone comfortable with regression analysis and dummy variables can eschew analysis of variance and covariance techniques.

14. Qualitative and Limited Dependent Variables

14.1 Dichotomous Dependent Variables

When the dependent variable is qualitative in nature and must be represented by a dummy variable, special estimating problems arise. Examples are the problem of explaining whether or not an individual will buy a car, whether an individual will be in or out of the labour force, whether an individual will use public transport or drive to work, or whether an individual will vote yes or no on a referendum.

If the dependent variable is set up as a 0–1 dummy variable (for example, the dependent variable is set equal to 1 for those buying cars and equal to 0 for those not buying cars) and regressed on the explanatory variables, we would expect the predicted values of the dependent variable to fall mainly within the interval between 0 and 1, as illustrated in Fig. 14.1. This suggests that the predicted value of the dependent variable could be interpreted as the probability that that individual will buy a car, given that individual's characteristics (i.e., the values of the explanatory variables). This is in fact the accepted convention. In Fig. 14.1 the dots represent the sample observations; most of the high values of the explanatory variable x correspond to a dependent dummy variable value of unity (implying that a car was bought), whereas most of the low values of x correspond to a dependent dummy variable value of zero (implying that no car was bought). Notice that for extremely low values of x the regression line yields a negative estimated probability of buying a car, while for extremely high values of x the estimated probability is greater than 1. As should be clear from this diagram, R^2 is likely to be very low for this kind of regression, suggesting that R^2 should not be used as an estimation criterion in this context.

An obvious drawback to this approach is that it is quite possible, as illustrated in Fig. 14.1, to have estimated probabilities outside the 0–1 range. This embarrassment could be avoided by converting estimated probabilities lying outside the 0–1 range to either 0 or 1 as appropriate. This defines the *linear probability model*. Although this model is often used because of its computational ease, many researchers feel uncomfortable with it because outcomes are sometimes predicted with certainty when it is quite possible that they may not occur.

What is needed is some means of squeezing the estimated probabilities inside the 0–1 interval without actually creating probability estimates of 0

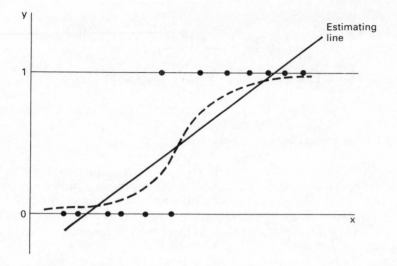

Fig. 14.1   The linear probability model

or 1, as shown by the dashed line in Figure 14.1. Many possible functions of this nature are available, the two most popular being the cumulative normal function and the logistic function. Using the cumulative normal function for this purpose creates the *probit* model; using the logistic function creates the *logit* model. Since these two functions are very similar, and since using the logistic function involves less computational cost, the *logit* model is usually employed in practice.

Estimation of these models falls into two basic categories.

(1) *Grouping possible*

This case occurs when there is a large number of observations capable of being grouped into sets of observations on identical individuals. This could arise in a large-sample survey, in which such grouping is often undertaken anyway (to reduce the number of observations to a manageable size). If there are enough observations in each group, a reliable estimate of the probability of an individual in that group buying a car can be produced by calculating the percentage of individuals in that group who bought a car.

(a) In the linear probability model, in which the estimated dependent variable is interpreted as the probability of buying a car, using the group-estimated probabilities as the dependent variable and regressing on the explanatory variables' group means should produce the desired estimates. The error term in this case is heteroskedastic (because the dependent variable observations are *estimated*), so some form of EGLS must be employed. Note that this approach does not avoid the problem of probability estimates of 0 or 1.

(b) In the logit model a linear function of the explanatory variables can be shown to be equal to the logarithm of the ratio of the probability of buying and of not buying a car. This logarithm can be calculated for each group from the group-estimated probabilities; regressing this new dependent variable on the explanatory variables' group means should produce the desired coefficient estimates. These estimates, in conjunction with the logistic function, can be used to create the estimated probabilities (which will by construction lie within the 0–1 range) of buying a car. Again, the error terms of this regression are heteroskedastic, so some form of GLS must be used.

(2) *Grouping not possible*

In small samples, or in situations with a large number of explanatory variables, it will not be possible legitimately to group observations or, if groups can be formed, to obtain a sufficiently large number of observations in each group to produce a reliable estimate of the probability of an individual in that group buying a car.

(a) Computational ease may dictate use of the linear probability model, in which case care must be taken to account for the heteroskedasticity (created by the unusual error term – it is such as to make the dependent variable 0 or 1).

(b) The logit (and probit) models must be estimated via a maximum likelihood technique, described in the General and Technical Notes to this section.

14.2 Polychotomous Dependent Variables

The preceding section addressed the problem of binary, or dichotomous, variables, for which there are only two choice categories. Categorical variables that can be classified into many categories are called polychotomous variables. For example, a commuter may be presented with a choice of commuting to work by subway, by bus or by private car, so there are three choices. Estimation in this context is undertaken by means of a generalization of the logit or probit models, called, respectively, the multinomial logit and the multinomial probit models. These generalizations are motivated by employing the random utility model.

In the random utility model the utility to a consumer of an alternative is specified as a linear function of the characteristics of the consumer and the attributes of the alternative, plus an error term. The probability that a particular consumer will choose a particular alternative is given by the probability that the utility of that alternative to that consumer is greater than the utility to that consumer of all other available alternatives. This makes good sense to an economist. The consumer picks the alternative that maximizes his or her utility. The multinomial logit and multinomial probit models follow from assumptions made concerning the nature of the error term in this random utility model.

If the random utility error terms are assumed to be independently and identically distributed as a Weibull distribution, the *multinomial logit* model results. The great advantage of this model is its computational ease; the probability of an individual selecting a given alternative is easily expressed (as described in the Technical Notes), and a likelihood function can be formed and maximized in straightforward fashion. The disadvantage of this model is that it is characterized by what is called the *independence of irrelevant alternatives* property. Suppose a new alternative, almost identical to an existing alternative, is added to the set of choices. One would expect that as a result the probability from this model of choosing the duplicated alternative would be cut in half and the probabilities of choosing the other alternatives would be unaffected. Unfortunately, this is not the case, implying that the multinomial logit model will be inappropriate whenever two or more of the alternatives are close substitutes.

If the random utility error terms are assumed to be distributed multivariate-normally, the *multinomial probit* model results. This model allows the error terms to be correlated across alternatives, thereby permitting it to circumvent the independence of irrelevant alternatives dilemma. Its disadvantage is its high computational cost, which becomes prohibitively high when there are more than four alternatives.

14.3   Limited Dependent Variables

Dependent variables are sometimes limited in their range. For example, data from the negative income tax experiment are such that income lies at or below some threshold level for all observations. As another example, data on household expenditure on automobiles has a lot of observations at 0, corresponding to households who choose not to buy a car. As a last example, data on wage rates may be obtainable only for those for whom their wage exceeds their reservation wage, others choosing not to work. If the dependent variable is limited in some way, OLS estimates are biased, even asymptotically.

The upper half of Fig. 14.2 illustrates why this is the case (ignore for now the lower half of this diagram). The relationship $y = \alpha + \beta x + \varepsilon$ is being estimated, where ε is a normally distributed error and observations with y values greater than k are not known (i.e., they are missing). These

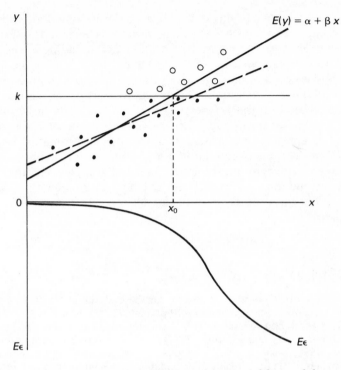

Fig. 14.2   A limited dependent variable model

unknown *y* values are denoted by small circles to distinguish them from known data points, designated by dots. Notice that for high values of *x* the known (dotted) observations below $E(y) = \alpha + \beta x$ are not fully balanced off by observations above $E(y) = \alpha + \beta x$, because some of these observations (the circled ones) are missing. This causes the resulting OLS regression line to be too flat, as shown by the dashed line.

Samples with limited dependent variables are classified into two general categories, censored and truncated regression models, depending on whether or not the values of *x* for the missing *y* data are known.

(1) *Censored sample*   In this case some observations on the dependent variable, corresponding to known values of the independent variable(s), are not observable. In Fig. 14.2, for example, the *y* values corresponding to the circled data points are not known, but their corresponding *x* values are known. In the example of automobile purchases noted earlier, it may be the case that data are available for both those who did buy a car and those who did not buy a car.

(2) *Truncated sample*   In this case values of the independent variable(s) are known only when the dependent variable is observed. In Fig. 14.2, for example, both the *y* and the *x* values corresponding to the circled data are not known. In the example of the negative income tax experiment noted earlier, no data of any kind are available for those above the income threshold; they were not part of the sample.

Estimation for both these types of problems is usually undertaken by maximum likelihood techniques. This avoids the asymptotic bias of OLS and by utilizing all the data generates more efficient estimates. For some problems, however, the computational cost of maximum likelihood estimation is so high that in the case of censored samples an alternative, two-stage, estimation technique is employed. These estimation methods are discussed in the general notes to this section.

General Notes

- The best, and most complete, reference for the material in this chapter and its possible extensions and modifications is Maddala (1983). Some textbook expositions are Pindyck and Rubinfeld (1981) chapter 10, Judge *et al.* (1985) chapter 18, and Fomby, Hill and Johnson (1984) chapter 16. Useful survey articles are Amemiya (1981, 1983). Readers should be warned that the subject matter of this chapter is one of the most technically demanding in econometrics; all references reflect this.

14.1   Dichotomous Dependent Variables

- Maximum likelihood estimation of the probit model is undertaken by interpreting a linear function of the independent variables as an index (called, say, 'buying potential'). If this 'buying potential' index for an individual exceeds that individual's personal critical value of this index, that individual will buy a car. Some individuals need little encouragement to buy cars, so that they will have low critical values; others buy cars only under extremely favourable circumstances and so will have high critical values. In the probit model these critical values are assumed to be distributed normally among individuals.

  Fig. 14.3 shows the probability density function of these critical values. For an individual with characteristics given by the row vector X_0, buying potential index is $X_0\beta$ where β is an unknown vector of parameters. The likelihood of this individual buying a car is given by the probability that his or her personal critical value is below $X_0\beta$. This is given in Fig. 14.3 by the dotted area, calculated as the cumulative density to the point $X_0\beta$. The likelihood of this person *not* buying a car is given by the probability that his or her personal critical value exceeds $X_0\beta$, measured by the lined area in Fig. 14.3 (equal to 1 minus the shaded area). For another individual, with a different row vector of characteristics X_1, these likelihoods would involve cumulating this density function to the point $X_1\beta$ rather than $X_0\beta$, so the dotted area will be of different size for different individuals.

  The likelihood function for the entire sample is formed by multiplying together all the expressions for the likelihoods for the individuals. Expressions

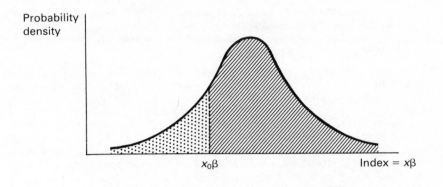

Fig. 14.3   Explaining probit and logit

measuring the dotted area would be used for those who actually bought a car, and expressions measuring the lined area, or 1 minus the dotted area), would be used for those who did not buy a car. Because each of these expressions requires calculation of an integral (the cumulative normal distribution), this likelihood function is computationally costly to maximize. Its maximization produces β^{MLE}. The buying index for an individual with a row vector of characteristics X_0 can then be estimated as $X_0\beta^{MLE}$ and the probability of that person buying a car is estimated as the cumulation of the normal distribution in Fig. 14.3 to the point $X_0\beta^{MLE}$.

- In the logit model, the personal critical values are distributed as a hyperbolic-secant-square (sech^2) distribution, the cumulative distribution of which is the logistic function. The logistic function is easy to calculate (see the Technical Notes), involving only the computation of an exponential, whereas the cumulative normal distribution is difficult to compute, involving the calculation of an integral.

14.2 Polychotomous Dependent Variables

- There are three ways of structuring the deterministic part of the random utility model.
  (1) Specify that the utility of an alternative to an individual is a linear function of the m attributes of that alternative. In this case m coefficients, identical for all individuals, must be estimated. With this specification it is possible to predict the probability that an individual will select a particular alternative, given only the attributes of that alternative; it is not possible to predict this probability given only the characteristics of that individual.
  (2) Specify that the utility of an alternative to an individual is a linear function of that individual's n characteristics, with a different set of parameters for each alternative. In thise case np coefficients must be estimated, where p is the number of alternatives. Using this specification, it is possible to predict the probability of an individual selecting a particular alternative, given only the characteristics of that individual; it is not possible to predict this probability given only the attributes of that alternative.

(3) Specify a combination of (1) and (2) above, namely a linear function of both the attributes of the alternatives and the characteristic of the individuals, with a different set of parameters for the characteristics (but not the attributes) for each alternative.

- The independence-of-irrelevant-alternatives problem arises from the fact that in the multinomial logit model the *relative* probability of choosing two existing alternatives is unaffected by the presence of additional alternatives. As an example, suppose a commuter is twice as likely to commute by subway as by bus and three times as likely to commute by private car as by bus, so that the probabilities of commuting by bus, subway and private car are 1/6, 2/6 and 3/6, respectively. Now suppose an extra bus service is added, differing from the existing bus service only in the colour of the buses. One would expect the probabilities of commuting by new bus, old bus, subway and private car to be 1/12, 1/12, 2/6 and 3/6, respectively. Instead, the multinomial logit model produces probabilities 1/7, 1/7, 2/7 and 3/7, to preserve the relative probabilities.

- A flexibility of the multinomial probit model is that the coefficients of the individual characteristics in the random utility model can be stochastic, varying (normally) over individuals to reflect individual's different tastes. This can be incorporated in the multinomial probit model through the covariances of the error terms; it cannot be made part of the multinomial logit model because the covariance between the error terms must be zero.

- Hausman and McFadden (1984) develop tests for the independence of irrelevant alternatives assumption. For more general specification tests see Davidson and MacKinnon (1984). Landwehr *et al.* (1984) suggest some graphical means of assessing logistic models.

14.3   Limited Dependent Variables

- An alternative way of explaining the OLS bias in the context of the limited dependent variable example of Fig. 14.2 is to note that the expected value of the error term ε varies with x. Consider the value x_0 in Fig. 14.2. For the corresponding y_0 to be observed, the related error ε_0 must be zero or negative, since if it were positive y would exceed k and would then be unobserved. This implies that for x_0 the expected value of the error term, $E\varepsilon$, is negative. Now consider values of x less than x_0. For y to be observed, ε can now take on small positive values, in addition to being negative or zero, so $E\varepsilon$ becomes less negative. For y to remain observed, the maximum value of ε is given by the vertical distance from the line $y = \alpha + \beta x$ to the horizontal line at $y = k$, a value rising as x falls. So although $E\varepsilon$ remains negative, it approaches zero as x falls. When x is greater than x_0 the opposite occurs. As x becomes larger and larger, for y to be observed ε must lie below a larger and larger negative number. Thus as x gets larger and larger, $E\varepsilon$ becomes more and more negative. This relationship between x and $E\varepsilon$ is shown in the lower half of Fig. 14.2.

  $E\varepsilon$ can be interpreted as an omitted variable in the specification of the original equation, the correct specification of which is $y = \alpha + \beta x + E\varepsilon + u$ where u is a traditional error term with mean zero. Because the omitted regressor $E\varepsilon$ is correlated with x, the OLS estimate of β is biased.

- Interpreting the OLS bias as resulting from the omission of the regressor $E\varepsilon$ suggests a means of generating estimates that improves on OLS. If for each observation an estimate $\hat{E}\varepsilon$ could be produced, y could be regressed on an intercept, x, and $\hat{E}\varepsilon$. This would in effect solve the omitted variable problem and replace it with a measurement errors problem (since $\hat{E}\varepsilon$ is an estimate of $E\varepsilon$); if $\hat{E}\varepsilon$ is a good estimate of $E\varepsilon$, this should produce estimates with less bias. This two-stage estimator is inferior to maximum likelihood estimation, but is used whenever the latter's computational cost becomes too high. This method can be used for the case of censored data, but not for the case of truncated data; the limit observations (on x) are needed to estimate $E\varepsilon$ (see the Technical Notes).

- The likelihood functions for censored and truncated samples are quite different. This can be illustrated with the help of Fig. 14.4, which graphs the density function of the error ε from Fig. 14.2. Consider a particular value x_3 of x. For y_3 to be observable, ε_3 must lie to the left of $k - \alpha - \beta x_3$; for y_3 unobservable, ε_3 must lie to the right of $k - \alpha - \beta x_3$. This result follows from the discussion of $E\varepsilon$ above.

  Suppose first we have a censored sample. If x_3 corresponds to an observable y, then there will be a specific ε_3 and the likelihood for that observation is given by L_3 in Fig. 14.4, the height of the density function for ε at ε_3. But if x_3 corresponds to an unobservable (i.e., missing) value of y, we have no specific ε_3; all we know is that ε_3 must lie to the right of $k - \alpha - \beta x_3$. The likelihood of this observation is thus the probability that ε_3 exceeds $k - \alpha - \beta x_3$, given by the lined area in Fig. 14.4, and calculated as 1 minus the density function cumulated to the point $k - \alpha - \beta x_3$. The likelihood for each observation in the sample may be calculated in one of these two ways, depending on whether the y value is observed or unobserved. Multiplying together all of these likelihood expressions, some of which are densities and some of which are cumulative densities, creates the likelihood for the censored sample.

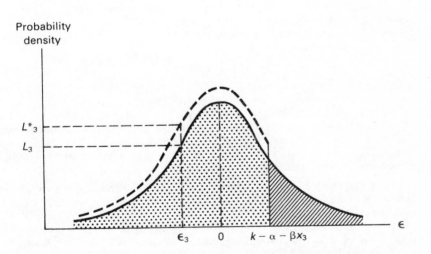

Fig. 14.4   Explaining the likelihood for censored and truncated models

Suppose now we have a truncated sample. For every possible value of x_3 in the sample the associated error must come from the left of $k - \alpha - \beta x$ in Fig. 14.4. Consequently the lined area should not be viewed as part of the density of ε_3. Because of this, ε_3 can be viewed as being drawn from the truncated normal distribution given by the dashed curve in Fig. 14.4. This dashed curve is obtained by dividing the height of the original normal distribution by the dotted area, forcing the area under the dashed curve to equal 1. Thus the likelihood of the observation y_3 is given in Fig. 14.4 by L_3^*. Note that L_3^* is a complicated function of the data, consisting of the height of the normal density function at the observation (y_3, x_3), divided by that density function cumulated to the point $k - \alpha - \beta x_3$. Each observation will give rise to a different dashed curve from which the likelihood of that observation can be calculated. Multiplying together all these likelihood expressions creates the likelihood function for the entire sample.

- The censored-sample example of Fig. 14.2 is often called the Tobit model, first introduced to econometrics by Tobin (1958) who structured his model such that y was observed whenever it exceeded $k = 0$. The estimated coefficients from this type of model must be interpreted with care. McDonald and Moffit (1980) show that the change in the expected value of y resulting from a change in an explanatory variable is not just the coefficient of that explanatory variable: the required calculation must account for the probability of being above/below the limit and changes therein. They discuss and illustrate the implications of this for the use and interpretation of results of studies employing this type of model. Hall (1984) reviews software available for estimation of these types of models.

- The example of Fig. 14.2 is an unsophisticated model of censored/truncated samples, because k is a known, fixed value. It would be more realistic, in the case of automobile purchases, for example, to specify that a household's expenditure was positive if what it could afford exceeded the price of the cheapest acceptable car, and 0 otherwise. Here the limit is both stochastic and unobservable. It is customary to specify that this limit is a linear function of some explanatory variables plus an error term, and the problem is interpreted as one of self-selection: An individual selects himself or herself into the sample on the basis of this second equation. The resulting OLS bias is called self-selection bias.
  To be more specific, we have

$$y = \alpha + \beta x + \varepsilon \tag{1}$$
$$p = \gamma + \delta z + u \tag{2}$$

with y being observed only if $y \geq p$. The likelihood function for this model is discussed by Maddala (1983) pp. 174–7. A variant of this model occurs when y is observed when $p \geq 0$. See Maddala (1983) p. 231 for the likelihood function for this case. These likelihood functions are examples of cases for which high computational cost leads some people to adopt the two-stage method noted earlier (for the censored-sample version).

- A popular example of the self-selection problem is the study of labour supply behaviour of married women. Many married women choose not to work and thus their wages are not observed (i.e., they self-select themselves out of the sample). If the choice not to work is related to the wage they would have earned had they worked, self-selection bias results. Wales and Woodland (1980) have an excellent exposition of self-selection bias in this context, as well as discussion of appropriate estimation procedures.

Technical Notes

14.1 Dichotomous Dependent Variables

- If the linear probability model is formulated as $Y = X\beta + \varepsilon$ where Y is interpreted as the probability of buying a car, the heteroskedastic nature of the error term is easily derived by noting that if the individual buys a car (probability $X\beta$) the error term takes the value $(1 - X\beta)$ and that if the individual does not buy a car (probability $(1 - X\beta)$) the error term takes the value $-X\beta$.

- The logistic function is given as $f(\theta) = e^{\theta}/(1 + e^{\theta})$. It varies from zero to one as θ varies from $-\infty$ to $+\infty$, and looks very much like the cumulative normal distribution. Note that it is much easier to calculate than the cumulative normal, which requires evaluating an integral. Suppose θ is replaced with an index $x\beta$, a linear function of (for example) several characteristics of a potential buyer. Then the logistic model specifies that the probability of buying is given by

$$\text{Prob(buy)} = \frac{e^{x\beta}}{1 + e^{x\beta}} .$$

This in turn implies that the probability of not buying is

$$\text{Prob(not buy)} = 1 - \text{Prob(buy)} = \frac{1}{1 + e^{x\beta}} .$$

The likelihood function is formed as

$$L = \prod_{i} \frac{e^{x_i\beta}}{1 + e^{x_i\beta}} \prod_{j} \frac{1}{1 + e^{x_j\beta}}$$

where i refers to those who bought and j refers to those who did not buy. Maximizing this likelihood with respect to the vector β produces the MLE of β. For the nth individual, then, the probability of buying is estimated as

$$\frac{e^{x_n\beta^{\text{MLE}}}}{1 + e^{x_n\beta^{\text{MLE}}}} .$$

The formulae given above for the logit model imply that

$$\frac{\text{Prob(buy)}}{\text{Prob(not buy)}} = e^{x\beta}$$

so that

$$\ln\left[\frac{\text{Prob(buy)}}{\text{Prob(not buy)}} \right] = x\beta .$$

This is the rationale behind the grouping method described earlier.

14.2 Polychotomous Dependent Variables

- The Weibull distribution, also known as the type I extreme-value distribution, has the convenient property that the cumulative density of the difference between any two random variables with this distribution is given by the logistic function. Suppose, for example, that the utility of option A to an individual with a row vector of characteristics x_0

is $x_0\beta_A + \varepsilon_A$ and of option B is $x_0\beta_B + \varepsilon_B$ where ε_A and ε_B are drawn independently from a Weibull distribution. This individual will choose option A if

$$x_0\beta_B + \varepsilon_B < x_0\beta_A + \varepsilon_A$$

or, alternatively, if

$$\varepsilon_B - \varepsilon_A < x_0(\beta_A - \beta_B).$$

The probability that this is the case is given by the cumulative density of $\varepsilon_B - \varepsilon_A$ to the point $x_0(\beta_A - \beta_B)$. Since the cumulative density of $\varepsilon_B - \varepsilon_A$ is given by the logistic function we have

$$\text{Prob(choose option A)} = \frac{e^{x_0(\beta_A - \beta_B)}}{1 + e^{x_0(\beta_A - \beta_B)}}.$$

This shows, for the binary case, the relationship between the random utility function and the logit model. A similar result for the polychotomous case can be derived (see Maddala (1983) pp. 59–61), producing the multinomial logit model, a generalization of the binary logit.

● A proper derivation of the multinomial logit is based on the random utility model. The resulting generalization of the binary logit can be illustrated in less rigorous fashion by specifying that the ratio of the probability of taking the kth alternative to the probability of taking some standard alternative is given by $e^{x\beta_k}$ where β_k is a vector of parameters relevant for the kth alternative. This is a direct generalization of the earlier result that Prob(buy)/Prob(not buy) $= e^{x\beta}$. Note that this ratio is unaffected by the presence of other alternatives; this reflects the independence of irrelevant alternatives phenomenon.

As an example of how this generalization operates, suppose there are three alternatives A, B and C, representing commuting alone (A), by bus (B), and by carpool (C). The model is specified as

$$\frac{\text{Prob(A)}}{\text{Prob(C)}} = e^{x\beta_A} \quad \text{and} \quad \frac{\text{Prob(B)}}{\text{Prob(C)}} = e^{x\beta_B}.$$

Here carpooling is chosen as the 'standard' or base alternative; only two such ratios are necessary since the remaining ratio, Prob(A)/Prob(B), can be derived from the other two. Using the fact that the sum of the probabilities of the three alternatives must be unity, a little algebra reveals that

$$\text{Prob(A)} = \frac{e^{x\beta_A}}{1 + e^{x\beta_A} + e^{x\beta_B}}$$

$$\text{Prob(B)} = \frac{e^{x\beta_B}}{1 + e^{x\beta_A} + e^{x\beta_B}}$$

$$\text{Prob(C)} = \frac{1}{1 + e^{x\beta_A} + e^{x\beta_B}}.$$

The likelihood function then becomes

$$L = \prod_i \frac{e^{x_i\beta_A}}{1 + e^{x_i\beta_A} + e^{x_i\beta_B}} \prod_j \frac{e^{x_j\beta_B}}{1 + e^{x_j\beta_A} + e^{x_j\beta_B}} \prod_k \frac{1}{1 + e^{x_k\beta_A} + e^{x_k\beta_B}}$$

where the subscripts i, j, and k refer to those commuting alone, by bus and by carpool, respectively. This expression, when maximized with respect to β_A and β_B, yields β_A^{MLE} and β_B^{MLE}. For any particular individual, his or her characteristics can be used, along with β_A^{MLE} and β_B^{MLE}, to estimate Prob(A), the probability that that person will commute to work alone, Prob(B), the probability that that person will commute to work by bus, and Prob(C), the probability that he or she will carpool it. Extension of this procedure to more than three alternatives is straightforward.

- The commuter example can be used to describe more fully the independence-of-irrelevant-alternatives phenomenon. Suppose we were to use the same data to estimate a logit model expanded to discriminate between commuting on a red bus (RB) versus commuting on a blue bus (BB). In the original example these two alternatives had been lumped together. Now there are four alternatives, A, RB, BB and C. Assuming everyone is indifferent between blue and red buses, it would seem logical that, when estimated, the expanded model should be such that for any individual each of the estimated probabilities of commuting alone, taking the bus (either red or blue) and carpooling it should remain unchanged, with the probability of riding the bus broken in half to estimate each of the two bus line alternatives. Unfortunately, this is not the case: adding an irrelevant alternative changes the probabilities assigned to all categories.

  The key to understanding why this comes about is to recognize that the number of people in the data set who commute by bus, relative to the number of people in the data set who, say, carpool it, is irrelevant from the point of view of calculating the estimate of β_B. It is the differences in these people's characteristics that detemine the estimate of β_B. If the people riding the bus are now arbitrarily divided into two categories, those riding red buses and those riding blue buses, there will be a change in the number of people in a bus category relative to the carpool category, but there will be no change in the nature of the differences in the characteristics of people in the bus categories versus people in the carpool category. Consequently, the estimate of β_{RB} (where Prob(RB)/Prob(C) $= e^{x\beta_{RB}}$) will be virtually the same as the original estimate of β_B, as will the estimate of β_{BB}.

  For the nth individual, before the introduction of the irrelevant alternative, the probability of commuting alone is estimated as

$$\text{Prob(A)} = \frac{e^{x_n \beta_A^{MLE}}}{1 + e^{x_n \beta_A^{MLE}} + e^{x_n \beta_B^{MLE}}}$$

a probability we would hope would remain unchanged when the irrelevant alternative is introduced. But it does change; by setting $\beta_B^{MLE} = \beta_{RB}^{MLE} = \beta_{BB}^{MLE}$ it becomes approximately

$$\text{Prob(A)} = \frac{e^{x_n \beta_A^{MLE}}}{1 + e^{x_n \beta_A^{MLE}} + 2\, e^{x_n \beta_B^{MLE}}} \cdot$$

Because of this problem, the multivariate logit methodology can be used only when the categories involved are all quite different from one another.

14.3 Limited Dependent Variables

- How does one go about estimating $E\varepsilon$ to operationalize the two-stage estimator discussed in the general notes to this section? Consider once again the example of Fig. 14.2 as reflected in its supplementary graph Fig. 14.4. For any value x_3 of x, the corresponding error term ε_3 for an observed y_3 has in effect been drawn from the truncated normal distribution shown in Fig. 14.4 as the dashed curve, cut off at the point $k - \alpha - \beta x_3$. Thus $E\varepsilon$ is the expected value of this truncated normal distribution. A standard formula for the calculation of $E\varepsilon$ can be used if it is known how many standard deviations $k - \alpha - \beta x_3$ represents. Estimation of $(k - \alpha - \beta x_3)/\sigma$, where σ^2 is the variance of the normal distribution, therefore allows estimation of $E\varepsilon$.

  In a censored sample the data on y can be interpreted as dichotomous, with y taking the value 1 if observed and 0 if unobserved. Then a probit analysis can be done on these data, generating for x_3, say, an estimate of the probability that y_3 is observed. (Note: this cannot be done for a truncated sample, since the x values for the unobserved y values are also missing – this explains why the two-stage method can be used only with censored samples.) Given an estimate of this probability, the dotted area in Fig. 14.4, it is easy to find the corresponding number of standard deviations of the standard normal giving rise to that probability, yielding the required estimate of $(k - \alpha - \beta x_3)/\sigma$.

For this example, maximum likelihood estimation is not costly, so the two-stage method is not used. The principles illustrated, however, are employed to generate $\hat{E}\varepsilon$ for more difficult cases.

15. Forecasting

15.1 Introduction

Up to now, this book has for the most part focused on the estimation of parameters, neglecting what to some is an equally important goal of econometricians, the production of good economic forecasts. The purpose of this chapter is to provide a brief overview of economic forecasting; no effort is made to describe forecasting methods, since textbooks doing this abound.

Economic forecasting methods can be classified into two very broad categories.

(1) *Causal forecasting/econometric models* Once estimates of the parameters of an economic model are available, the model can be employed to forecast the dependent variable if the associated values of the independent variables are given. It is this forecasting method, relying on the causal interpretation of the economic model in question, that is usually meant by the terminology 'econometric forecast'. The model used can range in sophistication from a single equation with one or two explanatory variables to a large simultaneous-equation model with scores of variables.

(2) *Time-series models* Time series can be characterized as consisting of a time trend, a seasonal factor, a cyclical element and an error term. A wide variety of techniques is available to break up a time series into these components and thereby generate a means of forecasting future behaviour of the series. These methods are based on the supposition that history provides some guide as to what to expect in the future. The most sophisticated of these time-series techniques is called Box–Jenkins analysis; it has become so common in economic forecasting that it is usually what is referred to when economists (as opposed to business forecasters) talk about the time-series method.

15.2 Causal Forecasting/Econometric Models

Suppose the model $Y_t = \alpha + \beta X_t + \varepsilon_t$ is assumed to satisfy the CLR model assumptions, and data for T periods are used to estimate α and β using OLS. If the value of X in time period $T + 1$ is given as X_{T+1}, then Y_{T+1} is forecast as $\hat{Y}_{T+1} = \alpha^{OLS} + \beta^{OLS} X_{T+1}$. Four potential sources of error exist when using $\hat{Y}_{T+1}$ to forecast Y_{T+1}.

(1) *Specification error*   It may not be true that the assumptions of the CLR model are met, in particular that all the relevant explanatory variables are included, that the functional form is correct, and that there has been no change in regime.

(2) *Conditioning error*   The value of X_{T+1}, on which the forecast is conditioned, may be inaccurate.

(3) *Sampling error*   The estimates α^{OLS} and β^{OLS}, rather than the true (unknown) values of α and β, are used in calculating $\hat{Y}_{T+1}$.

(4) *Random error*   The calculation of $\hat{Y}_{T+1}$ implicitly estimates ε_{T+1} as zero when its true value may differ considerably from zero.

Although each of these four sources of error plays a role in making $\hat{Y}_{T+1}$ diverge from Y_{T+1}, only sources (3) and (4) above are used to derive the forecast interval, shown in Fig. 15.1. This interval covers the actual value being forecast in, say, 95% of repeated samples (assuming no specification or conditioning errors); in Fig. 15.1 it is given for each value of X as the vertical distance between the two 95% confidence bands. The interval is smallest at the average value of the given data set used to estimate α and β; as predictions are made for values of X further and further away from this average, these intervals become larger and larger. Inside the X data set we have information on the behaviour of Y and so can be fairly confident about our forecasts; outside the data set the opposite is the case.

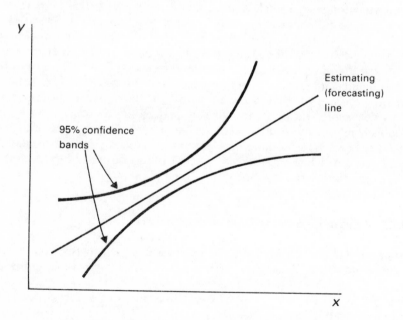

Fig. 15.1   Confidence intervals for forecasting

If error sources (1) and (2), the specification and conditioning errors, are absent, $\hat{Y}_{T+1}$ is the best linear unbiased forecast and the forecast interval in Fig. 15.1 is 'tighter' than that of any alternative linear unbiased forecast. This is due to the fact that in that circumstance α^{OLS} and β^{OLS} are BLUE. From this it should be clear that the two main objectives of econometrics – obtaining good parameter estimates and generating good forecasts – are tied closely together, at least in so far as the error sources (1) and (2) above can be ignored. The influence of these specification and conditioning errors, particularly the former, prompts many econometricians to adjust estimates from their models in light of information about factors in the economy whose influences are not incorporated in their model. In fact, this 'judgemental modification' of econometric models, consisting of a blend of qualitative information and the forecaster's experience (and often referred to as 'tender loving care'), is viewed as an essential ingredient of the process of forecasting from an econometric model. Examples are forecast modifications undertaken in light of a major strike, an application of moral suasion by a policy authority, or the announcement of a future oil price increase.

15.3 Time-series Analysis

The main competitor to econometric models for forecasting purposes is time-series analysis, also known as Box–Jenkins analysis. Rather than making use of explanatory variables to produce forecasts, the key to forecasting with econometric models, time-series models rely only on the past behaviour of the variable being predicted. Thus it is in essence no more than a sophisticated method of extrapolation. Whenever specification or conditioning errors render econometric models impractical (which some claim is most of the time), the time-series approach can be of value.

Suppose Y is the variable to be forecast. A Box–Jenkins analysis begins by transforming Y to ensure that it is 'stationary', namely that its stochastic properties are invariant with respect to time (i.e., that the mean of Y_t, its variance, and its covariance with other values of Y do not depend on time). Most economic time-series are not such that their stochastic properties are invariant over time; GNP, for example, is non-stationary because of its growth trend (i.e., the mean of GNP changes over time). The usual transformation undertaken to create stationarity is differencing; usually one or two differencing operations lead to stationarity. This creates a new series Y^* which becomes the input for the Box–Jenkins analysis.

The general model for Y^* is written as

$$Y_t^* = \phi_1 Y_{t-1}^* + \phi_2 Y_{t-2}^* + \ldots + \phi_p Y_{t-p}^* + \varepsilon_t + \theta_1 \varepsilon_{t-1} + \theta_2 \varepsilon_{t-2} + \ldots + \theta_q \varepsilon_{t-q}$$

where the ϕ and θ are unknown parameters and the ε are independent and identically distributed normal errors. Note that this model expresses Y^* in terms only of its own past values along with current and past errors. This model is called an ARIMA (p,d,q) model for Y. Here p is the number of lagged values of Y^*, representing the order of the *autoregressive* (AR) dimension of the model, d is the number of times Y is differenced to produce Y^*, and q is the number of lagged values of the error term, representing the order of the *moving average* (MA) dimension of the model. The acronym ARIMA stands for *autoregressive integrated moving average*. The 'integrated' means that to obtain a forecast for Y it is necessary to integrate over (sum up) the forecast Y^* because the Y^* are differenced values of Y.

There are three basic steps to the development of an ARIMA model:

(1) *Identification* The values of p,d and q must be determined; i.e., a particular model must be selected.
(2) *Estimation* The unknown parameters, the ϕ and the θ, must be estimated.
(3) *Diagnostic checking* The resulting model must be checked for its adequacy and revised if necessary.

By far the most crucial of these steps is the first – identification, or model selection. This step requires the researcher to use his or her personal judgement (in conjunction with an examination of the autocorrelations and partial autocorrelations of the data) to determine what model the data suggest is the appropriate one to employ. Thus in a sense the Box–Jenkins method is an art form, requiring considerable experience on the part of a researcher to be able to select the correct model.

15.4   Forecasting Accuracy

There are several ways of measuring forecasting accuracy and thereby comparing one forecasting technique with another.

(a) *Mean absolute deviation (MAD)* This is the average of the absolute values of the forecast errors. It is appropriate when the cost of forecast errors is proportional to the absolute size of the forecast error. This criterion is also called MAE (mean absolute error).
(b) *Root mean square error (RMSE)* This is the square root of the average of the squared values of the forecast errors. This measure implicitly weights large forecast errors more heavily than small ones and is appropriate to situations in which the cost of an error increases as the square of that error. This 'quadratic loss function' is the most popular in use.
(c) *Mean absolute percentage error (MAPE)* This is the average of the absolute values of the percentage errors; it has the advantage of being

dimensionless. It is more appropriate when the cost of the error is more closely related to the percentage error than to the numerical size of the error.

(d) *Coefficient of determination (R²)*   This measure gives the proportion of the variation in the variable being forecast that is captured by the forecasts. This is an undeservedly popular means of evaluating forecasting equations; the R^2 measure relates to the ability of the forecasting equation to explain the data used to develop the forecasting equation, not new data forecasted.

(e) *Percentage of turning points forecast*   Interest focuses on this criterion if it is the turning points as opposed to the numerical accuracy of the forecasts that are of relevance for the purpose served by the forecasts.

The relative accuracy of time-series versus econometric forecasting techniques is a controversial subject. Many claim that time-series methods outperform causal methods, mainly because of specification and conditioning errors inherent in the econometric approach. Others claim that this is true only for very short-range forecasts, and that econometric forecasts are superior for longer-range forecasting when one would expect extrapolation methods to fare less well than methods capable of accounting for substantive changes in other variables.

Recognition of the advantages of both methods has led to efforts to combine them. This has been accomplished in two basic ways, depending on which of the two techniques one wishes to have dominate.

(1) *Econometric dominance*   The variable to be explained is modelled in causal fashion and then the residuals from the resulting regression are predicted via a time-series analysis.

(2) *Time-series dominance*   Current and lagged values of an explanatory variable are included on the right-hand side of the general Box–Jenkins model, creating what is called a 'transfer function model'. Estimation is undertaken via a variant of the Box–Jenkins technique rather than by a regression.

In general, the idea of combining forecasting techniques is a good one. Research has indicated that the 'best' forecast is one formed as an average of a variety of forecasts, each generated by a completely different technique. If the principles on which these different forecasts are based are sufficiently different from one another, an average (or a weighted average, if more confidence is placed in some of these forecasts than others) of these forecasts, called an *amalgamated forecast*, could prove superior to any single forecasting technique. This is because the errors involved in these separate forecasts will tend to be cancelled out when they are averaged. Research has shown that this approach to forecasting is quite successful.

General Notes

15.1   Introduction

- When estimating parameter values, the failures of econometrics are shielded from public view by the fact that the true parameter values are unknown and thus cannot be compared with their estimated values. This protection does not exist when econometrics is used for forecasting – eventually predicted and actual values can be directly compared. Unfortunately for econometricians, most such comparisons have not shown their forecasts to be particularly accurate. This has prompted jokes from critics, such as 'If an economist is someone who guesses wrong about the economy, an econometrician is someone who uses a computer to guess wrong about the economy'. Economists reply with 'We only forecast to show the world that we have a sense of humour.'

   Joking aside, economists' forecasting record is not good. Martin Feldstein, chairman of the US Council of Economic Advisors, was quoted (*Time*, 27 August 1984, p. 46) as saying 'One of the great mistakes of the past 30 years of economic policy has been an excessive belief in the ability to forecast.' Nobel prize-winner Wassily Leontief (1971) p. 3 noted that 'in no other field of empirical enquiry has so massive and sophisticated a statistical machinery been used with such indifferent results.' Non-economists are much blunter in their assessment, as evidenced by US Treasury Secretary Donald Regan's statement (*Time*, 27 August 1984, p. 46) that, 'If you believe them, then you also believe in the tooth fairy.'

   One way of defending economic forecasts is to appeal to Alice-in-Wonderland logic:

   > '. . . how can you possibly award prizes when everybody missed the target?' said Alice.
   > 'Well,' said the Queen, 'Some missed by more than others, and we have a fine normal distribution of misses, which means we can forget the target.'

   Even if forecasts are poor, there are none better, and perhaps a poor forecast is better than none at all. Not everyone believes that economic forecasts are as poor as they are made out to be, however, or that the quality of what some claim to be poor forecasts is so bad that they cannot be useful. Klein (1984) has a good exposition of how forecasts are used and examples of their success in this regard. Armstrong *et al.* (1978) is a source of interesting debate on this subject.

- Not all forecasting methods can be neatly classified into one of the two categories structured here. A prominent example is the leading indicator approach; Klein and Moore (1983) have a good survey of its use.

- The discussion of this chapter is couched entirely in terms of forecasting time-series data. For forecasting cross-sectional data, only the econometric approach can be used.

15.2   Causal Forecasting/Econometric Models

- A variant of causal forecasting is *simulation*. The impact on the economy of a policy change is simulated by using the econometric model to forecast into the future. Challen and Hagger (1983) have a good discussion.

- For further discussion of the role played by the conditioning error, see Johnston (1984) pp. 198–200, Ashley (1983) and Feldstein (1971).

- Forecasting unknown values is called *ex ante* forecasting; forecasting known values is called *ex post* forecasting.

- Many critics of econometric forecasting claim that, for example, the model and parameter estimates used relate to the 1970s, for which data are available, but not to the 1980s, for which forecasts are required. Streissler (1970) even goes so far as to define econometrics as dealing with predictions of the economic past. Both Streissler (1970) and Rubner (1970) severely criticize economic forecasting. In the macroeconomic context the problem of regime changes is particularly nettlesome, as noted by Lucas (1976), since the behaviour of rational individuals should change whenever the policy environment within which they live changes.

- Forecast intervals are sometimes used to test the specification of a model – if the actual value falls within the forecast interval, the model specification is confirmed.

- An intuitive explanation for why the confidence interval widens as X moves farther away from its average value in the data set in Fig. 15.1 is as follows. Suppose the error term for one of the data points were slightly different. This would change slightly the estimates of α and β. If this is visualized in Fig. 15.1, it should be clear that the predicted value of Y at the mid-point of the data set will change by a small amount, because the new estimating line will cut the old near that point. It will diverge markedly from the old the further one goes beyond the bounds of the data set.

- The best linear unbiased forecast in the context of the GLS model differs from that of the CLR model in two ways. First, the GLS estimates are used instead of the OLS estimates, and second, if the errors are autocorrelated, the estimated values of past errors can be used to help predict future errors. For example, if $\varepsilon_t = \rho\varepsilon_{t-1} + u_t$, then the error in the $(T + 1)$th time period would be predicted as $\hat{\rho}\hat{\varepsilon}_T$, rather than 0. See Goldberger (1962). Many econometricians claim that failure to account for autocorrelated errors (characteristic of simultaneous equation model estimation) is a significant factor leading to poor forecasts.

- Young (1982) and Challen and Hagger (1983) pp. 184–90 have good discussions of judgemental adjustment/tender loving care. See also Howrey *et al.* (1974) and Evans *et al.* (1972).

- Belsley (1984a) has a good discussion of the impact of multicollinearity on forecasting.

- Salkever (1976) presents a computationally attractive way of calculating forecasts, forecast errors and confidence intervals.

15.3   Time-series Analysis

- Makridakis (1976, 1978) and Anderson (1977) provide an extensive survey of time-series methods (not just Box–Jenkins).

- Pankratz (1983), Hoff (1983) and McCleary and Hay (1980) are introductory texts for the Box–Jenkins approach. Pindyck and Rubinfeld (1981) also have a good exposition. Newbold (1983) has a good overview. Makridakis *et al.* (1982) report the results of a forecasting competition using a wide variety of competing time-series techniques, all of which are briefly described therein. One notable result of this study is that Box–Jenkins models did not perform as well (relatively) as expected. One suggestion for their improvement is the use of transfer function models.

- Differencing is not the only transformation employed to generate stationarity. Sometimes, for example, logarithms are taken before differencing.

- An ARIMA model in which no differencing is required is called an ARMA model. An AR and an MA model are ARMA models with q and p equal to zero, respectively.

- Although a true Box–Jenkins analysis requires judgemental input at the identification/model selection stage, there do exist some computer-directed automatic model-selection methods, cited in Hill and Fildes (1984) and Libert (1984).

- In econometric models economic theory usually provides a model and then it is imposed on the data. In contrast, Box–Jenkins models allow the data to determine the model. In allowing the data to do this, however, parsimony, in the form of small p and q values, is a guiding principle. Because a non-zero p value implies a model with an infinite q value, and a non-zero q value implies a model with an infinite p value, a combination of small p and q values can create an amazingly wide variety of time-series structures.

- A large shock to a time series can be captured in a Box–Jenkins analysis by employing a dummy variable to create an *intervention* model.

- Jenkins (1979) pp. 88–94 has an excellent comparison of time-series and econometric forecasting methods, stressing the advantages of the former. Time series and econometric models can be reconciled by viewing the former as variants of the latter embodying (plausible?) restrictions. For discussion and references see Anderson *et al.* (1983).

15.4   Forecasting Accuracy

- Criteria for selecting a forecasting method are discussed in Dhrymes et al. (1972) and Granger and Newbold (1973). See also Maddala (1977) pp. 343–7, and Granger and Newbold (1977) pp. 278–89. For a survey of characteristics of various measures of forecasting accuracy, see Armstrong (1978) pp. 319–29.

- 'Normative forecasting' is an approach to forecasting in which evaluation of a forecast in terms of its accuracy becomes less important than its utility in producing 'good' decisions or policies. For example, a deliberately exaggerated forecast of pollution would score well on this criterion if it induced people to take the appropriate measures to solve the actual problem.

- Cooper (1972) shows that one-quarter of predictions from a simple autoregressive scheme out-forecast seven econometric models of the US economy, and Nelson (1972) uses a Box–Jenkins model to out-forecast a major US econometric model. These studies and their critiques are reviewed by Granger and Newbold (1977) pp. 289–300. McNees (1982) presents a convincing case in favour of econometric forecasting models.

- Mahmoud (1984) is an excellent survey of studies on accuracy in forecasting. His general conclusions are that quantitative methods out-perform qualitative (subjectively oriented) methods so long as there are adequate data and no obvious regime changes have taken place; that simple methods are as accurate as sophisticated methods; and that amalgamating forecasts offers an improvement over the best of the individual forecasting methods.

- Amalgamating, or combining, forecasts is discussed by Granger and Newbold (1977) pp. 268–78. Granger and Ramanathan (1984) suggest that when amalgamating forecasts one should not force the weights of the weighted average to sum to unity, but should allow a constant term to play a role.

- Once the *univariate* Box–Jenkins model discussed in the body of this chapter is modified to create a transfer function model, it is natural to ask if further modification is possible to create, if desired, a simultaneous-equation version of Box–Jenkins. Such a *multivariate* Box–Jenkins model is possible, but is probably not worth the extra computational cost, as noted by Riise and Tjosthein (1984).

- Armstrong (1978) p. 86 presents a graph reflecting his findings that a small amount of forecasting expertise dramatically improves the accuracy of forecasts but thereafter further expertise does not improve (and may even worsen) forecasts. He concludes that for forecasting the cheapest expert should be hired. Why then is it the case that the most expensive forecasters using the most complex forecasting methods tend to be hired? His explanation for this (p. 399) is the 'rain dance theory':

> The rain dance has something for everyone. The dancer gets paid. The clients get to watch a good dance. The decision-maker gets to shift the problem onto someone else in a socially acceptable way. (Who can blame him? He hired the best dancer in the business.)

Technical Notes

15.2 Causal Forecasting/Econometric Models

- The variance of the forecast error, from which the confidence interval is constructed, is given by the formula $\sigma^2 + \sigma^2 X_0' (X'X)^{-1} X_0$ where X_0 is a vector of regressor observations corresponding to the value of the dependent variable that is to be forecast. The first term in this expression results from estimating the error term as zero; the second term results from the use of OLS estimates rather than the true parameter values. (Notice that the variance–covariance matrix of the OLS estimator, $\sigma^2(X'X)^{-1}$, appears in this second term).

15.3 Time-series Analysis

- *Autocorrelation coefficients* play a prominent role in Box–Jenkins analysis. The autocorrelation between Y_t and Y_{t+k} is given as the covariance between Y_t and Y_{t+k} divided by their common variance. When viewed as a function of k it is referred to as the autocorrelation function. The graph of an estimate of this function, sometimes called a *correlogram*, is used as a visual aid when a researcher is trying to select an appropriate model.

- For a stationary time series the autocorrelation function falls off to zero rather quickly, a fact used to determine whether or not a series is stationary.

- There are two main diagnostic checks used in Box–Jenkins analysis.

(1) *Overfitting* The model is re-estimated for a value of p or q one greater than that used for the selected model. The coefficient (ϕ or θ) on this extra lag should test insignificantly different from zero.

(2) *Autocorrelation of residuals* If the selected model is correct, the residuals from this model (the $\hat{\varepsilon}_t$ in terms of the model in the body of this chapter) should be "white noise", implying that their autocorrelations should be zero for *all* lags (k). If the sample size is large, the *Box–Pierce statistic* is used for this purpose.

- The Box–Pierce statistic is given as $Q = n\Sigma^M \hat{r}_k^2$ where n is the sample size, M is the number of autocorrelations being tested against zero, and $\hat{r}_k$ is an estimate of the autocorrelation at lag k. For a small sample size a variant of this statistic, due to Ljung and Box (1978) is employed, given by $Q^* = n(n+2)\Sigma^M (n-k)^{-1} \hat{r}_k^2$. Both statistics are distributed as a chi-square with degrees of freedom equal to M minus the number of parameters estimated in the model.

15.4 Forecasting Accuracy

- A popular method of evaluating a predictor is to regress the actual changes on the predicted changes and a constant. If the intercept estimate tests insignificantly different from 0 and the slope coefficient tests insignificantly different from 1, the predictor is said to be a good one. (More than one predictor may satisfy his criterion, however, in which case some additional criterion must be introduced – see Granger and Newbold, 1973.)

  In this context the mean square error of a predictor can be broken down into three parts. The first, called the *bias proportion*, corresponds to that part of the MSE resulting from a tendency to forecast too high or too low, reflected by the extent to which the intercept term in the aforementioned regression is non-zero. The second, called the *regression proportion*, corresponds to that part of the MSE resulting from other systematic influences, reflected by the extent to which the slope coefficient in the aforementioned regression differs from 1. The third, called the *disturbance proportion*, measures that part of the MSE resulting from an unpredictable error (measured by the variance of the residuals from the aforementioned regression). This decomposition (see Theil, 1966, pp. 26–36) provides useful information to someone attempting to evaluate a forecasting method. (An alternative decomposition, also due to Theil, into bias, variance and covariance proportions has been shown by Granger and Newbold, 1973, to have questionable meaning.)

- A common statistic found in the forecasting context is Theil's inequality (or 'U') statistic (see Theil, 1966, pp. 26–36), given as the square root of the ratio of the mean square error of the predicted change to the average squared actual change. For a perfect forecaster, the statistic is zero; a value of unity corresponds to a forecast of 'no change'. (Note that an earlier version of this statistic has been shown to be defective; see Bliemel, 1973.)

Glossary

This glossary contains common econometric terms that are not explained in the body of this book. Terms not included here appear in the index.

a.c.f. – autocorrelation function, used in the identification stage of time series (Box–Jenkins) analysis.

a priori information – extraneous information.

aggregation (grouping) – the use of group sums or group means for regression purposes instead of individual observations. Although theoretically this leads to a loss in efficiency because of the loss in information arising from the data aggregation, in applications this is not necessarily so, since aggregation can to a certain extent cancel out errors in measurement or mis-specifications of micro-relationships. See Grunfeld and Griliches (1960). Care must be taken in determining the basis on which grouping is undertaken since different results are usually obtained with different grouping rules. See Maddala (1977) pp. 66–9. Note that heteroskedasticity results if each group does not contain the same number of observations. Johnston (1972) pp. 228–38 has a general discussion of grouping.

analogy principle – that population parameters be estimated by sample statistics that have the same property in the sample as the parameters do in the population. See Goldberger (1968b) chapter 2 for a modification of this principle which produces the OLS estimates. See also *method of moments*.

ANOVA – analysis of variance.

beta coefficient – the coefficient estimate from a regression in which the variables have been standardized. It can be calculated by multiplying the usual coefficient estimate by the standard error of its regressor and dividing by the standard error of the regressand, and can be interpreted as the number of standard error changes in the dependent variable resulting from a standard error change in the independent variable. It is sometimes used as a measure of the relative strength of regressors in affecting the dependent variable.

bunch map analysis – a method developed by Frisch for analysing multicollinearity. See Malinvaud (1966) pp. 32–6.

canonical correlation – an analysis whereby linear combinations of two sets of variables are found such that the correlation between the two linear combinations is maximized. These linear combinations can be interpreted as indices representing their respective sets of variables. For example, an economist may be seeking an index to represent meat consumption, where there is a variety of differently priced meats, along with a corresponding price index.

classical – an adjective used to describe statisticians who are not Bayesians.

collinearity – multicollinearity.

confluence analysis – see *bunch map analysis*.

contemporaneous – an adjective used to indicate 'in the same time period.'

correlation coefficient – a measure of the linear association between two variables, calculated as the square root of the R^2 obtained by regressing one variable on the other (and signed to indicate whether the relationship is positive or negative). See also *partial correlation coefficient, multiple correlation coefficient,* and *Fisher's* z.

correlation matrix – a matrix displaying the correlation coefficients beween different elements of a vector (the *ij*th element contains the correlation coefficient between the *i*th and the *j*th elements of the vector; all the diagonal elements are ones, since a variable is perfectly correlated with itself). Most computer regression packages produce this matrix for the vector of regressors since it is useful in analysing multicollinearity.

covariance matrix – variance–covariance matrix.

degenerate distribution – a distribution concentrated entirely at one point.

degrees of freedom – the number of free or linearly independent sample observations used in the calculation of a statistic.

discriminant analysis – a means of assigning a new observation to a specific group. Suppose, for example, we wanted to know if a new country possesses good development potential. Using data on other countries known to have or not have good development potential, a rule is constructed (by choosing a linear combination of countries' characteristics and a critical value for this linear combination) to decide, on the basis of the new country's characteristics, whether or not it has good development potential. This rule (the discriminant function) is chosen as the one that best 'discriminates' between the classifications. See Johnston (1972) pp. 334–40.

dominant variables – independent variables that account for so much of the variation in a dependent variable that the influence of other variables cannot be estimated. For an example in the context of material inputs dominating capital and labour in determining output, see Rao and Miller (1971) pp. 40–3.

double k-class estimator – a generalized version of the *k*-class estimator.

dummy variable trap – forgetting to omit the dummy variable for one category when an intercept is included, since if a dummy is included for all categories an exact linear relaionship will exist between the dummies and the intercept.

Fisher's z – hypotheses concerning the population correlation coefficient ρ can be tested by using the fact that $z = \frac{1}{2}\ln[(r + 1)/(r - 1)]$, where r is the sample correlation coefficient, is approximately normally distributed (around the value of z calculated with $r = \rho$) with standard error $1/\sqrt{(T - 3)}$.

goodness of fit – the magnitude of R^2.

grouping – see *aggregation.*

information matrix – the inverse of the Cramer–Rao lower bound.

Janus coefficient – a measure of the accuracy of forecasts, calculated by taking the ratio of the average of the squared forecast errors for extra-sample data to the average of the squared forecast errors for sample data. See Koutsoyiannis (1977) p. 496.

method of moments – an estimation method in which the sample moments are equated to the population moments and the parameters are solved for. For an example see Koutsoyiannis (1977) pp. 543–4. See also *analogy principle.*

minimum variance bound – Cramer–Rao bound.

missing observations – an estimation problem that arises when some data are unavailable, for example if a survey respondent answers some but not all questions, or if one variable is measured annually whereas all others are measured quarterly. Several solutions for this problem, such as using estimates of the missing observations, are discussed in Maddala (1977) pp. 201–7.

multiple correlation coefficient – the square root of the coefficient of determination, R^2, from a multiple regression.

outlier – an observation that differs greatly from comparable observations.

p.a.c.f. – partial autocorrelation function, used in the identification stage of time-series (Box–Jenkins) analysis.

partial correlation coefficient – a measure of the linear association between two variables when specified other variables are held constant. It is calculated as the correlation coefficient between the residuals obtained when the two variables in question are regressed on the variables to be held constant. See Goldberger (1968b) chapter 4.

partial regression coefficient – a regression coefficient whose calculation accounts for the influence of other regressors. 'Gross' or 'simple' regression coefficients, calculated ignoring the influence of other regressors, are seldom encountered. See Goldberger (1968b) chapter 3.

precision – the accuracy of an estimator as measured by the inverse of its variance.

predetermined variable – exogenous or lagged endogenous variable.

prior information – extraneous information.

risk function – the expected value of a loss function in Bayesian estimation; in classical analyses, usually interpreted as the sum of the MSEs of the parameter estimates.

sampling error– the error in estimating a parameter caused by the fact that in the sample at hand all the disturbances are not zero.

serial correlation – autocorrelation.

Slutsky Theorem – the result that the probability limit of a nonlinear function of a variable is equal to the nonlinear function of the probability limit of that variable, i.e., that plim $f(x) = f(\text{plim } x)$.

spectral analysis – a technique whereby a time series is decomposed into a sum of periodic functions (sine curves, for example) plus an error term. Estimation involves finding the amplitude, period and phase of these curves. See Farley and Hinich (1969) for an elementary discussion.

spurious correlation – correlation induced by the method of handling the data and not present in the original data.

stock-adjustment model – partial-adjustment model.

sufficient statistic – an estimator that uses all the information contained in the sample in the sense that we would make the same parameter estimate whether we were told the whole set of observations or only the value of the sufficient statistic.

threshold loss function – a loss function taking the value 0 if the error is less than some critical or threshold level, and a constant value if the error is greater than or equal to this critical level. It captures losses of a dichotomous nature, such as death resulting from an overdose.

truncated squared error loss – a loss function equal to the squared error, but with a maximum loss for any observation. It is used as a means of handling outliers.

Bibliography

ADAMS, G. (1965) 'Prediction with Consumer Attitudes: The Time Series – Cross Section Paradox' *Review of Economics and Statistics* vol. 47, pp. 367–78.

AIGNER, D. (1971) *Basic Econometrics* Englewood Cliffs, NJ: Prentice-Hall.

AIGNER, D. J. (1974) 'MSE Dominance of Least Squares with Errors of Observation' *Journal of Econometrics* vol. 2, pp. 365–72.

AIGNER, D. J. and G. G. JUDGE (1977) 'Application of Pre-test and Stein Estimators to Economics Data' *Econometrica* vol. 45, pp. 1279–88.

AMEMIYA, T. (1980) 'Selection of Regressors' *International Economic Review* vol. 21, pp. 331–54.

AMEMIYA, T. (1981) 'Qualitative Response Models: A Survey' *Journal of Economic Literature* vol. 19, pp. 1483–1536.

AMEMIYA, T. (1983) 'Tobit Models: A Survey' *Journal of Econometrics* vol. 24, pp. 3–61.

AMES, E. and S. REITER (1961) 'Distributions of Correlation Coefficients in Economic Time Series' *Journal of the American Statistical Association* vol. 56, pp. 637–56.

ANDERSON, O. D. (1977) 'A Commentary on 'A Survey of Time Series' *International Statistical Review* vol. 45, pp. 273–97.

ANDERSON, R. G., J. M. JOHANNES, and R. H. RASCHE (1983) 'A New Look at the Relationship between Time-series and Structural Equation Models' *Journal of Econometrics* vol. 23, pp. 235–51.

ANDREWS, D. F. (1971) 'A Note on the Selection of Data Transformations' *Biometrika* vol. 58, pp. 249–54.

ARMSTRONG, J. S. (1978) *Long-Range Forecasting: From Crystal Ball to Computer* New York: John Wiley.

ARMSTRONG, J. S. et al. (1978) 'Symposium on Forecasting with Econometric Methods' *Journal of Business* vol. 51, pp. 547–600.

ASHLEY, R. (1983) 'On the Usefulness of Macroeconomic Forecasts as Inputs to Forecasting Models' *Journal of Forecasting* vol. 2, pp. 211–23.

ASHLEY, R. (1984) 'A Simple Test for Regression Parameter Stability' *Economic Inquiry* vol. 22, pp. 253–68.

BACON, R. W. (1977) 'Some Evidence on the Largest Squared Correlation Coefficient from Several Samples' *Econometrica* vol. 45, pp. 1997–2001.

BAKAN, D. (1966) 'The Test of Significance in Psychological Research' *Psychological Bulletin* vol. 66, pp. 423–37.

BALTAGI, B. H. and J. M. GRIFFIN (1984) 'Short and Long-run Effects in Pooled Models' *International Economic Review* vol. 25, pp. 631–45.

BARTELS, R. (1977) 'On the Use of Limit Theorem Arguments in Economic Statistics' *American Statistician* vol. 31, pp. 85–7.

BEACH, C. M. and J. G. MACKINNON (1978a) 'A Maximum Likelihood Procedure for Regressions with Autocorrelated Errors' *Econometrica* vol. 46, pp. 51–8.

BEACH, C. M. and J. G. MACKINNON (1978b) 'Full Maximum Likelihood Estimation of Second-order Autoregressive Error Models' *Journal of Econometrics* vol. 7, pp. 187–98.

216

BEATON, A. E., D. B. RUBIN and J. L. BARONE (1976) 'The Acceptability of Regression Solutions: Another Look at Computational Accuracy' *Journal of the American Statistical Association* vol. 71, pp. 158–68.

BELSLEY, D. A. (1984a) 'Collinearity and Forecasting' *Journal of Forecasting* vol. 3, pp. 183–96.

BELSLEY, D. A. (1984b) 'Demeaning Conditioning Diagnostics Through Centering' *American Statistician* vol. 38, pp. 73–93.

BELSLEY, D. A., E. KUH and R. E. WELSCH (1980) *Regression Diagnostics: Identifying Influential Data and Sources of Collinearity* New York: John Wiley.

BERA, A. K. and C. M. JARQUE (1982) 'Model Specification Tests: A Simultaneous Approach' *Journal of Econometrics* vol. 20, pp. 59–82.

BERNDT, E. R. and N. E. SAVIN (1977) 'Conflict Among Criteria for Testing Hypotheses in the Multivariate Regression Model' *Econometrica* vol. 45, pp. 1263–78.

BIBBY, J. and H. TOUTENBURG (1977) *Prediction and Improved Estimation in Linear Models* New York: John Wiley.

BISHOP, R. V. (1979) 'The Construction and Use of Causality Tests' *Agricultural Economics Research* vol. 31, pp. 1–6.

BLIEMEL, F. (1973) 'Theil's Forecast Accuracy Coefficient: A Clarification *Journal of Marketing Research* vol. 10, pp. 444–6.

BLYTH, C. R. (1972) 'Subjective vs. Objective Methods in Statistics' *American Statistician* vol. 26, pp. 20–2.

BREUSCH, T. S. (1978) 'Testing for Autocorrelation in Dynamic Linear Models' *Australian Economic Papers* vol. 17, pp. 334–55.

BREUSCH, T. S. and A. R. PAGAN (1979) 'A Simple Test for Heteroskedasticity and Random Coefficient Variation' *Econometrica* vol. 47, pp. 1287–94.

BREUSCH, T. S. and A. R. PAGAN (1980) 'The Lagrange Multiplier Test and its Application to Model Specification in Econometrics' *Review of Economic Studies* vol. 47, pp. 239–53.

BRIDGE, J. (1971) *Applied Econometrics* Amsterdam: North Holland.

BROWN, R., J. DURBIN, and J. EVANS (1975) 'Techniques for Testing the Constancy of Regression Relationships Over Time' *Journal of the Royal Statistical Society* vol. B37, pp. 149–63.

BROWN, T. M. (1960) 'Simultaneous Least Squares: A Distribution-free Method of Equation System Structure Estimation' *International Economic Review* vol. 1, pp. 173–91.

BRUNNER, K. (1973) Review of B. Hickman (ed.) *Econometric Models of Cyclical Behavior* in *Journal of Economic Literature* vol. 11, pp. 926–33.

BUSCHE, K. and P. KENNEDY (1984) 'On Economists' Belief in the Law of Small Numbers' *Economic Inquiry* vol. 22, pp. 602–3.

BUSE, A. (1973) 'Goodness of Fit in Generalized Least Squares Estimation' *American Statistician* vol. 27, pp. 106–8.

BUSE, A. (1982) 'The Likelihood Ratio, Wald and Lagrange Multiplier Tests: An Expository Note' *American Statistician* vol. 36, pp. 153–7.

CARTER, R. (1973) 'Least Squares as an Exploratory Estimator' *Canadian Journal of Economics* vol. 6, pp. 108–14.

CASELLA, G. (1983) 'Leverage and Regression Through the Origin' *American Statistician* vol. 37, pp. 147–52.

CASSIDY, H. J. (1981) *Using Econometrics: A Beginner's Guide* Reston, Va.: Reston.

CHALLEN, D. W. and A. J. HAGGER (1983) *Macroeconomic Systems: Construction, Validation and Applications* New York: St. Martin's Press.

CHANG, S. (1984) *Practitioners' Guide to Econometrics*   Lanham, Md: University Press of America.

CHRIST, C. (1966) *Econometric Models and Methods*   New York: John Wiley.

COHEN, J. and P. COHEN (1975) *Applied Multiple Regression/Correlation Analysis for the Behavioral Sciences*   Hillside, N.J.: Laurence Erlbaum Associates.

CONLISK, J. (1971) 'When Collinearity is Desirable'   *Western Economic Journal* vol. 9, pp. 393–407.

COOPER. R. (1972) 'The Predictive Performance of Quarterly Econometric Models of the United States' in Hickman (1972).

COPAS, J. (1966) 'Monte Carlo Results for Estimation in a Stable Markov Time Series'   *Journal of the Royal Statistical Society*   vol. A129, pp. 110–6.

CRAMER, J. (1971) *Empirical Econometrics*   Amsterdam: North Holland.

DASTOOR, N. K. (1981) 'A Note o the Interpretation of the Cox Procedure for Non-nested Hypotheses'   *Economics Letters*   vol. 8, pp. 113–19.

DAVIDSON, J., D. HENDRY, F. SRBA and S. YEO (1978) 'Econometric Modelling of the Aggregate Time-series Relationship between Consumers' Expenditure and Income in the United Kingdom'   *Economic Journal*   vol. 88, pp. 661–92.

DAVIDSON, R. and J. G. MACKINNON (1983) 'Small Sample Properties of Alternative Forms of the Lagrange Multiplier Test'   *Economics Letters*   vol. 12, pp. 269–75.

DAVIDSON, R. and J. G. MACKINNON (1984) 'Convenient Specification Tests for Logit and Probit Models'   *Journal of Econometrics*   vol. 25, pp. 241–62.

DESAI, M. (1976) *Applied Econometrics*   London: Philip Allan.

DHRYMES, P. H. (1973) 'Restricted and Unrestricted Reduced Forms: Asymptotic Distribution and Relative Efficiency'   *Econometrica*   vol. 41, pp. 119–34.

DHRYMES, P. et al. (1972) 'Criteria for Evaluation of Econometric Models'   *Annals of Economic and Social Measurement*   vol. 1, pp. 291–324.

DIELMAN, T. E. (1983) 'Pooled Cross-sectional and Time Series Data: A Survey of Current Statistical Methodology'   *American Statistician*   vol. 37, pp. 111–22.

DOWLING, J. and F. GLAHE (1970) *Readings in Econometric Theory*   Boulder, Colorado: Colorado Associated University Press.

DRAPER, N. R. and R. C. VAN NOSTRAND (1979) 'Ridge Regression and James Stein Estimation: Review and Comments'   *Technometrics*   vol. 21, pp. 451–65.

DRÈZE, J. (1983) 'Nonspecialist Teaching of Econometrics: A Personal Comment and Personalistic Lament'   *Econometric Reviews*   vol. 2, pp. 291–9.

DUFOUR, J. M. (1980) 'Dummy Variables and Predictive Tests for Structural Change   *Economic Letters*   vol. 6, pp. 241–7.

DUFOUR, J. M. (1982) 'Recursive Stability of Linear Regression Relationships'   *Journal of Econometrics*   vol. 19, pp. 31–76.

DURBIN, J. (1953) 'A Note on Regression when there is Extraneous Information about one of the Coefficients'   *Journal of the American Statistical Assocation* vol. 48, pp. 799–808.

DURBIN, J. (1970) 'Testing for Serial Correlation in Least Squares Regression When Some of the Regressors are Lagged Dependent Variables'   *Econometrica*   vol. 38, pp. 410–21.

DUTTA, M. (1975) *Econometric Methods*   Cincinnati: South-Western.

EDWARDS, J. B. (1969) 'The Relation between the F-Test and R^2'   *American Statistician*   vol. 23, p. 28.

EFRON, B. and C. MORRIS (1977) 'Stein's Paradox in Statistics'   *Scientific American*   vol. 236 (May), pp. 119–27.

ENGLE, R. (1974) 'Specification of the Disturbances for Efficient Estimation' *Econometrica* vol. 42, pp. 135–46.

EPPS, T. W. and M. L. EPPS (1977) 'The Robustness of Some Standard Tests for Autocorrelation and Heteroskedasticity when Both Problems are Present *Econometrica* vol. 45, pp. 745–53.

EVANS, M. (1969) *Macroeconomic Activity* New York: Harper and Row.

EVANS, M., Y. HAITOVSKY, and G. TREYZ (1972) 'An Analysis of the Forecasting Properties of US Econometric Models' in Hickman (1972).

FAIR, R. C. (1970) 'The Estimation of Simultaneous Equation Models with Lagged Endogenous Variables and First-order Serially Correlated Errors' *Econometrica* vol. 38, pp. 507–16.

FAIR, R. C. (1973) 'A Comparison of Alternative Estimators of Microeconomic Models' *International Economic Review* vol. 14, pp. 261–77.

FAIR, R. C. and D. M. JAFFEE (1972) 'Methods of Estimation for Markets in Disequilibrium' *Econometrica* vol. 40, pp. 497–514.

FARLEY, J. and HINICH (1969) 'Spectral Analysis' *Journal of Advertising Research* vol. 9, pp. 47–50.

FARRAR, D. and R. GLAUBER (1967) 'Multicollinearity in Regression Analysis: The Problem Revisited' *Review of Economics and Statistics* vol. 49, pp. 92–107; reprinted in Dowling and Glahe (1970).

FEIGE, E. L. (1975) 'The Consequences of Journal Editorial Policies and a Suggestion for Revision' *Journal of Political Economy* vol. 83, pp. 1291–6.

FELDSTEIN, M. (1971) 'The Error of Forecast in Econometric Models when the Forecast-period Exogenous Variables are Stochastic' *Econometrica* vol. 39, pp. 55–60.

FELDSTEIN, M. (1973) 'Multicollinearity and the Mean Square Error of Alternative Estimators *Econometrica* vol. 41, pp. 337–46.

FELDSTEIN, M. (1974) 'Errors in Variables: A Consistent Estimator with Smaller MSE in Finite Samples' *Journal of the American Statistical Association* vol. 69, pp. 990–6.

FIENBERG, S. E. and A. ZELLNER (eds) (1974) *Studies in Bayesian Econometrics and Statistics in Honor of Leonard J. Savage* Amsterdam: North Holland.

FISHCHOFF, B. and R. BEYTH-MAROM (1983) 'Hypothesis Evaluation from a Bayesian Perspective' *Psychological Review* vol. 90, pp. 239–60.

FISHER, F. (1966) *The Identification Problem* New York: McGraw-Hill.

FISHER, W. (1976) 'Normalization in Point Estimation' *Journal of Econometrics* vol. 4, pp. 243–52.

FOMBY, T. B., R. C. HILL and S. R. JOHNSON (1984) *Advanced Econometric Methods* New York: Springer–Verlag.

FORSUND, F. R., C. A. K. LOVELL, and P. SCHMIDT (1980) 'A Survey of Frontier Production Functions and of their Relationship to Efficiency Measurement' *Journal of Econometrics* vol. 13, pp. 5–25.

FROMM, G. and G. SCHINK (1973) 'Aggregation and Econometric Models' *International Economic Review* vol. 14, pp. 1–32.

GALLANT, A. R. (1975) 'Nonlinear Regression' *American Statistician* vol. 29, pp. 73–81.

GALPIN, J. S. and D. M. HAWKINS (1984) 'The Use of Recursive Residuals in Checking Model Fit in Linear Regression' *American Statistician* vol. 38, pp. 94–105.

GEARY, R. and C. LESER (1968) 'Significance Tests in Multiple Regression' *The*

American Statistician   vol. 22, pp. 20–1.

GERSOVITZ, M. and J. G. MACKINNON (1978) 'Seasonality in Regression: An Application of Smoothness Priors'   *Journal of the American Statistical Association*   vol. 73, pp. 264–73.

GILES, D. (1973) *Essays on Econometric Topics: From Theory to Practice*   Research Paper no. 10, Reserve Bank of New Zealand, Wellington, New Zealand.

GLEJSER, H. (1969) 'A New Test for Heteroskedasticity'   *Journal of the American Statistical Association*   vol. 64, pp. 316–23.

GODFREY, L. G. (1976) 'Testing for Serial Correlation in Dynamic Simultaneous Equation Models'   *Econometrica*   vol. 44, pp. 1077–84.

GODFREY, L. G. (1978) 'Testing Against General Autoregressive and Moving Average Error Models When the Regressors Include Lagged Dependent Variables'   *Econometrica*   vol. 46, pp. 1293–1302.

GODFREY, L. G. and M. R. WICKENS (1981) 'Testing Linear and Log-Linear Regressions for Functional Form'   *Review of Economic Studies*   vol. 48, pp. 487–96.

GOLDBERGER, A. S. (1962) 'Best Linear Unbiased Prediction in the Generalized Linear Regression Model'   *Journal of the American Statistical Association* vol. 57, pp. 369–75.

GOLDBERGER, A. S. (1964) *Econometric Theory*   New York: John Wiley.

GOLDBERGER, A. S. (1968a)   'The Interpretation and Estimation of Cobb–Douglas Functions'   *Econometrica*   vol. 35, pp. 464–72.

GOLDBERGER, A. S. (1968b) *Topics in Regression Analysis*   New York: Macmillan.

GOLDFELD, S. and R. QUANDT (1972) *Nonlinear Methods in Econometrics*   Amsterdam: North Holland.

GOLDFELD, S. and R. QUANDT (1976) *Studies in Nonlinear Estimation*   Cambridge, Mass.: Ballinger.

GOODHART, C. A. E. (1978) 'Problems of Monetary Management: the UK Experience' in A. S. Courakis (ed.),*Inflation, Depression and Economic Policy in the West: Lessons from the 1970s*   Oxford: Basil Blackwell.

GRANGER, C. and P. NEWBOLD (1973) 'Some Comments on the Evaluation of Economic Forecasts'   *Applied Economics*   vol. 5, pp. 35–47.

GRANGER, C. W. J. and P. NEWBOLD (1974) 'Spurious Regressions in Econometrics'   *Journal of Econometrics*   vol. 2, pp. 111–20.

GRANGER, C. and P. NEWBOLD (1976) 'R^2 and the Transformation of Regression Variables'   *Journal of Econometrics*   vol. 4, pp. 205–10.

GRANGER, C. and P. NEWBOLD (1977) *Forecasting Economic Time Series*   London: Academic Press.

GRANGER, C. and R. RAMANATHAN (1984) 'Improved Methods of Combining Forecasts'   *Journal of Forecasting*   vol. 3, pp. 197–204.

GREENBERG, E. and C. E. WEBSTER (1983) *Advanced Econometrics: A Bridge to the Literature*   New York: John Wiley.

GREENWALD, B. C. (1983) 'A General Analysis of Bias in the Estimated Standard Errors of Least Squares Coefficients'   *Journal of Econometrics*   vol. 22, pp. 323–38.

GRIFFITHS, W. E. and P. A. A. BEESLEY (1984) 'The Small-sample Properties of Some Preliminary Test Estimators in a Linear Model with Autocorrelated Errors'   *Journal of Econometrics*   vol. 25, pp. 49–61.

GRILICHES, Z. and M. D. INTRILIGATOR (eds) (1983) *Handbook of Econometrics* (Vol. I) Amsterdam: North Holland.

GRILICHES, Z. and M. D. INTRILIGATOR (eds) (1984) *Handbook of Econometrics* (Vol. II) Amsterdam: North Holland.

GRILICHES, Z. and P. RAO (1969) 'Small-sample Properties of Several Two-stage Regression Methods in the Context of Autocorrelated Errors' *Journal of the American Statistical Association* vol. 64, pp. 253–72.

GRUNFELD, Y. and Z. GRILICHES (1960) 'Is Aggregation Necessarily Bad?' *Review of Economics and Statistics* vol. 42, pp. 1–13; reprinted in Dowling and Glahe (1970).

GUJARATI, D. (1978) *Basic Econometrics* New York: McGraw-Hill.

HAESSEL, W. (1978) Measuring Goodness of Fit in Linear and Nonlinear Models' *Southern Economic Journal* vol. 44, pp. 648–52.

HALL, B. H. (1984) 'Software for the Computation of Tobit Model Estimates' *Journal of Econometrics* vol. 24, pp. 215–22.

HALVORSEN, R. and R. PALMQUIST (1980) 'The Interpretation of Dummy Variables in Semilogarithmic Equations' *American Economic Review* vol. 70, pp. 474–5.

HANNAN, E. and R. TERRELL (1968) 'Testing for Serial Correlation after Least Squares Regression' *Econometrica* vol. 36, pp. 133–50.

HARTWIG, F. and B. E. DEARING (1979) *Exploratory Data Analysis* Beverly Hills Ca.: Sage.

HARVEY, A. C. (1980) 'On Comparing Regression Models in Levels and First Differences' *International Economic Review* vol. 21, pp. 707–20.

HARVEY, A. C. (1981) *The Econometric Analysis of Time Series* Oxford: Philip Allan.

HARVEY, A. C. and P. COLLIER (1977) 'Testing for Functional Misspecification in Regression Analysis' *Journal of Econometrics* vol. 6, pp. 103–19.

HATANAKA, M. (1974) 'An Efficient Two-step Estimator for the Dynamic Adjustment Model with Autoregressive Errors' *Journal of Econometrics* vol. 2, pp. 199–220.

HAUSMAN, J. A. (1978) 'Specification Tests in Econometrics' *Econometrica* vol. 46, pp. 1251–71.

HAUSMAN, J. A. and D. McFADDEN (1984) 'Specification Tests for the Multinomial Logit Model' *Econometrica* vol. 52, pp. 1219–40.

HAWKINS, D. M. (1980) 'A Note on Fitting a Regression Without an Intercept Term' *American Statistician* vol. 34, p. 233.

HEBDEN, J. (1983) *Applications of Econometrics* Oxford: Philip Allan.

HENDRY, D. F. (1973) 'On Asymptotic Theory and Finite Sample Experiments' *Economica* vol. 40, pp. 210–17.

HENDRY, D. F. (1980) 'Econometrics – Alchemy or Science?' *Economica* vol. 47, pp. 387–406.

HENDRY, D. F. (1984) 'Monte Carlo Experimentation in Econometrics', chapter 16 in Griliches and Intriligator (1984).

HENDRY, D. F. and G. E. MIZON (1978) 'Serial Correlation as a Convenient Simplification, Not a Nuisance: A Comment on a Study of the Demand for Money by the Bank of England' *Economic Journal* vol. 88, pp. 549–63.

HENDRY, D. F. and K. F. WALLIS (eds) (1984) *Econometrics and Quantitative Economics* Oxford: Basil Blackwell.

HENSHAW, R. (1966) 'Testing Single Equation Least Squares Regression Models for Autocorrelated Disturbances' *Econometrica* vol. 34, pp. 646–60.

HEY, J. (1983) *Data in Doubt* Oxford: Martin Robertson.

HICKMAN, B. (1972) *Econometric Models of Cyclical Behavior* New York: Columbia University Press.

HILDRETH, C. and J. HOUCK (1968) 'Some Estimators for a Linear Model with Random Coefficients' *Journal of the American Statistical Association* vol. 63, pp. 584–95.

HILL, G. and R. FILDES (1984) 'The Accuracy of Extrapolation Methods: An Automatic Box–Jenkins Package Sift' *Journal of Forecasting* vol. 3, pp. 319–23.

HILL, R. C. and R. F. ZIEMER (1982) 'Small Sample Performance of the Stein Rule in Nonorthogonal Designs' *Economics Letters* vol. 10, pp. 285–92.

HILL, R. C. and R. F. ZIEMER (1984) 'The Risk of General Stein-like Estimators in the Presence of Multicollinearity' *Journal of Econometrics* vol. 25, pp. 205–16.

HILL, R. C., R. F. ZIEMER and F. C. WHITE (1981) 'Mitigating the Effects of Multicollinearity Using Exact and Stochastic Restrictions: The Case of an Agricultural Production Function in Thailand: Comment *American Journal of Agricultural Economics* vol. 63, pp. 298–9.

HOFF, J. C. (1983) *A Practical Guide to Box–Jenkins Forecasting* Belmont, Cal.: Lifetime Learning.

HOGARTH, R. M. (1975) 'Cognitive Processes and the Assessment of Subjective Probability Distributions' *Journal of the American Statistical Association* vol. 70, pp. 271–94.

HONDA, Y. (1982) 'On Tests of Equality Between Sets of Coefficients in Two Linear Regressions When Disturbance Variances are Unequal' *Manchester School* vol. 50, pp. 116–25.

HOWREY, E. et al. (1974) 'Notes on Testing the Predictive Performance of Econometric Models' *International Economic Review* vol. 15, pp. 366–83.

INTRILIGATOR, M. (1978) *Econometric Models, Techniques and Applications* Englewood Cliffs, NJ: Prentice–Hall.

JENKINS, G. M. (1979) *Practical Experiences with Modelling and Forecasting Time Series* St Helier: Gwilym Jenkins and Partners (Overseas) Ltd.

JOHNSON, H. G. (1971) 'The Keynesian Revolution and the Monetarist Counter-revolution' *American Economic Review* vol. 61, pp. 1–14.

JOHNSON, L. W. (1978) 'Regression with Random Coefficients' *OMEGA* vol. 6, pp. 71–81.

JOHNSTON, J. (1972) *Econometric Methods* (2nd edn) New York: McGraw-Hill.

JOHNSTON, J. (1984) *Econometric Methods* (3rd edn) New York: McGraw-Hill.

JONES, J. (1977) *Introduction to Decision Theory* Homewood, Ill.: Irwin.

JUDGE, G. G. and M. E. BOCK (1978) *The Statistical Implications of Pre-test and Stein-rule Estimators in Econometrics* Amsterdam: North Holland.

JUDGE, G. G., W. E. GRIFFITHS, R. C. HILL and T. C. LEE (1980) *The Theory and Practice of Econometrics* New York: John Wiley.

JUDGE, G. G., W. E. GRIFFITHS, R. C. HILL, H. LUTKEPOHL and T. C. LEE (1985) *The Theory and Practice of Econometrics* (2nd edn) New York: John Wiley.

KADANE et al. (1980) 'Interactive Elicitation of Opinion for a Normal Linear Model' *Journal of the American Statistical Association* vol. 75, pp. 845–54.

KADIYALA, K. (1968) 'A Transformation Used to Circumvent the Problem of Autocorrelation' *Econometrica* vol. 36, pp. 93–6.

KADIYALA, K. (1972) 'Regression with Non-Gaussian Stable Disturbances: Some

Sampling Results' *Econometrica* vol. 40, pp. 719–22.

KANE, E. (1968) *Economic Statistics and Econometrics* New York: Harper and Row.

KENNEDY, P. E. (1981a) 'Estimation with Correctly Interpreted Dummy Variables in Semilogarithmic Equations' *American Economic Review* vol. 71, p. 802.

KENNEDY, P. E. (1981b) 'The "Ballentine": A Graphical Aid for Econometrics' *Australian Economic Papers* vol. 20, pp. 414–16.

KENNEDY, P. E. (1983) 'Logarithmic Dependent Variables and Prediction Bias' *Oxford Bulletin of Economics and Statistics* vol. 45, pp. 389–92.

KENNEDY, P. E. (1984) 'Non-nested Hypothesis Tests: A Diagrammatic Exposition' Simon Fraser University Discussion Paper.

KENNEDY, P. E. (1985a) 'A Rule of Thumb for Mixed Heteroskedasticity' *Economic Letters,* forthcoming.

KENNEDY, P. E. (1985b) 'Interpreting Dummy Variables' *Review of Economics and Statistics,* forthcoming.

KEYNES, J. M. (1940) 'On Method of Statistical Research: Comment' *Economic Journal* vol. 50, pp. 154–6.

KHAZZOOM, J. (1976) 'An Indirect Least Squares Estimator for Overidentified Equations' *Econometrica* vol. 44, pp. 741–50.

KING, M. L. and D. E. A. GILES (1984) 'Autocorrelation Pre-testing in the Linear Model: Estimation, Testing and Prediction' *Journal of Econometrics* vol. 25, pp. 35–48.

KLEIN, L. R. (1984) 'The Importance of the Forecast' *Journal of Forecasting* vol. 3, pp. 1–9.

KLEIN, P. and G. MOORE (1983) 'The Leading Indicator Approach to Economic Forecasting – Retrospect and Prospect' *Journal of Forecasting* vol. 2, pp. 119–35.

KMENTA, J. (1971) *Elements of Econometrics* New York: Macmillan; 2nd edn 1986.

KMENTA, J. (1972) 'Summary of the Discussion' in K. Brunner (ed.) *Problems and Issues in Current Econometric Practice* Columbus: Ohio State University Press, pp. 262–84.

KMENTA, J. and R. GILBERT (1968) 'Small Sample Properties of Alternative Estimators of Seemingly Unrelated Regressions' *Journal of the American Statistical Association* vol. 63, pp. 1180–1200.

KOENKER, R. (1981) 'A Note on Studentizing a Test for Heteroskedasticity' *Journal of Econometrics* vol. 17, pp. 107–12.

KOENKER, R. (1982) 'Robust Methods in Econometrics' *Econometric Reviews* vol. 1, pp. 213–55.

KOENKER, R. and G. BASSETT (1978) 'Regression Quantiles' *Econometrica* vol. 46, pp. 33–50.

KOUTSOYIANNIS, A. (1977) *Theory of Econometrics* (2nd edn) London: Macmillan.

KRASKER, W. S., E. KUH and R. E. WELSCH (1983) 'Estimation for Dirty Data and Flawed Models', chapter 11 in Griliches and Intriligator (1983).

KUH, E. and J. MEYER (1957) 'How Extraneous are Extraneous Estimates?' *Review of Economics and Statistics* vol. 39, pp. 380–93; reprinted in Dowling and Glahe (1970).

LAHIRI, K. and D. EGY (1981) 'Joint Estimation and Testing for Functional Form and Heteroskedasticity' *Journal of Econometrics* vol. 15, pp. 299–307.

LANDWEHR, J. M., D. PREGIBON and A. C. SHOEMAKER (1984) 'Graphical Methods for Assessing Logistic Regression Models' *Journal of the American Statistical Association* vol. 79, pp. 61–83.

LAYSON, S. K. and T. G. SEAKS (1984) 'Estimation and Testing for Functional Form in First Difference Models' *Review of Economics and Statistics* vol. 66, pp. 338–43.

LEAMER, E. E. (1978) *Specification Searches: Ad Hoc Inference with Non-experimental Data* New York: John Wiley.

LEAMER, E. E. (1981) 'The Determinants of Reading Scores: An Analysis Built on Explicit Prior Information' Department of Economics, University of California at Los Angeles.

LEAMER, E. E. (1983a) 'Let's Take the Con out of Econometrics' *American Economic Review* vol. 73, pp. 31–43.

LEAMER, E. E. (1983b) 'Model Choice and Specification Analysis', chapter 5 in Griliches and Intriligator (1983).

LEAMER, E. E. (1984) 'A Bayesian Analysis of the Determinants of Inflation' Department of Economics, University of California at Los Angeles.

LEAMER, E. E. and H. LEONARD (1983) 'Reporting the Fragility of Regression Estimates' *Review of Economics and Statistics* vol. 65, pp. 306–17.

LEECH, D. (1975) 'Testing the Error Specification in Nonlinear Regression' *Econometrica* vol. 43, pp. 719–25.

LEONTIEF, W. (1971) 'Theoretical Assumptions and Nonobserved Facts' *American Economic Review* vol. 612, pp. 1–7.

LESER, C. E. V. (1974) *Econometric Techniques and Problems* (2nd edn) London: Griffen.

L'ESPERANCE, W. and D. TAYLOR (1975) 'The Power of Four Tests of Autocorrelation in the Linear Regression Model' *Journal of Econometrics* vol. 3, pp. 1–21.

LEVI, M. (1973) 'Errors in the Variables Bias in the Presence of Correctly Measured Variables' *Econometrica* vol. 41, pp. 985–6.

LEVI, M. (1977) 'Measurement Errors and Bounded OLS Estimates' *Journal of Econometrics* vol. 6, pp. 165–71.

LIBERT, G. (1984) 'The M-Competition with a Fully Automatic Box–Jenkins Procedure' *Journal of Forecasting* vol. 3, pp. 325–8.

LIN, K. and J. KMENTA (1982) 'Ridge Regression under Alternative Loss Criteria' *Review of Economics and Statistics* vol. 64, pp. 488–94.

LINDLEY, D. V., A. TVERSKY and R. BROWN (1979) 'On the Reconciliation of Probability Assessments' *Journal of the Royal Statistical Society* vol. A142, pp. 146–80.

LIU, T. C. (1960) 'Underidentification, Structural Estimation, and Forecasting' *Econometrica* vol. 28, pp. 855–65.

LJUNG, G. M. and G. E. P. BOX (1978) 'On a Measure of Lack of Fit in Time Series Models' *Biometrika* vol. 65, pp. 297–303.

LOVELL, M. C. (1983) 'Data Mining' *Review of Economics and Statistics* vol. 65, pp. 1–12.

LUCAS, R. E. (1976) 'Econometric Policy Evaluation: A Critique' *Carnegie–Rochester Conferences on Public Policy* vol. 1, pp. 19–46.

McCALLUM, B. T. (1972) 'Relative Asymptotic Bias from Errors of Omission and Measurement' *Econometrica* vol. 40, pp. 757–8.

McCARTHY, M. (1971) 'Notes on the Selection of Instruments for Two-stage Least Squares and K-class Type Estimators of Large Models' *Southern Economic Journal* vol. 37, pp. 251–9.

McCLEARY, R., and R. A. HAY (1980) *Applied Time Series Analysis for the Social Sciences* London: Sage.

MacDONALD, G. M. and J. G. MacKINNON (1985) 'Convenient Methods for Estimation of Linear Regression Models with MA(1) Errors' *Canadian Journal of Economics* vol. 18, pp. 106–16.

McDONALD, J. F. and R. A. MOFFITT (1980) 'The Uses of Tobit Analysis' *Review of Economics and Statistics* vol. 62, pp. 318–21.

MacKINNON, J. G. (1983) 'Model Specification Tests Against Nonnested Alternatives' *Econometric Reviews* vol. 2, pp. 85–110.

McNEES, S. (1982) 'The Role of Macroeconomic Models in Forecasting and Policy Analysis in the United States' *Journal of Forecasting* vol. 1, pp. 37–48.

McNOWN, R. F. and K. R. HUNTER (1980) 'A Test for Autocorrelation in Models with Lagged Dependent Variables' *Review of Economics and Statistics* vol. 62, pp. 313–17.

MACHLUP, F. (1974) 'Proxies and Dummies' *Journal of Political Economy* vol. 82, p. 892.

MADDALA, G. S. (1971) 'Generalized Least Squares with an Estimated Variance–Covariance Matrix' *Econometrica* vol. 39, pp. 23–33.

MADDALA, G. (1974) 'Some Small Sample Evidence on Tests of Significance in Simultaneous Equations Models' *Econometrica* vol. 42, pp. 841–51.

MADDALA, G. S. (1977) *Econometrics* New York: McGraw-Hill.

MADDALA, G. S. (1983) *Limited-Dependent and Qualitative Variables in Econometrics* Cambridge: Cambridge University Press.

MAHMOUD, E. (1984) 'Accuracy in Forecasting: A Survey' *Journal of Forecasting* vol. 3, pp. 139–59.

MAKRIDAKIS, S. (1976) 'A Survey of Time Series' *International Statistical Review* vol. 44, pp. 29–70.

MAKRIDAKIS, S. (1978) 'Time-series Analysis and Forecasting: An Update and Evaluation' *International Statistical Review* vol. 46, pp. 255–78.

MAKRIDAKIS, S. et al. (1982) 'The Accuracy of Extrapolation (Time Series) Methods: Results of a Forecasting Competition' *Journal of Forecasting* vol. 1, pp. 111–53 and commentary, vol. 2, pp. 259–311.

MALINVAUD, E. (1966) *Statistical Methods of Econometrics* Amsterdam: North Holland.

MAYER, L. S. (1980) 'The Use of Exploratory Methods in Economic Analysis: Analyzing Residential Energy Demand' in J. Kmenta and J. B. Ramsey (eds) *Evaluation and Econometric Models* New York: Academic Press, pp. 15–45 and commentary by V.K. Smith, pp. 123–8.

MAYER, T. (1975) 'Selecting Economic Hypotheses by Goodness of Fit' *Economic Journal* vol. 85, pp. 877–83.

MAYES, D. G. (1981) *Applications of Econometrics* Englewood Cliffs, NJ: Prentice-Hall.

MESSER, K. and H. WHITE (1984) 'A Note on Computing the Heteroskedasticity-consistent Covariance Matrix Using Instrumental Variable Techniques' *Oxford Bulletin of Economics and Statistics* vol. 46, pp. 181–4.

MIKHAIL, W. M. (1975) 'A Comparative Monte Carlo Study of the Properties of Econometric Estimators' *Journal of the American Statistical Association* vol. 70, pp. 94–104.

MILLER, D. M. (1984) 'Reducing Transformation Bias in Curve Fitting' *American Statistician* vol. 38, pp. 124–6.

MITTELHAMMER, R. C. and D. L. YOUNG (1981) 'Mitigating the Effects of Multicollinearity Using Exact and Stochastic Restrictions: The Case of an

Aggregate Agricultural Production Function in Thailand: Reply' *American Journal of Agricultural Economics* vol. 63, pp. 301–4.

MIYAZAKI, S. and W. E. GRIFFITHS (1984) 'The Properties of Some Covariance Matrix Estimators in Linear Models with AR(1) Errors' *Economics Letters* vol. 14, pp. 351–6.

MIZON, G. E. (1984) 'The Encompassing Approach in Econometrics', chapter 6 in Hendry and Wallace (1984).

MONTGOMERY, D. and D. MORRISON (1973) 'A Note on Adjusting R^2' *Journal of Finance* vol. 28, pp. 1009–13.

MOREY, M. J. (1984) 'The Statistical Implications of Preliminary Specification Error Testing' *Journal of Econometrics* vol. 25, pp. 63–72.

MORGENSTERN, O. (1963) *On the Accuracy of Economic Observations* Princeton, NJ: Princeton University Press.

MOSTELLER, F., A. F. SIEGAL, E. TRAPIDO and C. YOUTZ (1981) 'Eye Fitting Straight Lines' *American Statistician* vol. 35, pp. 150–2.

MUNDLAK, Y. (1978) 'On the Pooling of Time Series and Cross Section Data' *Econometrica* vol. 46, pp. 69–85.

MURPHY, J. (1973) *Introductory Econometrics* Homewood Ill.: Irwin.

NARULA, S. C. and J. F. WELLINGTON (1982) 'The Minimum Sum of Absolute Errors Regression: A State of the Art Survey' *International Statistical Review* vol. 50, pp. 317–26.

NELSON, C. (1972) 'The Prediction Performance of the FRB–PENN Model of the US Economy' *American Economic Review* vol. 62, pp. 902–17.

NEWBOLD, P. (1983) 'ARIMA Model Building and the Time Series Analysis Approach to Forecasting' *Journal of Forecasting* vol. 2, pp. 23–35.

NICHOLLS, D. F., A. R. PAGAN, and R. D. TERRELL (1975) 'The Estimation and Use of Models with Moving Average Disturbance Terms: A Survey' *International Economic Review* vol. 16, pp. 113–34.

NOVICK, M. R. and P. H. JACKSON (1974) *Statistical Methods for Educational and Psychological Research* New York: McGraw-Hill.

NOVICK, M. et al. (1983) 'The Computer-Assisted Data Analysis (CADA) Monitor' CADA Research Group, University of Iowa.

ORCUTT, G. and H. WINOKUR (1969) 'First Order Autoregression: Inference Estimation and Prediction' *Econometrica* vol. 37, pp. 1–14.

OXLEY, L. T. and C. J. ROBERTS (1982) 'Pitfalls in the Application of the Cochrane–Orcutt Technique' *Oxford Bulletin of Economics and Statistics* vol. 44, pp. 227–40.

PAGAN, A. R. (1984) 'Model Evaluation by Variable Addition', chapter 5 in Hendry and Wallis (1984).

PANKRATZ, A. (1983) *Forecasting with Univariate Box–Jenkins Models: Concepts and Cases* New York: John Wiley.

PARK, R. (1966) 'Estimation with Heteroskedastic Error Terms' *Econometrica* vol. 34, p. 888.

PARK, R. E. and B. M. MITCHELL (1980) 'Estimating the Autocorrelated Error Model with Trended Data'. *Journal of Econometrics* vol. 13, pp. 185–201.

PARKE, W. R. (1982) 'An Algorithm for FIML and 3SLS Estimation of Large Nonlinear Models' *Econometrica* vol. 50, pp. 81–95.

PEACH, J. T. and J. L. WEBB (1983) 'Randomly Specified Macroeconomic Models:

Some Implications for Model Selection' *Journal of Economic Issues* vol. 17, pp. 697–720.

PIERCE, D. A. (1980) 'A Survey of Recent Developments in Seasonal Adjustment' *American Statisitician* vol. 34, pp. 125–34.

PINDYCK, R. S. and D. L. RUBINFELD (1981) *Econometric Models and Economic Forecasts* (2nd ed) New York: McGraw-Hill.

PLOSSER, C. I., G. W. SCHWERT and H. WHITE (1982) 'Differencing as a Test of Specification' *International Economic Review* vol. 23, pp. 535–52.

POIRIER, D. (1976) *The Econometrics of Structural Change* Amsterdam: North Holland.

PRESS, J. (1980) 'Bayesian Computer Programs', chapter 27 in A. Zellner (ed.) *Bayesian Analysis in Econometrics and Statistics: Essays in Honor of Harold Jeffreys* Amsterdam: North Holland.

QUANDT, R. E. (1982) 'Econometric Disequilibrium Models' *Econometric Reviews* vol. 1, pp. 1–96 with commentary.

QUANDT, R. E. (1983) 'Computational Problems and Methods', chapter 12 in Griliches and Intriligator (1983).

RAJ, B. and A. ULLAH (1981) *Econometrics: A Varying Coefficients Approach* London: Croom Helm.

RAMSEY, J. B. (1969) 'Tests for Specification Error in Classical Linear Least Squares Regression Analysis' *Journal of the Royal Statistical Society* vol. B31, pp. 250–71.

RAMSEY, J. B. and R. GILBERT (1972) 'Some Small Sample Properties of Tests for Specification Error' *Journal of the American Statistical Association* vol. 67, pp. 180–6.

RAMSEY, J. and P. ZAREMBKA (1971) 'Specification Error Tests and Alternative Functional Forms of the Aggregate Production Function' *Journal of the American Statistical Association* vol. 66, pp. 471–7.

RAO, P. (1971) 'Some Notes on Misspecification in Multiple Regressions' *American Statistician* vol. 25, pp. 37–9.

RAO, P. and R. MILLER (1971) *Applied Econometrics* Belmont, Cal.: Wadsworth.

RAVEH, A. (1984) 'Comments on Some Properties of X–11' *Review of Economics and Statistics* vol. 66, pp. 343–8.

RHODES, G. (1975) 'Non-theoretical Errors and Testing Economic Hypotheses' *Economic Inquiry* vol. 13, pp. 437–44.

RIISE, T. and D. TJOSTHEIN (1984) 'Theory and Practice of Multivariate ARMA Forecasting' *Journal of Forecasting* vol. 3, pp. 309–17.

ROBB, A. L. (1980) 'Accounting for Seasonality with Spline Functions' *Review of Economics and Statistics* vol. 62, pp. 321–3.

ROTHENBERG, T. (1973) *Efficient Estimation with A Priori Information* New Haven, Conn.: Yale University Press.

ROTHENBERG, T. and C. LEENDERS (1964) 'Efficient Estimation of Simultaneous Equation System' *Econometrica* vol. 32, pp. 57–76.

RUBNER, A. (1970) *Three Sacred Cows of Economics* London: MacGibbon and Kee.

RUTEMILLER, H. and D. BOWERS (1968) 'Estimation in a Heteroskedastic Regression Model' *Journal of the American Statistical Association* vol. 63, pp. 552–7.

SALKEVER, D. (1976) 'The Use of Dummy Variables to Compute Predictions, Prediction Errors, and Confidence Intervals' *Journal of Econometrics* vol. 4, pp. 393–7.

SAMUELSON, P. (1965) 'Research in Macroeconomics' mimeo, Cambridge, Mass.

SANINT, L. R. (1982) 'Applying Principal Components Regression Analysis to Time Series Demand Estimation' *Agricultural Economics Research* vol. 34, pp. 21–7.

SAVAGE, L. (1954) *The Foundations of Statistics* New York: John Wiley.

SAVIN, N. E. and K. J. WHITE (1978) 'Estimation and Testing for Functional Form and Autocorrelation' *Journal of Econometrics* vol. 8, pp. 1–12.

SEAKS, T. G. and S. K. LAYSON (1983) 'Box–Cox Estimation with Standard Econometric Problems' *Review of Economics and Statistics* vol. 65, pp. 160–4.

SHABAN, S. A. (1980) 'Change-point Problem and Two-phase Regression: An Annotated Bibliography' *International Statistical Review* vol. 48, pp. 83–93.

SHOURIE, A. (1972) 'The Use of Macroeconomic Regression Models of Developing Countries for Forecasts and Policy Prescription: Some Reflections on Current Practice' *Oxford Economic Papers* vol. 24, pp. 1–35.

SILVEY, S. (1969) 'Multicollinearity and Imprecise Estimation' *Journal of the Royal Statistical Society* vol. B31, pp. 539–52.

SMITH, G. and W. BRAINARD (1976) 'The Value of A Priori Information in Estimating a Financial Model' *Journal of Finance* vol. 31, pp. 1299–1322.

SMITH, G. and F. CAMPBELL (1980) 'A Critique of Some Ridge Regression Methods' *Journal of the American Statistical Association* vol. 75, pp. 74–103 and commentary following.

SMITH, V. K. (1973) *Monte Carlo Methods: Role for Econometrics* Lexington, Mass.: Lexington Books.

SNEE, R. D. (1977) 'Validation of Regression Models: Methods and Examples' *Technometrics* vol. 19, pp. 415–28.

SPITZER, J. J. (1982) 'A Primer on Box–Cox Estimation' *Review of Economics and Statistics* vol. 64, pp. 307–13.

SPITZER, J. J. (1984) 'Variances Estimates in Models with the Box–Cox Transformation: Implications for Estimation and Hypotheses-testing' *Review of Economics and Statistics* vol. 66, pp. 645–52.

SRIVASTAVA, V. K. (1980) 'Estimation of Linear Single Equation and Simultaneous Equation Models under Stochastic Linear Constraints: An Annotated Bibliography' *International Statistical Review* vol. 48, pp. 79–82.

STAMP, J. (1929) *Some Economic Factors in Modern Life* London: King and Son.

STONE, R. (1945) 'The Analysis of Market Demand' *Journal of the Royal Statistical Society* vol. B7, p. 297.

STREISSLER, E. (1970) *Pitfalls in Econometric Forecasting* London: Institute of Economic Affairs.

SUITS, D. (1984) 'Dummy Variables: Mechanics vs Interpretation' *Review of Economics and Statistics* vol. 66, pp. 177–80.

SUITS, D. B., A. MASON and L. CHAN (1978) 'Spline Functions Fitted by Standard Regression Methods' *Review of Economics and Statistics* vol. 60, pp. 132–9.

SZROETER, J. (1978) 'A Class of Parametric Tests for Heteroskedasticity in Linear Econometric Models' *Econometrica* vol. 46, pp. 1311–28.

TAYLOR, L. D. (1974) 'Estimation by Minimizing the Sum of Absolute Errors' in P. Zarembka (ed) *Frontiers in Econometrics* New York: Academic Press.

TAYLOR, W. (1976) 'Prior Information on the Coefficients When the Disturbance

Covariance Matrix is Unknown *Econometrica* vol. 44, pp. 725–39.

THEIL, H. (1957) 'Specification Errors and the Estimation of Economic Relationships' *Review of the International Statistical Institute* vol. 25, pp. 41–51; reprinted in Dowling and Glahe (1970).

THEIL, H. (1963) 'On the Use of Incomplete Prior Information in Regression Analysis' *Journal of the American Statistical Association* vol. 58, pp. 401–14.

THEIL, H. (1966) *Applied Economic Forecasting* Amsterdam: North Holland.

THEIL, H. (1971) *Principles of Econometrics* New York: John Wiley.

THEIL, H. and A. S. GOLDBERGER (1961) 'On Pure and Mixed Statistical Estimation in Economics' *International Economic Review* vol. 2, pp. 65–78.

THEIL, H. and A. NAGAR (1961) 'Testing the Independence of Regression Disturbances' *Journal of the American Statistical Association* vol. 56, pp. 793–806; reprinted in Dowling and Glahe (1970).

THURSBY, J. G. (1979) 'Alternative Specification Error Tests: A Comparative Study' *Journal of the American Statistical Association* vol. 74, pp. 222–5.

THURSBY, J. G. (1981) 'A Test Strategy for Discriminating Between Autocorrelation and Misspecification in Regression Analysis' *Review of Economics and Statistics* vol. 63, pp. 117–23.

THURSBY, J. G. (1982) 'Misspecification, Heteroskedasticity, and the Chow and Goldfeld–Quandt Tests' *Review of Economics and Statistics* vol. 64, pp. 314–21.

THURSBY, J. and P. SCHMIDT (1977) 'Some Properties of Tests for Specification Error in a Linear Regression Model' *Journal of the American Statistical Association* vol. 72, pp. 635–41.

TIAO, G. C. and G. E. P. BOX (1973) 'Some Comments on "Bayes" Estimators' *American Statistician* vol. 27, pp. 12–14.

TINTNER, G. (1953). 'The Definition of Econometrics *Econometrica* vol. 21, pp. 31–40.

TOBIN, J. (1958) 'Estimation of Relationships for Limited Dependent Variables' *Econometrica* vol. 26, pp. 24–36.

TORO-VIZCARRONDO, C., and T. D. WALLACE (1968) 'A Test of the Mean Square Error Criterion for Restrictions in Linear Regression' *Journal of the American Statistical Association* vol. 63, pp. 558–72.

TSE, Y. K. (1984) 'Testing Linear and Log-Linear Regressions with Autocorrelated Errors' *Economics Letters* vol. 14, pp. 333–7.

UHL, N. and T. EISENBERG (1970) 'Predicting Shrinkage in the Multiple Correlation Coefficient' *Educational and Psychological Measurement* vol. 30, pp. 487–9.

VALAVANIS, S. (1959) *Econometrics* New York: McGraw-Hill.

VANDAELE, W. (1981) 'Wald, Likelihood Ratio, and Lagrange Multiplier Tests as an F Test' *Economics Letters* vol. 8, pp. 361–5.

VARIAN, H. R. (1974) 'A Bayesian Approach to Real Estate Assessment', pp. 195–208 in Fienberg and Zellner (1974).

VINOD, H. (1973) 'Generalization of the Durbin–Watson Statistic for Higher-order Autoregressive Processes' *Communications in Statistics* vol. 2, pp. 115–44.

VINOD, H. D. and A. ULLAH (1981) *Recent Advances in Regression Methods* New York: Marcel Dekker.

WALDMAN, D. M. (1983) 'A Note on Algebraic Equivalence of White's Test and a Variation of the Godfrey/Breusch-Pagan Test for Heteroskedasticity' *Economics Letters* vol. 13, pp. 197–200.

WALLACE, T. (1972) 'Weaker Criteria and Tests for Linear Restrictions in Regression' *Econometrica* vol. 40, pp. 689–98.

WALLACE, T. D. (1977) 'Pretest Estimation in Regression: A Survey' *American Journal of Agricultural Economics* vol. 59, pp. 431–43.

WALLACE, T. D. and V. ASHAR (1972) 'Sequential Methods in Model Construction' *Review of Economics and Statistics* vol. 54, pp. 172–8.

WALLACE, T. D. and C. TORO-VIZCARRONDO (1969) 'Tables for the Mean Square Error Test for Exact Linear Restrictions in Regression' *Journal of the American Statistical Association* vol. 64, pp. 1649–63.

WALLIS, K. (1967) 'Lagged Dependent Variables and Serially Correlated Errors: A Reappraisal of Three-pass Least Squares' *Review of Economics and Statistics* vol. 49, pp. 555–67.

WALLIS, K. (1972) 'Testing for Fourth Order Autocorrelation in Quarterly Regression Equations' *Econometrica* vol. 40, pp. 617–36.

WALLIS, K. (1979) *Topics in Applied Economics* (2nd edn) London: Gray Mills.

WALLSTEN, T. S. and D. V. BUDESCU (1983) 'Encoding Subjective Probabilities: A Psychological and Psychometric Review' *Management Science* vol. 29, pp. 151–73.

WATT, P. A. (1979) 'Tests of Equality Between Sets of Coefficients in Two Linear Regressions When Disturbance Variances are Unequal: Some Small Sample Properties' *Manchester School* vol. 47, pp. 391–6.

WATTS, D. (1973) 'Transformations Made Transparently Easy, or, So That's What a Jacobian Is!' *American Statistician* vol. 27, pp. 22–5.

WAUD, R. (1968) 'Misspecification in the "Partial Adjustment" and "Adaptive Expectations" Models' *International Economic Review* vol. 9, pp. 204–17.

WEBER, J. D. (1973) *Historical Aspects of the Bayesian Controversy* Tucson: Division of Economic and Business Research, University of Arizona.

WHITE, H. (1980) 'A Heteroskedasticity-consistent Covariance Matrix Estimator and a Direct Test for Heteroskedasticity' *Econometrica* vol. 48, pp. 817–38.

WHITE, H. (1982) 'Maximum Likelihood Estimation of Misspecified Models' *Econometrica* vol. 50, pp. 1–18.

WHITE, H. (1984) *Asymptotic Theory for Econometrics* Orlando: Academic Press.

WICKENS, M. R. (1972) 'A Note on the Use of Proxy Variables' *Econometrica* vol. 40, pp. 759–61.

WILTON, D. (1975) 'Structural Shift with an Interstructural Transition Function' *Canadian Journal of Economics* vol. 8, pp. 423–32.

WONNACOTT, R. and T. WONNACOTT (1970) *Econometrics* New York: John Wiley.

WORKING, (1927) 'What Do Statistical Demand Curves Show?' *Quarterly Journal of Economics* vol. 41, pp. 212–35.

WORSWICK, G. D. N. (1972) 'Is Progress in Science Possible?' *Economic Journal* vol. 82, pp. 73–86.

WYNN, R. and K. HOLDEN (1974) *An Introduction to Applied Econometric Analysis* London: Macmillan.

YOUNG, R. (1982) 'Forecasting with an Econometric Model: The Issue of Judgemental Adjustment' *Journal of Forecasting* vol. 1, pp. 189–204.

ZAMAN, A. (1984) 'Avoiding Model Selection by the Use of Shrinkage Techniques' *Journal of Econometrics* vol. 25, pp. 73–85.

ZELLNER, A. (1962) 'An Efficient Method of Estimating Seemingly Unrelated

Regressions and Tests for Aggregation Bias' *Journal of the American Statistical Association* vol. 57, pp. 348–68; reprinted in Dowling and Glahe (1970).

ZELLNER, A. (1968) *Readings in Economic Statistics and Econometrics* Boston: Little, Brown.

ZELLNER, A. (1971) *An Introduction to Bayesian Inference in Econometrics* New York: John Wiley.

ZELLNER, A. (1974) 'The Bayesian Approach and Alternatives in Econometrics', pp. 39–54 in Fienberg and Zellner (1974).

ZELLNER, A. (1978) 'Estimation of Functions of Population Means and Regression Coefficients Including Structural Coefficients: A Minimum Expected Loss (MELO) Approach' *Journal of Econometrics* vol. 8, pp. 127–58.

ZELLNER, A. (1981) 'Philosophy and Objectives of Econometrics'. pp. 24–34 in D. Currie, R. Nobay and D. Peel. *Macroeconomic Analysis: Essays in Macroeconomics and Econometrics* London: Croom Helm.

ZELLNER, A. and J. F. RICHARD (1973) 'Use of Prior Information in the Analysis and Estimation of Cobb–Douglas Production Function Models' *International Economic Review* vol. 14, pp. 107–19.

ZIEMER, R. F. (1984) 'Reporting Econometric Results: Believe It or Not?' *Land Economics* vol. 60, pp. 122–7.

Index